Anonymous

Anecdotes of Luther and the Reformation

Anonymous

Anecdotes of Luther and the Reformation

ISBN/EAN: 9783337126858

Printed in Europe, USA, Canada, Australia, Japan

Cover: Foto ©Lupo / pixelio.de

More available books at **www.hansebooks.com**

ANECDOTES OF LUTHER

AND

THE REFORMATION.

"We have heard with our ears, O God, our fathers have told us what work Thou didst do in their days, in the times of old."—Psalm XLIV.

London:

HODDER AND STOUGHTON,

27, PATERNOSTER ROW.

MDCCCLXXXIII.

PREFACE.

THE celebration of the four hundredth anniversary of Luther's birth has been judged to be a fitting time for issuing a collection of anecdotes illustrative of the rise and progress of the Reformation.

Many of the pieces included in the following pages were prepared for periodicals during the last twelve years; and are, in the main, reproduced as they originally appeared. Others have been specially written out for the present volume; while such as are given in the words of others have their source sufficiently indicated.

It is quite natural that the four hundredth birthday of Luther should be honoured in Germany; and it is also an omen for good that the celebration of a national festival should attract the notice of other nations, and draw forth a sympathy, as well as excite an interest, sufficiently unique to create uneasy feelings at Rome. Hitherto history has been supposed to testify against the pope; but such are the straits to which the papacy is now driven, that the self-styled successor of St. Peter challenges opponents to meet him in this very arena. The archives of the Vatican are to be thrown open to literary inquirers who shall dare to tell the truth. If the truth is really allowed to come out, we need have no anxiety concerning the result; for one of the things against which Protestants have continually protested has been the suppression or the garbling of facts by Jesuits, who hold that even lying itself is a virtue when practised in the interest of their cause. Not that this is to be wondered at when the pope himself is found uttering sentiments more worthy of a semi-pagan priest than of a Christian bishop. 'We, meanwhile, in order that we may have light and counsel,' lately said Leo XIII., addressing a band of pilgrims, 'have ordered that the Virgin, who is called the Queen of the Rosary, shall be called to our aid.' The Reformation has still a mighty work to accomplish in the world when priestcraft deals out such superstition as this to its crowd of slaves.

The selection of anecdotes will be found to be

sufficiently comprehensive to embrace something like the entire ground of the sixteenth century awakening; and the persons referred to include the chief of the actors who laboured to make the Reformation permanent at home and abroad.

G. H. P.

LONDON, *October*, 1883.

THE BIBLE, WHEN FIRST PRINTED.

NO one can really tell when the Scriptures were first brought to our favoured British Isles; and if any portions were ever translated into the language of the ancient Britons, they would be swept away in that hurricane of persecution which characterised the reign of Diocletian in the opening of the fourth century. According to references in old authors the Gospels once existed in the ancient British language, but on that point we are unable to speak with certainty. After the Saxons embraced Christianity we may suppose that they possessed portions of the Scripture in their own dialect, even before Bede and Alfred at successive periods undertook the work of translation. When, however, the long Dark Ages succeeded, these old versions, with no printing press to multiply them, lapsed into disuse, and were, of course, obsolete when Wickliff, as the pioneer of the Reformation, made the first translation into English at the latter end of the fourteenth century. When at length the printing press was invented, the first book it sent forth was very properly the Latin Bible, a copy of which would now realise sufficient money to purchase a small estate. We have to remember that, in its earlier stages, printing was a very costly business; and, not dreaming of meeting their expenses by sales, practisers of the art frequently issued books under the patronage of some grandee. Thus the first Bible printed in Polish, in the sixteenth century—copies of which are now among the scarcest treasures of the universe—was issued at the expense of Prince Radzivil, who for this purpose subscribed ten thousand golden crowns. The work carried on in this way in centuries preceding our own was probably greater than we are sometimes disposed to think, the principal drawback being that such producers looked to the wealthy for custom instead of supplying cheap copies to the poor, who, however, were for the most part unable to read. Just after the Revolution, France showed such a dearth of Bibles that people sent over for the purpose searched for four days among the booksellers of Paris without coming upon a single copy; but happily the French were not altogether a fair sample of other nations. We learn something of what had been done from the fact that a century ago the then unique collection of Bibles belonging to the Duke of Wirtemberg included between five and six thousand articles, the German and Teutonic versions alone showing one thousand one hundred and fifty-eight different editions. About seventy years ago a writer endeavoured to prove that a free circulation of the Scriptures was quite in accordance with the spirit of Romanism; but such special pleaders read history upside down. Rome has shown a good deal of enterprise in repressing the Scriptures by fire and sword, but virtually no enterprise in scattering them. The representative Pius IV. assures us that 'more harm than benefit' arises from reading the Word in the vulgar tongue. That is the spirit of this apostasy throughout, so that we need hardly wonder when the murdered victims of Popery are even more numerous than those who during the same period have perished in war.

THE BIRTH OF LUTHER.

No trifling disputes among the learned have there been on the date of Luther's birth, chiefly agitated by Roman

Catholic writers, after he appeared, as they term him *the grand heresiarch*. In this they turned astrologers, falsifying the day and hour of his birth, that they might draw his character to their liking; believing, or pretending to believe, that no man could have effected such a singular revolution in the Church unless he had been under the influence of the devil. Some maintained that he was born on the 22nd of October, 1483, specifying even the hour and the minute, as Floramond de Remond and the famous Jerome Cardan declare; while a writer named Gauricus, a Romish prelate, says it was on the 22nd of October, 1484, at ten minutes past one, p.m.—thus differing from his contemporaries a whole year, though he found his astrological reveries to coincide completely with those of Remond and Cardan. It is amusing to see the inference which Gauricus, in common with the others, draws from this calculation. This is strange and indeed terrible! Five planets, Jupiter, Venus, Mars, Saturn, and Mercury, to which may be added the Sun and Moon, being in conjunction under Scorpio in the ninth station of the heavens, which the Arabians allotted to religion, made this Luther a sacrilegious heretic, a most bitter and profane enemy to the Christian faith. From the horoscope being directed to the conjunction of Mars, he died without any sense of religion. His soul, most impious, sailed to hell, there to be scourged for ever with the fiery whips of Alecto, Tisiphone, and Megæra.

'I have often,' says Melancthon, quoted by Audin, 'asked Margaret at what hour of what day it was her son Martin came into the world; she recollected the hour and the day perfectly, but had forgotten the year. She stated that she was brought to bed on the 10th of November, at eleven o'clock in the evening, at Eisleben, whither she had gone to buy provisions at the fair that was held every year in that place, and the child was baptized the next day, after the name of the saint whose festival they were celebrating at the time, St. Martin. Luther's brother James, an honest, worthy man, believed that the year of Martin's birth was 1483.'—*Michelet's* '*Life of Luther,*' in *Bohn's Standard Library.*

LUTHER'S YOUTH.

In the month of May 1497, two scholars wended their way along the high-road from Mansfeldt to Bernburg, knapsacks on their backs, sticks in their hands, and great tears rolling down their cheeks: they were Martin Luther, aged fourteen, and his comrade, Hans Reineke, about the same. Both had just quitted the paternal roof, and were proceeding on foot to Magdeburg, to avail themselves of the *currend schulen*, celebrated seminaries in the middle ages which still subsist. Here each boy paid his board and education by means of alms collected from the richer townsmen, under whose windows they used to sing twice a week, and of money they earned as choristers. Martin quitted this place in 1498, and directed his steps towards Eisenach.

At Eisenach, Luther studied grammar, rhetoric, poetry, under a famous master, J. Trebonius, rector of the convent of the Bare-footed Carmelites. It was the custom of Trebonius to give his lessons with head uncovered, to honour, as he said, the consuls, chancellors, doctors, and masters who would one day proceed from his school. The young scholar's ready comprehension, his natural eloquence, his rare power of elocution, his skill in composition, both prose and poetical, soon made him the object of his master's especial favour.

In the registers of the university we find, under the year 1501, the name of Luther, there written by the rector,

Jodocus Truttvetter—*Martinus Ludher, ex Mansfield.* In 1502, the name appears, Martinus Luder, Baccalaureus philosophiæ. Luther's instructors at Erfurt were Jodocus Truttvetter, whose death he afterwards accused himself of having hastened by his rebellion against scholastic theology; Jerome Emser, who explained the poetics of Reuchlin; Gerard Hecker, an Augustine monk, who afterwards became a convert to Protestantism, and introduced the Reformation into his convent; Bartholomew Usinger surnamed Arnoldi, who vigorously opposed the new doctrine; John Grevenstein, who loudly protested against the execution of John Huss, and regarded the curate of Bethleem as a martyr; and John Bigand, who remained throughout life zealously attached to his pupil.—*Audin, quoted by Michelet.*

EARLY HARDSHIPS.

All things connected with Luther are sufficiently extraordinary to show that from his birth he was destined to become the hero of a great mission. His parents, though so poor, must have been extraordinary people; for their parts must have been far above the average, and the ambition they entertained for their gifted son was in the highest degree creditable. Yet though he contrived to get to the university of Erfurt, he was compelled to beg sufficient for his support. Who would have foreseen the future written in the stars? Luther himself once asked, with the bias of one who half believed in astrology. When he turned from the law to become a monk he gave his parents more trouble than he was ever likely to occasion the pope. He attained his twentieth year before he even saw a Bible; and, though a university student versed in the learning of those days, he was not aware that the Gospels and Epistles extended further than the portions used in the service. Was such an one likely to shake the Papacy? Yes, there was something ominous in the joyful avidity with which he read the complete Bible for the first time in the library at Erfurt.

LUTHER'S EARLY EDUCATION.

The reformer was probably as fortunate in his earliest preceptors as any child could hope to be in that severe age, but that is not saying very much. That his father was a remarkable peasant is sufficiently shown in the fact that he was a reader of books; but while he and his wife desired the best things for their son, they were strict even to harshness, while the schoolmaster they patronized believed in chastisement more heartily than in anything else. He seems to have sought to make up for all other personal deficiencies by the vigour with which he thrashed his pupils.

When he first left home, Martin went to Magdeburg, and there, in the Franciscan school, his education proceeded. It was here that he and his companions commenced the practice of begging,—a practice continued in Eisenach a year later; and it was here that Ursula, the wife of Conrad Catta, dispensed a charity which has immortalized her name. When he ultimately reached the university his father contributed to his support, but he was never ashamed to recall the days when he was a juvenile mendicant.

One of the professors to whom he was particularly indebted in these early days was John Trebonius, the courteous scholar, alluded to by Audin, who, on entering the room where his students were assembled, never failed to raise his hat. When asked to account for his apparent fastidiousness he said, 'Among these youths are men whom God will one day make burgomasters, chancellors, doctors, and magistrates; and though you do not see them with their badges of office, it is right, however, to show them respect.'

THE SCRIPTURES AN UNKNOWN BOOK.

The Papists of the sixteenth century seem to have made a virtue of their total ignorance of the contents of the Sacred Books. Robert Etienne, a scholar and printer who flourished in France, and who was born in 1503, speaking of the attainments of the doctors of the Paris Sorbonne in his earlier days, remarks: 'In these times, as I can affirm with truth, when I asked them in what part of the New Testament some matter was written, they used to answer that they had read it in St. Jerome or in the Decretals, but that they did not know what the New Testament was, not being aware that it was customary to print it after the Old. What I am going to state will appear almost a prodigy, and yet there is nothing more true nor better proven. Not long since a member of their college used daily to say, "I am amazed that these young people keep bringing up the New Testament to us. *I was more than fifty years old before I knew anything about the New Testament!*"'

LUTHER AS A MONK.

From what we know about Luther's early life we are able to infer that it was not considered the most creditable thing in the world for a youth of promise to bury himself in a monastery. When, after the death of his friend Alexis, young Luther decided on retiring into the monastery at Erfurt, the disappointment and chagrin of his father were excessive; and they show that such a step was not only regarded as one of self-sacrifice, but a wilful throwing away of every earthly prospect and advantage. Truly may we say that Luther knew not what he was doing when he entered the convent, but that he was being led by a way that he knew not. 'It was an action done in the spirit of the age, out of which he was soon to be instrumental in raising the Church,' says D'Aubigné. 'Though destined to become the teacher of the world, he was still its servile imitator. A new stone was placed upon the edifice of superstition by the very hand which was soon to overturn it.' The fact was, that at this time he was a self-seeker striving to save himself, and by a severe discipline alone could he be undeceived.

He needed to go through the discipline which he now imposed upon himself, otherwise he would never have thoroughly comprehended the controversy with Rome in which he was afterwards engaged. First we see him heartily welcomed by the monks as Brother Augustine; and the brethren showed their affection by relegating to the novice all the humiliating drudgery of which he was capable of bearing. Relieved of this by the intervention of the superior, he set himself to study; and while mastering the works of Occam, 'the Invincible Doctor,' and of Gerson, 'the most Christian Doctor,' he became also absorbed for the first time in the study of the Bible. Under such conditions, in the case of such a mind, light was sure to come. 'If ever monk had got to heaven by monkery, I had been that monk,' he afterwards remarked; but all was of no use. The light came at last, but not until the pilgrim had passed through dreadful sufferings and terrors.

What he had mistaken for the most genuine medicine turned out to be merely a nostrum of the greatest of earthly quacks —the Pope.

THE CRADLE OF THE REFORMATION.

After he entered the convent Luther was indebted to two friends more than to any others, John Braun, vicar of Eisenach, and Staupitz, who first introduced him to the Elector Frederick of Saxony, and otherwise drew out the future Reformer's gifts by the best of advice he was able to give.

The day on which the monk was consecrated priest was a high day, although the pleasure of the dinner which followed the service must have been marred by John Luther's asking his son if he had not read aught in Scripture about rendering obedience to father and mother. This ordination was a step in advance, however; for now, following Staupitz's advice, he became an itinerant preacher. The next advance was to accept from the Elector a professorship in the university of Wittemburg—the town in which the battle of the Reformation was to be fought and won. Besides lecturing to the students on the Inspired Word and on philosophy, Luther had now an opportunity of preaching in an old wooden chapel in the square of the town--a building used while the church of the Augustines was being erected, and which was only saved from falling down by props on both sides. This was long before the time had arrived for challenging the authority of the Pope and denouncing Indulgences. This old wooden shed was the cradle of the mighty movement which ere long would shake the world. Luther had not come to fulness of light; but even now he stood forth different from all other preachers of that age, and taught the Gospel with a clearness which augured death to popish pretensions. Nevertheless he still needed a journey to Rome fully to open his eyes and to complete his education.

LUTHER'S TABLE-TALK—ITS PRESERVATION.

The Table-talk of the Reformer was jotted down by a number of admirers in a Boswell-like fashion; and the first who translated this book into English was Captain Henry Bell, whose MS. was examined by Laud, and afterwards discussed by the Westminster Assembly in 1646. The Captain's story, by Hazlitt, is as follows:—

I, Captain Henry Bell, do hereby declare, both to the present age, and also to posterity, that being employed beyond the seas in state affairs divers years together, both by king James, and also by the late king Charles, in Germany, I did hear and understand, in all places, great bewailing and lamentation made, by reason of the destroying and burning of above four-score thousand of Martin Luther's books, entitled, 'His Last Divine Discourses.'

For after such time as God stirred up the spirit of Martin Luther to detect the corruptions and abuses of Popery, and to preach Christ, and clearly to set forth the simplicity of the Gospel, many kings, princes, and states, imperial cities, and Hans-towns, fell from the popish religion, and became Protestants, as their posterities still are, and remain to this very day.

And for the further advancement of the great work of reformation then begun, the aforesaid princes and the rest did then order, that the said Divine Discourses of Luther should forthwith be printed; and that every parish should have and receive one of the aforesaid printed books into every church throughout all their principalities and dominions, to be chained up, for the common people to read therein.

Upon which divine work, or Discourses, the Reformation, began before in Germany, was wonderfully promoted and increased, and spread both here in England and other countries besides.

' But afterwards it so fell out, that the pope then living, viz., Gregory XIII., understanding what great hurt and prejudice he and his popish religion had already received by reason of the said Luther's Divine Discourses, and also fearing that the same might bring further contempt and mischief upon himself, and upon the Popish Church, he therefore, to prevent the same, did fiercely stir up and instigate the emperor then in being, viz., Rudolphus II., to make an edict throughout the whole empire, that all the aforesaid printed books should be burnt; and also, that it should be death for any person to have or keep a copy thereof, but also to burn the same; which edict was speedily put in execution accordingly; insomuch that not one of all the said printed books, nor so much as any one copy of the same, could be found out nor heard of in any place.

Yet it pleased God, that, anno 1626, a German gentleman, named Casparus Van Sparr, with whom, in the time of my staying in Germany about king James's business, I became very familiarly known and acquainted, having occasion to build upon the old foundation of a house, wherein his grandfather dwelt at that time when the said edict was published in Germany for the burning of the aforesaid books, and digging deep into the ground, under the said old foundation, one of the said original books was there happily found, lying in a deep obscure hole, being wrapped in a strong linen cloth, which was waxed all over with beeswax, within and without; whereby the book was preserved fair, without any blemish.

And at the same time Ferdinandus II. being emperor in Germany, who was a severe enemy and persecutor of the Protestant religion, the aforesaid gentleman, and grandchild to him that had hidden the said books in that obscure hole, fearing that if the said emperor should get knowledge that one of the said books was yet forthcoming, and in his custody, whereby not only himself might be brought into trouble, but also the book in danger to be destroyed, as all the rest were so long before, and also calling me to mind, and knowing that I had the high Dutch tongue very perfect, did send the said original book over hither into England unto me; and therewith did write unto me a letter, wherein he related the passages of the preserving and finding out the said book.

And also he earnestly moved me in his letter, that for the advancement of God's glory, and of Christ's Church, I would take the pains to translate the said book, to the end, that *that* most excellent divine work of Luther might be brought again to light.

Whereupon I took the said book before me, and many times began to translate the same, but always I was hindered therein, being called upon about other business; insomuch that by no possible means I could remain by that work. Then, about six weeks after I had received the said book, it fell out, that I being in bed with my wife one night, between twelve and one of the clock, she being asleep, but myself yet awake, there appeared unto me an ancient man, standing at my bedside, arrayed all in white, having a long and broad white beard hanging down to his girdle steed, who taking me by my right ear, spake these words following unto me: 'Sirrah! will not you take time to translate that book which is sent unto you out of Germany? I will shortly provide for you both place and time to do it;' and then he vanished away out of my sight.

Whereupon being much thereby affrighted, I fell into an extreme sweat; insomuch, that my wife awaking, and finding me all over wet, she asked me what I ailed? I told her what I had seen and heard; but I never did heed nor regard visions nor dreams. And so the same fell soon out of my mind.

Then about a fortnight after I had seen that vision, on a Sunday, I went to Whitehall to hear the sermon; after which ended, I returned to my lodging, which was then at King-street, at Westminster, and sitting down to dinner with my wife, two messengers were sent from the whole council-board, with a warrant to carry me to the keeper of the Gatehouse, Westminster, there to be safely kept, until further order from the lords of the council; which was done without showing me any cause at all wherefore I was committed. Upon which said warrant I was kept ten whole years close prisoner, where I spent five years thereof about the translating of the said book; insomuch as I found the words very true which the old man, in the aforesaid vision, did say unto me—'I will shortly provide for you both place and time to translate it.'

Then after I had finished the said translation in the prison, the late archbishop of Canterbury, Dr. Laud, understanding that I had translated such a book, called 'Martin Luther's Divine Discourses,' sent unto me his chaplain, Dr. Bray, into the prison, with this message following:—

'Captain Bell, My lord grace of Canterbury hath sent me unto you, to tell you, that his grace hath understood that you have translated a book of Luther's; touching which book his grace, many years before, did hear of the burning of so many thousands in Germany, by the then emperor. His grace therefore doth desire you, that you would send unto him the said original book in Dutch, and also your translation; which, after his grace hath perused, shall be returned safely unto you.'

Whereupon I told Dr. Bray that I had taken a great deal of pains in translating the said book, and was very loath to part with it out of my hands; and, therefore, I desired him to excuse me to his grace, that I could not part from it; with which answer he at that time returned again to his master.

But the next day after he sent him unto me again, and bid him tell me that, upon his honour, the book should be as safe in his custody, if not safer than in mine own; for he would lock it up in his own cabinet, to the end no man might come unto it, but only himself. Thereupon, I knowing it would be a thing bootless for me to refuse the sending of them, by reason he was then of such great power, that he would have them *nolens volens*, I sent them both unto him. Then after he had kept them in his custody two months, and had daily read therein, he sent the said doctor unto me, to tell me that I had performed a work worthy of eternal memory, and that he had never read a more excellent divine work; yet saying that some things therein were fitting to be left out, and desired me not to think long, that he did not return them unto me so soon again. The reason was, because that the more he did read therein, the more desire he had to go on therewith; and so presenting me with ten livres in gold, he returned back again.

After which, when he had them in his custody one whole

year, and that I understood he had perused it all over, then I sent unto his grace, and humbly desired that his grace would be pleased to return me my books again. Whereupon he sent me word by the said Dr. Bray, that he had not as yet perused them so thoroughly over as he desired to do; then I stayed yet a year longer before I sent to him again.

In which time I heard for certain that it was concluded by the king and council that a parliament should forthwith be called; at which news I did much rejoice. And then I sent unto his grace an humble petition, and therein desired the returning of my book again; otherwise I told him I should be enforced to make it known, and to complain of him to the parliament, which was then coming on. Whereupon he sent unto me again safely both the said original book and my translation, and caused his chaplain, the said doctor, to tell me that he would make it known unto his majesty what an excellent piece of work I had translated, and that he would procure an order from his majesty to have the said translation printed, and to be dispersed throughout the whole kingdom, as it was in Germany, as he had heard thereof; and thereupon he presented me again with forty livres in gold.

And presently after I was set at liberty by warrant from the whole House of Lords, according to his majesty's direction in that behalf; but shortly afterwards the archbishop fell into his troubles, and was by the parliament sent unto the Tower, and afterwards beheaded. Insomuch that I could never since hear anything touching the printing of my book.

The House of Commons having then notice that I had translated the aforesaid book, they sent for me, and did appoint a committee to see it, and the translation, and diligently to make inquiry whether the translation did agree with the original or no; whereupon they desired me to bring the same before them, sitting then in the Treasury Chamber. And Sir Edward Dearing being chairman, said unto me, that he was acquainted with a learned minister beneficed in Essex, who had lived long in England, but was born in High Germany, in the Palatinate, named Mr. Paul Amiraut, whom the committee sending for, desired him to take both the original and my translation into his custody, and diligently to compare them together, and to make report unto the said committee whether he found that I had rightly and truly translated it according to the original; which report he made accordingly, and they being satisfied therein, referred it to two of the assembly, Mr. Charles Herle and Mr. Edward Corbet, desiring them diligently to peruse the same, and to make report unto them if they thought it fitting to be printed and published.

Whereupon they made report, dated the 10th of November, 1646, that they found it to be an excellent divine work, worthy the light and publishing, especially in regard that Luther, in the said Discourses, did revoke his opinion, which he formerly held, touching Consubstantiation in the Sacrament. Whereupon the House of Commons, the 24th of February, 1646, did give order for the printing thereof.

Thus having been lately desired to set down in writing the relation of the passages abovesaid concerning the said book, as well for the satisfaction of judicious and godly Christians as for the conservation of the perpetual memory of God's extraordinary providence in the miraculous preservation of the aforesaid Divine Discourses, and now bringing them again to light, I have done the same according to the plain truth thereof, not doubting but they will prove a notable advantage of God's glory, and the good and edification of the whole Church, and an unspeakable consolation of every particular member of the same.

THE LORD'S SUPPER DEGENERATES INTO THE MASS.

In the Primitive Church, they who attended the Lord's Supper brought oblations of bread, wine, and other necessaries, for the use of the altar, the clergy, and the poor. The ministry then had no other provision, and what was given on these occasions was for the use of the clergy in general. When other arrangements were made for their maintenance, these oblations fell off. But about the eighth century it would seem that a custom arose among those who still made oblations (the richer classes, we presume) of offering *money* at the Lord's Supper, instead of the articles formerly in use. The money, however, was still intended for the same excellent purpose as the original oblations. But, after a time, the officiating priest learned to rob his brethren and the poor, and to appropriate the money to his own use. These practices were, no doubt, severely reprobated at first, but they continued, and matters stood thus. As the money paid went to the officiating priest, the layman who gave it began to consider that he paid it *for* the celebration of the Lord's Supper. And the richer laity soon wished to have mass said at the most convenient times and places. The Church, to gratify them, ordained priests by wholesale, who were mere mass-readers, ranked no higher than servants, and officiated when their lord pleased. But when they were not in the houses of nobility, they celebrated mass for money whenever called on. Nay, they soon learned never to do it without money. This went to such lengths that it was found necessary to forbid the perpetual celebration of mass. One council restrained the priests thrice a day, and another, with still higher feelings, forbade them to receive money at all. They would say masses of the Trinity, and of the archangel Michael, etc., as they called them, to find where hidden things were to be found, etc. They frequently ordered penitents at confession to have masses said and paid for; and the masses were of very different prices. A *sung* mass naturally cost more than a *said* one. A mass at the altar of a favourite saint, or where a particular relic was kept, was sure to bring a high price.

Then came all the iniquities of masses for the dead. The *Requiem*, the service on the thirtieth day after the death (the *Trental*), and the anniversary of it, were all fruitful sources of profit. But, most of all, the priests were enriched by the perpetual foundations for masses to release the souls of the departed from purgatory. Then the popes began the system of granting *privileges* to altars and to priests. A mass, for instance, said at a given privileged altar might release a soul from purgatory at once, and not merely shorten its stay there. For such a benefit it was reasonable that a higher price should be charged than for gaining an indulgence for a few hundred days or years. The priesthood, in a word, made use of all the means in their hands to excite the hopes and fears of the superstitious; and the fruit of their exertions soon appeared in the numberless *foundations* for masses to be said for the benefit of the departed. They were, indeed, so enormous in number, that notwithstanding it was alike the policy and the wish of the Church of Rome to create large bodies of priests, who were to be maintained principally from this source, it became utterly impossible for them to say all the masses provided for by these pious foundations.—*Foreign Review.*

PROPHECIES OF THE REFORMATION.

In his 'Acts and Monuments,' Foxe tells us of 'divers sundry and good men' who, ' long before the time of Luther, prophesied of this reformation of the Church.'

Among the chief of these was John Huss, who foretold that a change would come in a hundred years. Then, while lying in prison at Constance, he dreamed a remarkable dream, *e.g.*, 'I pray you expound to me the dream which I had this night. I saw that in my church at Bethlehem, whereof I was parson, they desired and laboured to abolish all the images of Christ, and did abolish them. I, the next day following, rose up, and saw many other painters, who painted both the same, and many more images, and more fair, which I was glad to behold. Whereupon the painters with the great multitude of people said, Now let the bishops and priests come and put out these images if they can. At which thing done much people rejoiced in Bethlehem, and I with them. And rising up, I felt myself to laugh.' The meaning of this, according to Huss, was, 'The same life of Christ shall be painted up again by more preachers much better than I, and after a much better sort, so that a great number of people shall rejoice thereat.'

Jerome of Prague, who was burned in 1416, also said to his persecutors, 'I cite you all to answer before the Most High and Just Judge, after a hundred years.'

Then a monk named John Hilton is mentioned by Melancthon as having prophesied that one would appear in 1516 'who should utterly subvert all monkery.'

Theodoric, Bishop of Crotia, who wrote early in the 15th century, said 'that the see of Rome, which is so horribly polluted with simony and avarice, shall fall, and no more oppress men with tyranny as it hath done.' The Church was to be subverted by its own subjects, after which true piety was to flourish in the world as it had not done before.

There were many similar predictions; but beyond all Foxe says 'that in the year of our Lord 1516 (which was the same year when Martin Luther began), Pope Leo X. did create one and thirty cardinals; in which year and day of their creation, there fell a tempest of thunder and lightning in Rome, which so struck the church where the cardinals were made, that it removed the little child Jesus out of the lap of His mother, and the keys out of St. Peter's hand; which thing many then did interpret to signify and foreshow the subversion and alteration of the see of Rome.' There had been discovered a plot got up by certain members of the Sacred College to poison the Pope; and while one cardinal was executed and several others were imprisoned, this extraordinary stretch of authority in creating such a number of new members at one time shows his extreme anxiety to checkmate the conspirators. The most splendid and ostentatious of popes, he was at first amused at Luther's actions; but although he only lived to see middle age,—he died in 1523,—he lived long enough to see the Reformation firmly rooted in the German nation.

LUTHER AND TETZEL.

The friars of St. Augustine, Luther's own order, though addicted with no less obsequiousness than the other monastic fraternities to the papal see, gave no check to the publication of his uncommon opinions. Luther had by his piety and learning acquired extraordinary authority among his brethren: he professed the highest regard for the authority of the pope; his professions were at that time sincere; and as a secret enmity, excited by interest and emulation, subsists among all the monastic orders in the Romish Church, the Augustinians were highly pleased with his invectives against the Dominicans, and hoped to see them exposed to the hatred and scorn of the people. Nor was his sovereign, the Elector of Saxony, the wisest prince at that time in Germany, dissatisfied with this obstruction which Luther threw in the way of the publication of indulgences He secretly encouraged the attempt, and flattered himself that this dispute among the ecclesiastics themselves might give some check to the exactions of the Court of Rome, which the secular prince had long, though without success, been endeavouring to oppose.—*Robertson*.

LEO X. AND INDULGENCES.

It was from causes seemingly fortuitous, and from a source very inconsiderable, that all the mighty effects of the Reformation flowed. Leo X., when raised to the papal throne, found the revenues of the Church exhausted by the vast projects of his two ambitious predecessors, Alexander VI. and Julius II.; and his own temper, naturally liberal and enterprizing, rendered him incapable of that severe and patient economy which the situation of his finances required. On the contrary, his schemes for aggrandizing the family of Medici, his love of splendour, his taste for pleasure, and his magnificence in rewarding men of genius, involved him daily in new expenses, in order to provide a fund for which every device that the fertile invention of priests had fallen upon to drain the credulous multitude was tried. Among others, he had recourse to a sale of indulgences. According to the doctrine of the Romish Church, all the good works of the saints, over and above those which were necessary towards their own justification, together with the infinite merits of Jesus Christ, are deposited in one inexhaustible treasury. The keys of this were committed to St. Peter and to his successors the popes, who may open it at pleasure, and, by transferring a portion of this superabundant merit to any particular person for a sum of money, may convey to him either the pardon of his own sins, or a release for any one in whom he is interested from the pains of purgatory. Such indulgences were first invented in the eleventh century by Urban II., as a recompense for those who were in person upon the wild enterprize of conquering the Holy Land. They were afterwards granted to those who hired a soldier for that purpose; and, in process of time, were bestowed on such as gave money for accomplishing any pious work enjoined by the pope. Julius II. had bestowed indulgences on all who contributed towards building the Church of St. Peter at Rome; and as Leo was carrying on that magnificent and expensive fabric, his grant was founded on the same pretence.

The promulgating of these indulgences in Germany, together with a share in the profits arising from the sale of them, was assigned to Albert, Elector of Mentz and Archbishop of Magdeburg, who, as his chief agent for retailing them in Saxony, employed Tetzel, a Dominican friar, of licentious morals, but of an active spirit, and remarkable for his noisy and popular eloquence. He, assisted by the monks of his order, executed the commission with great zeal and success, but with little discretion or decency; and though by magnifying excessively the benefit of their indulgences, and by disposing of them at a very low price, they carried on for some time an extensive and lucrative traffic among the credulous multitude, the extravagance of their assertions and the irregularities in their conduct came at last to give general offence. The princes and nobles were irritated at seeing their vassals drained of so much wealth, in order to replenish the treasury of a profuse pontiff. Men of piety regretted the delusion of the people, who, being taught to rely for the pardon of their sins on the indulgences which they purchased, did not think it incumbent on them either to abound in faith or to practise holiness. Even the most unthinking were shocked at the scandalous behaviour of Tetzel and his associates, who often squandered in drunkenness, gaming, and low debauchery those sums which were piously bestowed in hopes of obtaining eternal happiness; and all began to wish that some check were given to this commerce, no less detrimental to society than destructive to religion.

Such was the favourable juncture, and so disposed were the minds of his countrymen to listen to his discourses, when Martin Luther first began to call in question the efficacy of indulgences, and to declaim against the vicious lives and false doctrines of those who promulgated them.—*Robertson.*

TETZEL ADVANCES THE CAUSE.

In the second chapter of Book III. of his *History of the Reformation*, D'Aubigné relates several anecdotes which show that this shameless trafficker in indulgences really opened the people's eyes to the true character of the Romish Church. At Magdeburg a wealthy widow asked her confessor about the subject, and was told that God forgave without selling pardons. On hearing of that decision Tetzel said that his opponent ought to be put out of the way.

The main bulk of the people, however, were too blinded by superstition to raise objections; and accordingly they gathered around the red cross which the impostor usually erected wherever he took his stand in a town, and gave him plentifully of their cash. Such was the man's grasping avarice, however, that, even after an unusual run of luck, he would invent some audacious story to work upon the people's emotions. One of these was forthcoming at Zwichau, where he assured his astonished auditors that during the night he had heard groans coming from the burial-ground—the appeal, as Tetzel explained, of a soul in purgatory crying to be delivered. In response to the pathetic appeals of the adventurer the faithful gave fresh supplies of money, which was spent in the evening on an entertainment.

In one instance, at least, Tetzel was caught in his own trap. He sold one gentleman an indulgence for sins to be committed —a free pardon—and the purchaser waylaid the inquisitor in a wood, and after giving him a mild chastisement with a stick, carried off the chest of money. The injured man carried his cause before the authorities; but when the Elector saw the document which the offender possessed, the case was dismissed. These men were the master-swindlers of Rome, who taught the people that the papacy was an imposture. 'Please God, I'll make a holt in his drum,' said Luther when he first heard of Tetzel; and when his people at Wittenberg showed him their licenses to sin, his answer was, 'Unless you repent, you will all perish.' Tetzel stamped with rage when he heard of this opposition, which was destined to broaden and deepen, and he declared he had the Pope's orders to burn all heretics.

LUTHER AND LEO X.

As people judged in the sixteenth century, Leo X. was the child of fortune; and certainly no king of Babylon was ever prouder of the splendour of his empire than he, nor more confident in the royal ability to keep the great inheritance intact. His father, Lorenzo de Medici, was called the Magnificent; and Leo became a priest at seven years of age; he held several benefices a year later, and at thirteen became a cardinal. He was a politician more than a divine, his ambition to regain states to the papal see which had been lost having been inordinate. Thus while his cause was failing in one direction it was gaining in another. Luther repelled the great Pope's assaults by calling him heretic and apostate, Antichrist and blasphemer; but Leo was absorbed with other matters than theology, and never lived to realize the full meaning of the reformer's language and tactics. 'Could I recover Parma and Piacenza for the Church, I would willingly lay down my life,' he once exclaimed; and his joy was boundless when, on a chill, malarious November evening, the news arrived that the states mentioned had returned to their allegiance. On the first of December following the Pope died with a suddenness which led many to suspect that he had been poisoned. At this time the Reformation was sweeping onward, but the papal exchequer was empty. 'Among all the individuals who have attracted the attention of mankind,' says Roscoe, ' there is perhaps no one whose chaacter has stood in so doubtful a light as that of Leo X.' 'The best possible pope for the age that was going out,' says another, 'he was the worst possible for the age that was coming in: hence the splendours of his administration were ephemeral, and its disasters lasting.'

OPEN-AIR PREACHERS.

While the Reformation was dispersing the fogs of Popery, open-air preachers, next to the printing-press, were principal agents in enlightening the people, who were perishing for lack of knowledge. There were doubtless many itinerants of whose names we have never heard, men who spent themselves in zealous and heroic service for no earthly reward. On the Continent, in the time of Luther, the crowds were sometimes too great for the largest cathedral to hold them; and things similar to what occurred elsewhere took place in England and Scotland. One of the most striking, affecting, and, we may hope, effective open-air addresses ever delivered was that given by the martyr Wishart at the gate of Dundee, at the time the plague was raging within the city, when the stricken and the healthy stood apart while listening to the words of life and truth.

In the ancient city of London open-air preaching was a recognised institution; and, as all readers of history are aware, the two chief stations were St. Paul's Cross and the ancient Spital Cross near Bethnal Green, the latter having disappeared during the tumult of the civil wars. There, until as late as the seventeenth century, the citizens were accustomed to keep their Hospital Sunday by listening to learned discourses and making collections for the sick. The old custom of preaching at this place, and beneath the shadow of the cathedral, is well known to all readers of the archæology of the city; and it is well explained by the Professor of Ecclesiastical History at King's College, London, in 'Classic Preachers of the English Church.'

'It is said to have been for a long time a custom on Good Friday, in the afternoon, for some learned men, by appointment of the prelates, to preach a sermon at Paul's Cross, treating of Christ's passion. On the next three Easter holidays, other learned men, by a like appointment, used to preach in the afternoon at the said Spital on the article of Christ's resurrection; and then, on the Sunday after Easter, before noon, another learned man at Paul's

Cross was to make a rehearsal of these four sermons, either commending or reproving, as was thought convenient; and he was then to make a sermon himself, which in all were five sermons in one.'

In those days, Spital fields were really what their name implied, so that the spot must have been an open and breezy area, where people might congregate without fear of inhaling the fever-breeding effluvia common to St. Paul's Churchyard. Only men of position were employed in such service, and 'A sermon preached at the Spital' may frequently be met with in old books.

In old times, Paul's Cross, especially, was a centre of information as well as of religious teaching; and hence intelligent and inquisitive citizens would almost have preferred neglect of business to the missing of a sermon on a high occasion. In many instances the divines were inspired by the ruling powers until their utterances were of a semi-official character which the people well knew how to interpret. In 1461, on the 4th of March, we even find the Bishop of Exeter proving the title of Edward IV. to the crown in opposition to the claim of his vanquished rival, Henry VI.

Other memorable scenes in connection with the preachers who did duty at this famous station were sometimes witnessed during the dark midnight century which preceded the sunrise of the Reformation. We find that one of the more notable divines who fell into trouble on account of teaching evangelical doctrine at Paul's Cross was Reynold Peacock, Bishop of Chichester. According to the quaint expression of Foxe, he was 'afflicted by the Pope's prelates for his faith and profession of the Gospel.' In Hall's 'Chronology' we are also told how 'this man began to move questions, not privately, but openly in the Universities, concerning the Annates or Peter-pence, and other jurisdictions and authorities pertaining to the See of Rome; and not only put forth the questions, but declared his mind and opinion in the same; wherefore he was for this cause abjured at Paul's Cross.' In those fearful days a faithful preacher was certain, sooner or later, to come to a martyr's end; and this appears to have been the case with this reformer, who stoutly defended himself before the Archbishop's court; then, under pressure and through fear of torture, recanted, only to repent in due course of his timidity, and to be again committed to prison, 'where,' says the martyrologist, ' it is uncertain whether he was oppressed with privy and secret tyranny, and there obtained the crown of martyrdom or no.' The probability is that he was murdered in prison.

In this same century it was common for persons accused of heresy to be compelled to do penance during sermon time at Paul's Cross. Thus, speaking of the 17th of January, 1496, Foxe tells of two men who ' bare faggots before the procession of Paul's, and stood before the preacher in the time of his sermon. And upon the Sunday following stood other two men at Paul's Cross all the sermon time; the one garnished with painted and written papers, the other bearing a faggot on his neck. After that in Lent season, upon Passion Sunday, one Hugh Glover bare a faggot before the procession of Paul's, and after, with a faggot, stood before the preacher all the sermon while at Paul's Cross. And on the Sunday next following, four men stood, and did their open penance at Paul's, as is aforesaid, in the sermon time; and many of their books were burnt before them, at the Cross.'

In the reign of Edward VI., or on September 1st, 1549, Bonner, Bishop of London, was appointed by the Government to preach at Paul's Cross; and because he 'did spend most part of his sermon about the carnal and papistical presence of Christ's body and blood in the sacrament of the altar, and also, contrary thereunto, did not only slenderly touch the rest of his articles, but of a rebellious and wilful carefulness did utterly leave out unspoken the whole last article, concerning the as effectual and as lawful authority of the King's Highness,' he was deprived and imprisoned.

Four years later, or in August 1553, when Bonner was restored to his see and honours, another scene characteristic of the times was witnessed by a large crowd around the old Cross. The restored bishop embraced the opportunity of crowing over his opponents; and for that purpose appointed that Master Bourn, a canon of Paul's, should preach to the people. To display his wit as well as his learning, 'Master Bourn' somewhat unadvisedly selected the same text which his patron Bonner had chosen four years before; and as Bonner then insulted the Government by omitting to support the royal supremacy, Bourn now outraged the public sentiment by reviling the memory of Edward VI. The Lord Mayor and his attendants feared the results, and not without good reason; for after a wave of angry murmurs had passed over the crowd, a gleaming dagger, hurled by a strong hand, was within an inch or two of striking down the preacher, who, however, retreated with precipitance, shielded by the future martyr, Thomas Bradford. This disturbance naturally had the effect of rendering the service unpopular, and timid people stayed away from the out-door services, especially when, on the following Sabbath, the Queen's guards were in attendance to protect the preacher for the day. And then, according to the old chronicler, 'when quiet men withdrew themselves from the sermon, order was taken by the mayor that the ancients of all companies should be present, lest the preacher should be discouraged by his small auditory.'

LUTHER IN THE WARTBURG.

The sudden removal of Luther to this old stronghold, while he was returning from the Diet of Worms, forms one of the most singular chapters in the history of providence with which readers of Church history are familiar. The reformer left the city at the instigation of his protector the Elector, who foresaw the storm which the Pope's bull and the action of Charles V. would occasion. Luther was taken prisoner in a friendly way in a wood just after he had left his parents; and while they allowed others to escape, the horsemen obliged their chief prisoner to assume the disguise of a cavalier. They took away his robe and gave him a false beard; and apparently willing to second the wishes of his captors, Luther allowed his hair to grow. 'You would hardly know me; indeed, I scarcely know myself,' he remarked; but all the while he enjoyed abundant liberty, and worked with the pen in a quieter and more effective manner than would perhaps have been possible had he been at large in the world. The mark in the wall of his study, caused, as tradition says, by the inkstand which the Reformer threw at the head of the evil one who appeared to him, is still shown. People said that his enemies had seized him; so that while he was really being sheltered from persecution by friends, the popular feeling his captivity engendered stimulated the progress of the Reformation generally.

He passed some of his time in the neighbouring woods in shooting game; but growing weary of the pastime of worrying innocent wild animals, he longed to be again at his legitimate work. Towards the end of his retirement he was staying at an inn near Jena, when he was joined by a student *en route* to Wittenberg, and several traders. While still unrecognized, Luther paid the whole reckoning; and it was not until the student departed that the party were bewildered by learning who had been their entertainer. They made many excuses for having behaved foolishly and so on, but, though now recognized, Luther did not openly disclose his name.

LUTHER AND THE FUGITIVE NUNS.

In the year 1523 the Reformer issued a work directed against the vows of celibacy taken by monks and nuns. This work soon found its way into some of the religious houses; and one of its effects was that nine nuns, who had escaped from a convent at Nimptschen, appeared at Wittenberg on the 5th of April to ask for advice. While strongly denouncing the custom of which they were the victims, Luther heartily sympathised with his visitors, and one of the nine, Catherine von Boro, afterwards became his wife. It appears that the girls' mode of escape was as marvellous as their change of view in regard to their religious obligations. It was determined to restore them to their parents, or, in the event of their being refused admission at home, friends promised to take care of them. Kate was a gentleman's daughter, and twenty-six years of age when she married, or sixteen years younger than her husband.

When Catherine was left a widow in 1547, she remained for a year at Wittenberg, but left the town for a time after its surrender to Charles V. When the place was restored to the Elector she returned, but left again in 1552, in consequence of the plague. She resolved on ending her days at Torgau, but, while travelling thither, the horses became restive, and being badly hurt, the widow died just before

Christmas in the year named. She appears to have been well provided for by friends, so that the stories about her and the children not having had sufficient bread appear to be quite in keeping with the other stories, invented by the papists, concerning the portents which happened at the time of the death of Luther himself.

LEO THE TENTH'S BULL.

When the bull of condemnation arrived in Germany, it found a whole nation in a state of ebullition. At Erfurt, the students took it from the booksellers' shops, tore it in pieces, and threw it into the water, saying, with more vehemence than point, 'It is a bull; let us see if it can swim.' Luther at once sent forth a pamphlet, *Against the execrable Bull of Antichrist*. On the 10th December, 1520, he publicly burnt the Pope's anathema at the gates of the town, amid the exulting shouts of the people; and on the same day wrote to Spalatin, his ordinary medium of communication with the Elector, 'This day, the 10th of December, in the year 1520, at nine o'clock in the morning, were burnt at Wittenberg, at the east gate, opposite the church of the Holy Cross, all the Pope's books, the Rescripts, the Decretals of Clement VI., the Extravagants, the new bull of Leo X., the *Somma Angelica*, the Chrysopasus of Eck, and some other productions of his and of Emser's. This is something new, I wot.' He adds in the report he drew up on the subject, 'If any one asks me why I act thus, I will answer him, that it is an old custom to burn bad books. The apostles burned books to the value of five thousand deniers.'

According to the tradition, he said, in throwing the book of the Decretals into the flames, ''Thou hast afflicted the holy of the Lord : may eternal fire afflict thee, and consume thee.'

All this was, indeed, as Luther said, something new. Hitherto most of the sects and heresies that had arisen from time to time had formed themselves in secret, and were only too happy if their existence remained unknown; but here was a simple monk placing himself on an equality with the Pope, and constituting himself the judge of the Church's supreme head. The chain of old tradition was thus broken, its continuity destroyed, the seamless robe torn.—*Michelet's 'Life of Luther,'* in *Bohn's Standard Library.*

LUTHER AND THE POPE.

Our manner of life is as evil as is that of the papists. Wickliffe and Huss assailed the immoral conduct of papists; but I chiefly oppose and resist their doctrine; I affirm roundly and plainly, that they preach not the truth. To this am I called; I take the goose by the neck, and set the knife to its throat. When I can show that the papists' doctrine is false, which I have shown, then I can easily prove that their manner of life is evil. For when the Word remains pure, the manner of life, though something therein be amiss, will be pure also. The Pope has taken away the pure Word and doctrine, and brought in another word and doctrine, which he has hanged upon the Church. I shook all Popedom with this one point, that I teach uprightly, and mix up nothing else. We must press the doctrine onwards, that breaks the neck of the Pope. Therefore the prophet Daniel rightly pictured the Pope, that he would be a king that would do according to his own will, that is, would regard neither spirituality nor temporality, but say roundly, 'Thus and thus will I have it. For the Pope derives his institution neither from divine nor from human right, but is a self-chosen human creature and intruder. Therefore the pope must needs confess that he governs neither by divine nor human command. Daniel calls him a god, *Maosim;* he had almost spoken it plainly out, and said *Mass*, which word is written, Deut. xxxvi. St. Paul read Daniel thoroughly, and uses nearly his words, where he says, The son of perdition will exalt himself above all that is called God, or that is worshipped, etc., 2 Thess. ii.

Whence comes it that the popes pretend 'tis they who form the Church, when all the while they are bitter enemies of the Church, and have no knowledge, certainly no comprehension, of the Holy Gospel? Pope, cardinals, bishops, not a soul of them has read the Bible; 'tis a book unknown to them. They are a pack of guzzling, stuffing wretches, rich, wallowing in wealth and laziness, resting secure in their power, and never, for a moment, thinking of accomplishing God's will. The Sadducees were infinitely more pious than the papists; from whose holiness God preserve us. May He preserve us, too, from security, which engenders ingratitude, contempt of God, blasphemy, and the persecution of divine things.

There are many that think I am too fierce against Popedom; on the contrary, I complain that I am, alas! too mild; I wish I could breathe out lightning against Pope and Popedom, and that every word were a thunderbolt.—*Table Talk, Hazlitt's Translation.*

LUTHER AND THE MONKS.

Some one asked how happened it St. James had been at Compostella. Dr. Martin replied, Just as it happens that the papists reckon up sixteen apostles, while Jesus Christ had but twelve. In many places, the papists boast of having some of the milk of the Virgin Mary, and of the hay in which Christ lay in the cradle. A Franciscan boasted he had some of this hay in a wallet he carried with him. A roguish fellow took out the hay, and put some charcoal in its place. When the monk came to show the people his hay, he found only the wood. However, he was at no loss: 'My brethren,' said he, 'I brought out the wrong wallet with me, and so cannot show you the hay; but here is some of the wood that St. Lawrence was grilled upon.'

Kings and princes coin money only out of metals, but the Pope coins money out of everything—indulgences, ceremonies, dispensations, pardons; 'tis all fish comes to his net. 'Tis only baptism escapes him, for children come into the world without clothes to be stolen or teeth to be drawn.

In Italy, the monasteries are very wealthy. There are but three or four monks to each; the surplus of their revenues goes to the Pope and his cardinals.

A gentleman being at the point of death, a monk from the next convent came to see what he could pick up, and said to the gentleman, 'Sir, will you give so and so to our monastery?' The dying man, unable to speak, replied by a nod of the head; whereupon the monk, turning to the gentleman's son, said, 'You see your father makes us this bequest.' The son said to the father, 'Sir, is it your pleasure that I kick this monk downstairs?' The dying man nodded as before; and the son forthwith drove the monk out of doors.

They once showed here, at Wittenberg, the drawers of St. Joseph and the breeches of St. Francis. The bishop of Mayence boasted he had a gleam of the flame of Moses' bush. At Compostella they exhibit the standard of the victory that Jesus Christ gained over death and the devil. The crown of thorns is shown in several places.

The cuckoo takes the eggs out of the linnet's nest, and puts her own in their place. When the young cuckoos grow big, they eat the linnet. The cuckoo, too, has a great antipathy towards the nightingale. The Pope is a cuckoo; he robs the Church of her true eggs, and substitutes in their place his greedy cardinals, who devour the mother that has nourished them. The Pope, too, cannot abide that nightingale, the preaching and singing of the true doctrine. —*Ibid.*

LUTHER AND THE PROPHETS.

In 1521 a man from Zwickau called upon me, of the name of Marcus. He was agreeable enough in his manners, and very courteous, but frivolous and shallow-pated. As I found he went on talking about things entirely foreign to the Scriptures, I interrupted him by saying that I acknowledged only the Word of God, and that if he sought to set up anything else, he must, in the first place, prove his mission by miracles. 'Miracles!' said he, 'you shall have miracles in seven years. God Himself could not deprive me of my faith,' he added; 'I can tell at once whether a person is one of the elect or not.' He then went on with a long rigmarole about *talent that must not be hidden*, and *unravelling*, and *tedium*, and *expecting*, and what not. I asked him what all this meant, and who understood him when he talked in this manner. He replied that he only preached to believing and skilled disciples. 'How know you that they are skilled?' asked I. 'I have only to look at them,' he replied; 'I can see their *talent* at a glance.' 'Well, my friend,' I rejoined, 'what *talent* do you see in me, for instance?' 'You are as yet only in the first degree of mobility,' he said, 'but there will come a time when you will be in the first degree of immobility, like myself.' Thereupon I cited to him several texts of Scripture, and so we parted. Some time after he wrote me a letter very friendly in its tone, and full of exhortations; I returned for an answer simply this, *Good-bye to thee, dear Marcus.*

On a later occasion I was visited by a turner, who also described himself as a prophet. He met me just at the door as I was going out, and accosting me in a confident tone, said, 'Mr. Doctor, I bring you a message from my father.' 'Who is your father?' I asked. 'Jesus Christ,' he replied. 'He is our common father,' said I; 'what did He order you to announce to me?' 'I was to announce to you, on the part of my father, that God is angry with the whole world.' 'Who told you this?' 'Yesterday, as I was going out of the Koswick gate, I saw in the air a little cloud of fire, a sufficient proof that God is angry.' He then told me of another sign: 'In a deep sleep,' said he, 'I saw a party of drunkards sitting round a table, crying one to another, " Drink! drink !" Above them was extended, menacingly, the hand of God. All at once, one of them threw a cup of beer at me, and I awoke.' 'Listen to me, my friend,' said I, calmly; 'you must not make a jest in this manner of the name and commands of God;' and I proceeded to reprimand him severely. When he saw how I took the affair up, he went away in a rage, muttering to himself, 'And yet there are some people who do not see what a fool this Luther is !'

Another time I had to do in the same way with a man from the Low Countries. He came and wanted to dispute with me about all sorts of things, *down to fire inclusively,* as he said. When I saw what a poor ignorant creature it was, I said to him, 'Hadn't we better dispute over a can or two of beer?' This quite irritated him, and he went away. The devil is a haughty spirit, and can't bear to be treated with contempt in any way.

Maître-Stiefel came to Wittenberg, and, in a private interview with Dr. Luther, gave him, set forth in twenty articles, his opinion respecting the day of judgment. He considered that it would be on St. Luke's day. He was told to remain silent on the subject, and by no means to give forth his opinions publicly. He was very nettled at this. 'Dear Doctor,' said he, 'I am astonished that you should forbid my preaching this matter, that you yourself should not believe what I tell you. I feel certain that I ought not to remain silent thereupon, though I should speak unwillingly, after what you have said.' Luther replied, 'Dear sir, you managed very well to remain silent upon the subject for ten years, under the reign of Popery; you may well keep quiet respecting it for the little time that remains.' 'But this morning, early,' urged Stiefel, 'as I was on my way, I saw a very fine rainbow, and I at once thought of the coming of Christ.' 'There will be no rainbow in the case,' returned Luther; 'in one instant, one enormous thunderbolt will destroy every living creature as one tremendous blast from the trump will awaken us all at the same moment; for it is no gentle breathing on a pipe that can make itself heard by those who are asleep in the tomb.'—*Translated by Michelet.*

LUTHER'S BIBLE.

It has been said of the Reformer's own copy of the *Biblia Sacra Germanica*, published in two vols., folio, in 1541:—'This copy must excite the deepest interest and most lively emotions in the breast of every Protestant. The manuscript notes prefixed to each volume seem to introduce us to the closest acquaintance of a bright assemblage of Reformers. We find Luther exhibiting in the privacy of retirement the same unshaken confidence in the Deity under the persecutions he was suffering as he nobly evinced in public. In a manuscript note in the second volume he transcribes the verse of the Twenty-third Psalm, and then adds a passage strongly indicative of his own exalted ideas of faith. He appears to have bequeathed this copy to Bugenhagen, who, on the 19th of May, 1556, wrote in it a pious distich and some religious sentiments, in which he denies the necessity of profane learning. The illustrious Melancthon was its next possessor. He writes a remarkable passage relative to the final consummation of all things, and intimates his belief that the end of the world is not far distant, adding, "May Jesus Christ, the Son of Almighty God, preserve and protect His poor flock, etc., 1557." The same year it passed into the hands of George Major, another Reformer, who has written in it a compendious exposition of his faith, signed with his name. In this version Luther omits the contested verse in St. John's Epistle, relative to the three heavenly witnesses.'

When he was engaged in translating the Scriptures, Luther referred to the extreme difficulty he experienced in making 'Jew writers speak German.' He added that they struggled against 'giving up their beautiful language to our barbarous idiom,' and then compared the process to trying to make a nightingale sing like the cuckoo.

THE BIBLE AND THE REFORMATION.

Dr. Jonas Justus remarked at Luther's table, 'There is in the Holy Scripture a wisdom so profound, that no man may thoroughly study it or comprehend it.' 'Ay,' said

Luther, 'we must ever remain scholars here; we cannot sound the depth of one single verse in Scripture; we get hold but of the A B C, and that imperfectly. Who can so exalt himself as to comprehend this one line of St. Peter, "Rejoice, inasmuch as ye are partakers of Christ's sufferings"? Here St. Peter would have us rejoice in our deepest misery and trouble, like as a child kisses the rod.'

I have many times essayed thoroughly to investigate the Ten Commandments, but at the very outset, 'I am the Lord thy God,' I stuck fast; that very one word, 'I,' put me to a *non-plus*. He that has but one word of God before him, and out of that word cannot make a sermon, can never be a preacher. I am well content that I know however little of what God's Word is, and take good heed not to murmur at my small knowledge.

No greater mischief can happen to a Christian people than to have God's word taken from them, or falsified, so that they no longer have it pure and clear. God grant we and our descendants be not witnesses of such a calamity.— *Table Talk.**

THE WORTH OF THE BIBLE.

Some one asked Luther for his Psalter, which was old and ragged, promising to give him a new one in exchange; but the doctor refused, because he was used to his own old copy, adding, 'A local memory is very useful, and I have weakened mine in translating the Bible.'

Oh! how great and glorious a thing it is to have before

---

* The extracts from the 'Table Talk' are from William Hazlitt's translation, published by Messrs. George Bell and Sons, in Bohn's Standard Library, a performance which leaves nothing more to be desired on the part of English readers.

one the Word of God! With that we may at all times feel joyous and secure; we need never be in want of consolation, for we see before us, in all its brightness, the pure and right way. He who loses sight of the Word of God falls into despair; the voice of heaven no longer sustains him; he follows only the disorderly tendency of his heart, and of world vanity, which lead him on to his destruction.

Before the Gospel came among us, men used to undergo endless labour and cost, and make dangerous journeys to St. James of Compostella, and where not, in order to seek the favour of God. But now that God, in His Word, brings His favour unto us gratis, confirming it with His sacraments, saying, *Unless ye believe, ye shall surely perish*, we will have none of it.

Forsheim said that the first of the five books of Moses was not written by Moses himself. Dr. Luther replied, 'What matters it, even though Moses did not write it? It is, nevertheless, Moses's book, wherein is exactly related the creation of the world. Such futile objections as these should not be listened to.'

The ungodly papists prefer the authority of the Church far above God's Word; a blasphemy abominable and not to be endured; wherewith, void of all shame and piety, they spit in God's face. Truly, God's patience is exceeding great, in that they be not destroyed; but so it always has been.—*Ibid.*

LUTHER AT AUGSBURG.

The Imperial Diet held at Augsburg, 1530, is worthy of all praise; for then and thence came the Gospel among the people in other countries, contrary to the will and expectation both of Emperor and Pope. God appointed the Imperial

Diet at Augsburg, to the end the Gospel should be spread further abroad and planted. They over-climbed themselves at Augsburg, for the papists openly approved there of our doctrine. Before that Diet was held, the papists had made the Emperor believe that our doctrine was altogether frivolous; and that when he came to the Diet, he should see them put us all to silence, so that none of us should be able to speak a word in the defence of our religion; but it fell out far otherwise; for we openly and freely confessed the Gospel before the Emperor and the whole empire, and confounded our adversaries in the highest degree. The Emperor discriminated understandly and discreetly, and carried himself princely in this cause of religion; he found us far otherwise than the papists had informed him; and that we were not ungodly people, leading most wicked and detestable lives, and teaching against the first and second tables of the ten commandments of God. For this cause the Emperor sent our confession and apology to all the universities; his council also delivered their opinions, and said, 'If the doctrine of these men be against the holy Christian faith, then his imperial majesty should suppress it with all his power. But if it be only against ceremonies and abuses, as it appears to be, then it should be referred to the consideration and judgment of learned people, or good and wise counsel.'

Oh! God's Word is powerful; the more it is persecuted, the more and further it spreads itself abroad. I would fain the papist confutation might appear to the world; for I would set upon that old torn and tattered skin, and so baste it, that the stitches thereof should fly about; but they shun the light. This time twelvemonth no man would have given a farthing for the Protestants, so sure the ungodly Papists were of us. For when my most gracious lord and master, the Prince Elector of Saxony, came before other princes to the Diet, the papists marvelled much thereat, for they verily believed he would not have appeared, because, as they imagined, his cause was too bad and foul to be brought before the light. But what fell out? Even this, that in their greatest security they were overwhelmed with the utmost fear and affright, because the Prince Elector, like an upright prince, appeared so early at Augsburg. The popish princes swiftly posted away to Inspruck, where they held serious counsel with Prince George and the Marquis of Baden, all of them wondering what the Prince Elector's so early approach to the Diet should mean; and the Emperor himself was astonished, and doubted whether he could come and go in safety; whereupon the princes were constrained to promise that they would stand, body, goods, and blood, by the Emperor, one offering to maintain 6,000 horse, another so many thousands of foot-soldiers, etc., to the end his majesty might be the better secured. Then was a wonder among wonders to be seen, in that God struck with fear and cowardliness the enemies of the truth. And although at that time the Prince Elector of Saxony was alone, and but only the hundredth sheep, the others being ninety and nine, yet it so fell out that they all trembled and were afraid. When they came to the point, and began to take the business in hand, there appeared but a very small heap that stood by God's Word. But that small heap brought with us a strong and mighty King, a King above all emperors and kings, namely, Christ Jesus, the powerful Word of God. Then all the papists cried out, and said, Oh, it is insufferable that so small and mean a heap should set themselves against the imperial power. But the Lord of hosts frustrates the councils of princes. Pilate had power to put our Blessed Saviour to death, but willingly he would not.

Annas and Caiaphas willingly would have done it, but could not.

The Emperor, for his own part, is good and honest; but the popish bishops and cardinals are undoubted knaves. And forasmuch as the Emperor now refuses to bathe his hands in innocent blood, the frantic princes bestir themselves, and scorn and contemn the good Emperor in the highest degree. The Pope also for anger is ready to burst in pieces, because the Diet should be dissolved without shedding of blood; therefore he sends the sword to the Duke of Bavaria, intending to take the crown from the Emperor's head, and set it upon the head of Bavaria; but he shall not accomplish it. In this manner ordered God the business, that kings, princes, yea, and the Pope himself, fell from the Emperor, and we joined him, which was a great wonder of God's providence, in that he whom the devil intended to use against us, God takes and uses for us. O wonder above all wonders!

LUTHER AND CAJETAN.

It was a critical time in Luther's history when, in 1518, he was summoned to appear before Cajetan, the Pope's legate, at Augsburg. He had challenged the whole power of the papacy, and now was called upon to answer for his temerity. As he had been a poor student, poverty still clung to him now that the serious business of life was opening before him. He well knew that the crisis was a most hazardous one, and, on the eve of his departure, the Reformer wrote to Melancthon to say that had become the talk of the entire town. When he set out from Wittenberg, he did so in a well-worn gown, and without money in his pocket; but he was encouraged not only by the favour of the Elector, but by the enthusiasm of the chief portion of the populace, who were waiting at the gates to cheer onward the representative of the now popular cause. 'Luther for ever!' cried the people; and the answer was, 'Christ and His Word for ever!' 'Courage, master, and may God help you,' said others; to which the response was, 'Amen,' as the traveller went on his way.

Nothing satisfactory to either side was likely to come of such a meeting, for neither side was disposed to compromise. The legate judged Luther to be a renegade who must yield to authority; and Luther himself soon judged that his best policy would be to retire whence he came.

The Cardinal at this time was in his 50th year, and was thus about fourteen years the senior of his rival. His real name was Thomas de Vio; but having won the bishopric of Cajeta from the Pope for the papal zeal shown in his book *Of the Power of the Pope*, he changed his name. He subsequently became Archbishop of Palermo, and only a few months before meeting with Luther, he had received a cardinal's hat from Leo X. He was a very active man of letters; and it is a remarkable fact, that in addition to his commentaries on Aristotle and Aquinas, he translated the greater portion of the Old and New Testaments.

LUTHER AND MONEY.

Whoso relies on his money prospers not. The richest monarchs have had ill fortune, have been destroyed and slain in the wars; while men with but small store of money have had great fortune and victory; as the Emperor Maximilian overcame the Venetians, and continued warring ten years with them, though they were exceedingly rich and powerful. Therefore we ought not to trust in money or wealth, or depend thereon. I hear that the prince elector,

George, begins to be covetous, which is a sign of his death very shortly. When I saw Dr. Gode begin to tell his puddings hanging in the chimney, I told him he would not live long, and so it fell out; and when I begin to trouble myself about brewing, malting, cooking, etc., then shall I soon die.

A covetous farmer, well known at Erfurt, carried his corn, to sell there in the market; but selling it at too dear a rate, no man would buy of him, or give him his price. He being thereby moved to anger, said, 'I will not sell it cheaper, but rather carry it home again, and give it to the mice.' When he had come home with it, an infinity of mice and rats flocked into his house, and devoured up all his corn. And next day going out to see his grounds, which were newly sown, he found that all the seed was eaten up, while no hurt at all was done to the grounds of his neighbours. This certainly was a just punishment from God, a merited token of His wrath.

Three rich farmers have lately, God be praised! hanged themselves: these wretches, that rob the whole country, deserve such punishments; for the dearth at this time is a wilful dearth. God has given enough, but the devil has possessed such wicked cormorants to withhold it. They are thieves and murderers of their poor neighbours. Christ will say unto them at the last day, 'I was hungry, and ye have not fed Me.' Do not think, thou that sellest thy corn so dear, that thou shalt escape punishment, for thou art an occasion of the deaths and famishing of the poor; the devil will fetch thee away. They that fear God and trust in Him pray for their daily bread, and against such robbers as thou, that either thou mayest be put to shame or be reformed.

A man that depends on the riches and honours of this world, forgetting God and the welfare of his soul, is like a little child that holds a fair apple in the hand, of agreeable exterior, promising goodness, but within 'tis rotten and full of worms.—*Table Talk.*

LEO THE TENTH'S BULL.

The form of the bull by which Luther and his doctrines were to be condemned gave rise to many debates and a great variety of opinion; and the authority of the pontiff was necessary to terminate a contest between the cardinals Pietro Accolti and Lorenzo Pucci the datary, each of whom had proposed the form of the bull, and were earnest in defence of their respective opinions. At length the model of Accolti was, with some variations, adopted; and this formidable document, which has been considered as the final separation of Luther and adherents from the Roman Church, and as the foundation of the celebrated council of Trent, was issued with the date of the fifteenth day of June, 1520.

By this bull the supreme pontiff, after calling upon Christ to arise and judge His own cause, and upon St. Peter, St. Paul, and all the hosts of saints to intercede for the peace and unity of the Church, selects forty-one articles from the assertions and writings of Luther as heretical, dangerous, and scandalous, offensive to pious ears, contrary to Christian charity, the respect due to the Roman Church, and to that obedience which is the sinew of ecclesiastical discipline. He then proceeds to condemn them, and prohibits every person, under pain of excommunication, from advancing, defending, preaching, or favouring the opinions therein contained. He also condemns the books published by Luther as containing similar assertions, and directs that they shall be sought out and publicly burnt. Proceeding then to the person of Luther, the pontiff declares that he has omitted no effort of paternal charity to reclaim him from his errors, that he has invited him to Rome, offered him a safe-conduct, and the payment of the expense of his journey, in the full confidence that he would, on his arrival, have acknowledged his errors, and have discovered, that in his contempt of the Roman court and his accusations against the holy pontiff, he had been misled by empty and malicious reports. That Luther had, notwithstanding this summons, contumaciously refused for upwards of a year to appear at Rome ; that he still persevered in his refusal ; and that, adding one offence to another, he had rashly dared to appeal to a future council, in defiance of the constitutions of Pius II. and Julius II., which had declared all such appeals heretical. That in consequence of these reiterated offences, the Pope might justly have proceeded to his condemnation, but that, being induced by the voice of his brethren, and imitating the clemency of the Omnipotent, who desireth not the death of a sinner, he had forgotten all the offences hitherto committed by Luther against himself and the holy see, had determined to treat him with the greatest lenity, and to endeavour, by mildness alone, to recall him to a sense of his duty, in which case he was still willing to receive him, like a repentant prodigal, into the bosom of the Church. He then proceeds to exhort Luther and his adherents to maintain the peace and unity of the Church of Christ ; prohibits them from preaching ; and admonishes them, within sixty days, publicly to recant their errors, and commit their writings to the flames ; otherwise he denounces them as notorious and pertinacious heretics ; he requires all Christian princes and powers to seize upon Luther and his adherents, and send them to Rome, or at least to expel them from their territories ; and he interdicts every place to which they may be allowed to resort ; and, lastly, he directs that this bull shall be read through all Christendom, and excommunicates those who may oppose its publication.—Roscoe, '*Life of Leo the Tenth*,' in *Bohn's Standard Library*.

LEO X. AND LUTHER.

After having just escaped with his life from the machinations of the College of Cardinals, it is not surprising that he gave himself little concern at the proceedings of Luther in Germany, or that he rejoiced that the danger, whatever it might be, was at least removed to a greater distance. 'We may now,' said he, 'live in quiet, for the axe is taken from the root, and applied to the branches.' In fact, the Church was at this period in its greatest credit and respectability. The personal character of the pontiff stood high throughout all Europe. He was surrounded at home, and represented abroad, by men of the greatest eminence. The sovereigns of Christendom vied with each other in manifesting their obedience to the holy see; even Luther himself had written to the Pope in the most respectful terms, transmitting to him, under the title of *Resolutiones*, a full explanation of his propositions, submitting not only his writings, but his life to his disposal, and declaring that he would regard whatever proceeded from him as delivered by Christ Himself. Under such circumstances how was it possible for Leo, unless he had been endowed with a greater portion of the prophetic spirit than had been conferred on any of his predecessors, to foresee that the efforts of an obscure monk in a corner of Germany would effect a schism in the hierarchy which would detach from its obedience to the Roman see one half of the Christian world? When, however, Leo found his interference necessary, his first impulse was rather to soothe and pacify Luther than to irritate him by severity to further acts of disobedience, for which purpose he wrote to John Staupitz, Vicar-General of the Augustines, directing him to endeavour to reconcile his refractory brother by admonitory letters, written by some persons of integrity and good sense, which he did not doubt would soon extinguish the newly-kindled flame. The effect which might have been produced on the mind of Luther by the moderation of the pontiff was, however, counteracted by the violence and intemperance of the interested zealots who undertook to defend the cause of the Church; and who also, as has been conjectured by more judicious writers, by prematurely representing Luther as a heretic, forced him at length to become one. The scholastic disputations or dogmatic assertions of Tetzel, Eccius, and Prierio were ill calculated to oppose the strong reasonings on which Luther relied in his dissent; but if they did not discredit his doctrines by their arguments, they exasperated his temper by their abuse to such a degree that he was no longer satisfied with defending victoriously the ground which he had already assumed, but, with an unsparing hand, to lay waste all that seemed to oppose his course. Leo addressed a monitory letter to Luther commanding him to appear at Rome within the space of sixty days and defend himself from the imputations charged against him in respect of his doctrines.—*Ibid.*

LUTHER AT WORMS.

Whilst Luther was passing to the assembly, he was surrounded with immense crowds, and even the roofs of the houses were almost covered with spectators. Among these, and even when he stood in the presence of the Diet, he had the satisfaction to hear frequent exhortations addressed to him to keep up his courage, to act like a man, accompanied by passages from Scripture, *Not to fear those who can kill the body only, but to fear Him who can cast both body and soul into hell.* And again, *When ye shall stand before kings, think not how you shall speak; for it shall be given to you in that same hour.* His adversaries were, however, gratified to find, that instead of replying, he had thought it necessary to ask time to deliberate; and the apologists of the Roman see affected to consider it as a proof that he possessed no portion of the Divine Spirit, otherwise he would not by his delay have given rise to a doubt whether he meant to retract his opinions. We are also informed that his conduct on this occasion fell so far short of what was expected from him, that the emperor said, 'This man will never induce me to become a heretic.' To observations of this kind the friends of Luther might have replied that the prohibition imposed upon him before the assembly prevented him from entering into a general vindication either of his opinions or his conduct. That with respect to his having exhibited no symptoms of divine inspiration, he had never asserted any pretensions to such an endowment; but, on the contrary, had represented himself as a fallible mortal, anxious only to discharge his duty, and to consult the safety of his own soul. And that as to the remark of the emperor, if, in fact, such an assertion escaped him, it proved no more than that he had been already prejudiced against Luther; and that, by a youthful impatience which he ought to have restrained, he had already anticipated his condemnation.

On the following day, Luther again appeared before the Diet, and being called upon to answer whether he meant to retract the opinions asserted in his writings, in reply he first observed that these writings were of different kinds and on different subjects. That some related only to the inculcation of piety and morality, which his enemies must confess to be innocent and even useful; and that he could not therefore retract these without condemning what both his friends and his foes must equally approve. That others were written against the papacy and the doctrines of the papists, which had been so generally complained of, particularly in Germany, and by which the consciences of the faithful had been so long ensnared and tormented; that he could not retract these writings without adding new strength to the cause of tyranny, sanctioning and perpetuating that impiety which he had hitherto so firmly opposed, and betraying the cause which he had undertaken to defend. That among his writings there was a third kind, in which he had inveighed against those who had undertaken to defend the tyranny of Rome, and attacked his own opinions, in which he confessed that he had been more severe than became his religion and profession. That, however, he did not consider himself as a saint, but as a man liable to error, and that he could only say, in the words of Jesus Christ, *If I have spoken evil, bear witness of the evil.* That he was at all times ready to defend his opinions and equally ready to retract any of them which might be proved from reason and Scripture, and not from authority, to be erroneous; and would even, in such case, be the first to commit his own books to the flames. That with respect to the dissensions which it had been said would be occasioned in the world by his doctrines, it was of all things the most pleasant to him to see dissensions arise on account of the Word of God. That such dissensions were incident to its very nature, course, and purpose, as was said by our Saviour, *I come not to send peace among you, but a sword.* He then with great dignity and firmness admonished the young emperor to be cautious in the commencement of his authority not to give occasion to those calamities which might arise from the condemnation of the Word of God, and cited the example of Pharaoh and of the kings of Israel, who had incurred the greatest dangers when they had been surrounded by their counsellors, and employed, as they supposed, in the establishment and pacification of their dominions. When Luther had finished, the orator of the assembly observed, in terms of reprehension, that he had not answered to the purpose; that what had been defined and condemned by the council ought not to be called in question, and that he must therefore give a simple and unequivocal answer, whether he would retract or not. Luther replied in Latin, in which language he had before spoken, in these terms:—'Since your majesty and the sovereigns now present require a simple answer, I shall reply thus, without evasion and without vehemence, Unless I be convinced by the testimony of Scripture or by evident reason (for I cannot rely on the authority of the pope and councils alone, since it appears that they have frequently erred and contradicted each other), and unless my conscience be subdued by the Word of God, I neither can nor will retract anything, seeing that to act against my own conscience is neither safe nor honest.' After which he added in his native German, '*Here I take my stand; I can do no other; God be my help! Amen.*' The orator made another effort to induce him to relax from his determination, but to no purpose, and, night approaching, the assembly separated; several of the Spaniards who attended the emperor having expressed their disapprobation of Luther by hisses and groans.—*Ibid.*

LUTHER'S REPLY TO THE BULL.

The first measure adopted by Luther in opposition to the pontifical decree was to renew his appeal to a general council. He soon afterwards published his animadversions upon the execrable Bull of Leo X., in which he in his turn admonishes the pope and his cardinals to repent of their errors, and to disavow their diabolical blasphemies and impious attempts; threatening them, that unless they speedily comply with his remonstrances, he and all other Christians shall regard the Court of Rome as the seat of Antichrist, possessed by Satan himself. He declares that he is prepared, in defence of his opinions, not only to receive with joy these censures, but to entreat that he may never be absolved from them, or be numbered among the followers of the Roman Church, being rather willing to gratify their sanguinary tyranny by offering them his life; that if they still persist in their fury, he shall proceed to deliver over both them and their bull, with all their decretals, to Satan, that, by the destruction of the flesh, their souls may be liberated in the coming of our Lord. These menaces he soon after carried into effect, as far as lay in his power. On the 10th day of December, 1520, he caused a kind of funeral pile to be erected without the walls of Wittenberg, surrounded by scaffolds, as for a public spectacle, and when the places thus prepared were filled by the members of the university and the inhabitants of the city, Luther made his appearance, with many attendants, bringing with him several volumes, containing the Decretals of the Popes, the constitutions called the Extravagants, the writings of Eccius and of Emser, another of his antagonists, and finally a copy of the bull of Leo X. The pile being then set on fire, he with his own hands committed the books to the flames, exclaiming at the same time, 'Because ye have troubled the holy of the Lord, ye shall be burnt with eternal fire.' On the following day he mounted the pulpit, and admonished his audience to be upon their guard against papistical decrees.

'The conflagration we have now seen,' said he, 'is a matter of small importance. It would be more to the purpose if the Pope himself, or, in other words, the papal see, were also burnt.' The example of Luther at Wittenberg was followed by his disciples in several other parts of Germany, where the papal bulls and decretals were committed to the flames with public marks of indignation and contempt. Such were the ceremonies that confirmed the separation of Luther and his followers from the Court of Rome. A just representation of that hostile spirit which has subsisted between them to the present day, and which, unfortunately for the world, has not always been appeased by the burning of heretical works on the one hand, nor of papal bulls and decretals on the other.—*Ibid.*

GERMAN SOLDIERS AND THE POPE.

Charles V. himself contributed to spread the name and doctrines of Luther in the peninsula by constantly pouring into that country fresh bands of lanzknechts, among whom there were many Protestants. It is well known that George von Freundsberg, the leader of the German troops in the service of the Constable de Bourbon, swore to strangle the Pope with the gold chain he wore round his neck. The author of a Lutheran history relates that one of these German soldiers openly promised that he would soon eat a piece of the Pope. He adds, that after the taking of Rome, some of the Germans turned a chapel into a stable, and collecting a number of the Pope's bulls, made litter of them for their horses. Then dressing themselves in sacerdotal habits, they proclaimed as pope one of their comrades, who thereupon holding a consistory with the rest, resigned the popedom to Luther. Luther, indeed, was solemnly proclaimed pope by the Germans on another occasion. A number of these troops assembled one day in the streets of Rome, on horses and mules. One of them named Grunwald, remarkable for his stature, was apparelled as pope, with a triple crown on his head, and mounted on a mule richly caparisoned. Other troopers were dressed as cardinals, with hats on their heads, the colours of their garments being scarlet or white, according to the persons whom each represented. They then formed, and proceeded through the streets to the sound of drums and fifes, surrounded by an immense crowd, and, in short, with all the pomp and circumstance usual in pontifical processions. Whenever they came opposite a cardinal's palace, Grunwald blessed the people in the accustomed form. By-and-by he got off his mule, and the soldiers, placing him in a chair, carried him the rest of the way on their shoulders. On arriving at the castle of St. Angelo, the mock pope took a large goblet filled with wine, and drank off its contents to the health of Clement, the rest of the party doing the same. He then administered the usual oath to his cardinals, adding that he called upon them to render homage to the emperor, their legitimate and only sovereign; he made them promise that they would no longer trouble the peace of the empire by their intrigues and machinations, but that, following the precepts of the Gospel and the example of Jesus Christ and His apostles, they would remain submissive to the civil power. After an harangue, in which he recapitulated the wars, the murders, the sacrileges, the crimes of all sorts of which the popes had been guilty, the pretended pontiff solemnly undertook to transfer, by way of will, his authority and power to Martin Luther. 'He alone,' said Grunwald, 'can remedy all these abuses, can put in order the bark of St. Peter, so that it may no longer be the sport of the winds and waves.' Then raising his voice, he exclaimed, 'Let all those who are of this opinion declare the same by holding up their hand;' whereupon the multitude of soldiers raised their hands, shouting, '*Long live Pope Luther!*' All this passed under the eyes of Pope Clement VII.—*M'Crie, etc., quoted by Michelet.*

WAS LEO X. POISONED?

It was the general opinion at the time, and has been confirmed by the suffrages of succeeding historians, that his death was occasioned by the excess of his joy on hearing of the success of his arms. If, however, after all the vicissitudes of fortune which Leo had experienced, his mind had not been sufficiently fortified to resist this influx of good fortune, it is probable that its effects would have been more sudden. On this occasion, it has been well observed that an excess of joy is dangerous only on a first emotion, and that Leo survived this intelligence eight days. It seems, therefore, not unlikely that this story was fabricated merely as a pretext to conceal the real cause of his death; and that the slight indisposition and temporary seclusion of the pontiff afforded an opportunity for some of his enemies to gratify their resentment or promote their own ambitious views by his destruction. Some circumstances are related which give additional credulity to this supposition. Before the body of the Pope was interred, Paris de Grassis, perceiving it to be much inflated, inquired from the consistory whether they would have it opened and examined, to which they assented. On performing this operation, the medical attendants reported that he had certainly died by poison. To this it is added, that during his illness the Pope had frequently complained of an internal burning, which was attributed to the same cause, 'whence,' says Paris de Grassis, 'it is certain that the Pope was poisoned.' In confirmation of this opinion, a singular incident is also recorded by the same officer, who relates in his diary that a few days before the indisposition of the pontiff, a person unknown and disguised called upon one of the monks in the monastery of St. Jerom, and requested him to inform the Pope that an attempt would be made by one of his confidential servants to poison him, not in his food but in his linen. The friar, not choosing to convey this intelligence to the Pope, who was then at Malliana, communicated it to the datary, who immediately acquainted the Pope with it. The friar was sent for to the villa, and having there confirmed in the presence of the pontiff what he had before related, Leo, with great emotion, observed, 'That if it was the will of God that he should die, he should submit to it; but that he should use all the precaution in his power.' We are further informed, that in the course of a few days he fell sick, and that with his last words he declared that he had been murdered, and could not long survive.—*Roscoe's* '*Leo the Tenth*' in *Bohn's Standard Library.*

LUTHER'S FAITH IN PRAYER.

'Just as a shoemaker makes a shoe, and a tailor a coat,' the reformer once remarked, 'so also ought the Christian to pray. The Christian's trade is praying. And the prayer of the Church works great miracles. In our days it has raised from the dead three persons—viz., myself, having been frequently sick unto death; my wife Catherine, who likewise was dangerously ill; and Melancthon, who was sick unto death at Weimar (1540). And though their rescue from sickness and other bodily dangers be but trifling miracles, nevertheless they must be exhibited for the sake of those whose faith is weak.' When these words were spoken, a great drought was afflicting the country, and hence Luther lifted his eyes to heaven and prayed, 'Lord God, Thou hast spoken through the mouth of Thy servant David, *The Lord is nigh unto all them that call upon Him, to all that call upon Him in truth. He will fulfil the desire of them that fear Him; He also will hear their cry and will save them.* Why wilt Thou not give us rain now, for which so long we have cried and prayed? Well then, if no rain, Thou art able to give us something better,—a peaceable and quiet life, peace and harmony. Now we have prayed so much, prayed so often, and our prayers not being granted, dear Father, the wicked will say, Christ, Thy beloved Son, hath told a falsehood, saying, Verily, verily, I say unto you, Whatsoever ye shall ask the Father in My name, He will give it you. Thus they will give both Thee and Thy Son the lie. I know that we sincerely cry to Thee, and with yearning. Why then dost Thou not hear us?' This was in the year 1532, and in the course of that night an abundant rain refreshed the face of nature.

THE HONEST MAN OF EISLEBEN.

A certain honest man, at Eisleben, complained to me of his great misery; he had bestowed on his children all his goods, and now in his old age they forsook and trod him under their feet. I said, Ecclesiasticus gives unto parents the best counsel, where he says, Give not all out of thy hands while thou livest, etc., for the children keep not promises. One father, as the proverb says, can maintain ten children, but ten children cannot, or at least will not, maintain one father. There is a story of a certain father that, having made his last will, he locked it up safe in a chest, and, together with a good strong cudgel, laid a note thereby, in these words, 'The father who gives his goods out of his hands to his children deserves to have his brains beat out with cudgels.' Here is another story: A certain father that was grown old had given over all his goods to his children, on condition they should maintain him; but the children were unthankful, and being weary of him, kept him very hard and sparingly, and gave him not sufficient to eat. The father, being a wise man, more crafty than his children, locked himself secretly into a chamber, and made a great ringing and jingling with gold crowns, which, for that purpose, a rich neighbour had lent him, as though he had still much money in store. When his children heard this, they gave him ever afterwards good entertainment, in hopes he would leave them much wealth; but the father secretly restored the crowns again to his neighbour, and so rightly deceived his children.—*Table Talk.*

PRINCE EBERHARD OF WIRTEMBERG.

At an imperial diet at Augsburg, certain princes there spoke in praise of the riches and advantages of their respective principalities. The Prince Elector of Saxony said, he had, in his country, store of silver mines, which brought him great revenues. The Prince Elector Palatine extolled his vineyards on the Rhine. When it became the turn of Eberhard, Prince of Wirtemberg, he said, 'I am, indeed, but a poor prince, and not to be compared with either of you; yet, nevertheless, I have also in my country a rich and precious jewel, namely, that if at any time I should ride astray in my country, and were left all alone in the fields, yet I could safely and securely sleep in the bosom of any one of my subjects, who all, for my service, are ready to venture body, goods, and blood.' And, indeed, his people esteemed him as a *pater patriæ*. When the other two princes heard this, they confessed that, in truth, his was the most rich and precious jewel.—*Ibid.*

LUTHER AND THE PHYSICIANS.

The physicians in sickness consider only of what natural causes the malady proceeds, and this they cure, or not, with their physic. But they see not that often the devil casts a sickness upon one without any natural causes. A higher physic must be required to resist the devil's diseases, namely, faith and prayer, which physic may be fetched out of God's Word. The 31st Psalm is good thereunto, where David says, 'Into Thine hand I commit my spirit.' This passage I learned, in my sickness, to correct; in the first translation, I applied it only to the hour of death; but it should be said, My health, my happiness, my life, misfortunes, sickness, death, etc., stand all in Thy hands. Experience testifies this; for when we think now we will be joyful and merry, easy and healthy, God soon sends what makes us quite the contrary.

When I was ill at Schmalcalden, the physicians made me take as much medicine as though I had been a great bull. Alack for him that depends upon the aid of physic. I do not deny that medicine is a gift of God, nor do I refuse to acknowledge science in the skill of many physicians; but, take the best of them, how far are they from perfection? A sound regimen produces excellent effects. When I feel indisposed, by observing a strict diet and going to bed early, I generally manage to get round again, that is, if I can keep my mind tolerably at rest. I have no objection to the doctors acting upon certain theories, but at the same time they must not expect us to be the slaves of their fancies. We find Avicenna and Galen, living in other times and in other countries, prescribing wholly different remedies for the same disorders. I won't pin my faith to any of them, ancient or modern. On the other hand, nothing can well be more deplorable than the proceeding of those fellows, ignorant as they are complaisant, who let their patients follow exactly their own fancies; 'tis these wretches who more especially people the graveyards. Able, cautious, and experienced physicians are gifts of God. They are the ministers of nature, to whom human life is confided; but a moment's negligence may ruin everything. No physician should take a single step but in humility and the fear of God; they who are without the fear of God are mere homicides. I expect that exercise and change of air do more good than all their purgings and bleedings; but when we do employ medical remedies, we should be careful to do so under the advice of a judicious physician. See what happened to Peter Lupinus, who died from taking internally a mixture designed for external application. I remember hearing of a great law-suit arising out of a dose of appium being given instead of a dose of opium.—*Ibid.*

LUTHER AND THE EVIL ONE.

He who will have, for his master and king, Jesus Christ, the Son of the virgin, who took upon Himself our flesh and our blood, will have the devil for his enemy.

It is very certain that, as to all persons who have hanged themselves or killed themselves in any other way, 'tis the devil who has put the cord round their necks, or the knife to their throats.

A man had a habit, whenever he fell, of saying, 'Devil take me.' He was advised to discontinue this evil custom, lest some day the devil should take him at his word. He promised to vent his impatience by some other phrase; but one day having stumbled, he called upon the devil, in the way I have mentioned, and was killed upon the spot, falling on a sharp-pointed piece of wood.

A pastor, near Torgau, came to Luther, and complained that the devil tormented him without intermission. The Doctor replied, 'He plagues and harasses me too, but I resist him with the arms of faith. I know of one person at Magdeburg who put Satan to the rout by spitting at him; but this example is not to be lightly followed, for the devil is a presumptuous spirit, and not disposed to yield. We run great risk when, with him, we attempt more than we can do. One man, who relied implicitly on his baptism, when the devil presented himself to him, his head furnished with horns, tore off one of the horns; but another man of less faith, who attempted the same thing, was killed by the devil.'

Henning, the Bohemian, asked Doctor Luther why the devil bore so furious a hatred to the human race? The Doctor replied, 'That ought not to surprise you; see what a hate Prince George bears me, so that, day and night, he is ever meditating how he shall injure me. Nothing would delight him more than to see me undergo a thousand tortures. If such be the hatred of man, what must the hatred of the devil be?'—*Ibid.*

THE POPE'S COOKS.

Philip Melancthon, on the authority of a person who had filled an important post at the Court of Clement VII., mentioned that every day after the Pope had dined or supped, his cup-bearer and cooks were imprisoned for two hours, and then, if no symptoms of poison manifested themselves in their master, were released. 'What a miserable life!' observed Luther; ' 'tis exactly what Moses has described in Deuteronomy, "And thy life shall hang in doubt before thee, and thou shalt fear day and night, and shall have none assurance of thy life. In the morning, thou shalt say, Would God it were even! and at even thou shalt say, Would God it were morning!"'—*Ibid.*

BAPTIZING A JEW.

In 1541, Doctor Menius asked Doctor Luther in what manner a Jew should be baptized? The Doctor replied, You must fill a large tub with water, and, having divested the Jew of his clothes, cover him with a white garment. He must then sit down in the tub, and you must baptize him quite under the water. The ancients, when they were baptized, were attired in white, whence the first Sunday after Easter, which was peculiarly consecrated to this ceremony, was called *dominica in albis*. This garb was rendered the more suitable from the circumstance that it was, as now, the custom to bury people in a white shroud; and baptism, you know, is an emblem of our death. I have no doubt that when Jesus was baptized in the river Jordan, He was attired in a white robe. If a Jew, not converted at heart, were to ask baptism at my hands, I would take him on to the bridge, tie a stone round his neck, and hurl him into the river; for these wretches are wont to make a jest of our religion. Yet, after all, water and the Divine Word being the essence of baptism, a Jew, or any other, would be none the less validly baptized that his own feelings and intentions were not the result of faith.—*Ibid.*

LUTHER AND THE STUDENT.

On one occasion the reformer paid a pastoral visit to a young scholar who was in his last illness, and one of the first inquiries made was, 'What do you think you can take to God, in whose presence you are so shortly to appear?' With striking confidence the youth at once replied, 'Everything that is good, dear father—everything that is good!' 'But how can you bring Him everything good, seeing that you are but a poor sinner?' anxiously asked the Doctor. 'Dear father,' at once added the young man, 'I will take to my God in heaven a penitent, humble heart, sprinkled with the blood of Christ.' 'Truly that is everything good,' answered Luther. 'Then go, dear son; you will be a welcome guest to God.'

A BIRD PREACHES TO LUTHER.

The Reformer had a quick eye to detect and read the lessons of nature. Thus, on a certain calm summer evening he happened to be standing at a window, when he observed a small bird quietly settle down for the night. 'Look how that little fellow preaches faith to us all,' remarked Luther. 'He takes hold of his twig, tucks his head under his wing, and goes to sleep, leaving God to think for him.'

LUTHER'S HOME.

He entered into domestic life by marrying Catherine von Bora, a lady who had been a nun, but who made him for many years an excellent and devoted wife. He lived as a family man in the very building in which he had lived as a friar—the Augustinian monastery—in a suite of rooms which was converted into a house for him. We will, if you please, go upstairs into the parlour which he and his family occupied, and which is yet preserved for the gratification of visitors. This is the room. Look round it for a moment. It is a very comfortable sitting-room, sufficiently large and lofty; and, indeed, a room which must have been very handsome. Overlooking the decayed state of the floor, it is handsome still. You notice the ornamental character of the window and of the ceiling. Observe also the furniture. There are two very old-fashioned chairs standing by the window. One has its back towards you,—a rather large chair, with arms; that was Luther's. There, sit down in it. A comfortable chair, is it not? although rude and inelegant. That chair now just before you, and facing the window, smaller and without arms, belonged to Luther's wife; and many a tidy piece of work no doubt did she do in it. Tidy, however, is not quite the word, for her needlework was beautiful. There is a specimen of it in the cupboard behind you—actually a portrait of her husband, wrought entirely with a needle and silk; it is a good likeness, too, and the work is exquisite. Now if you turn round, you will see a good-sized oak table, square and without leaves, old and decaying; that is Luther's table, at which he ate, and read, and wrote. And there in the corner is his stove, made after the old German fashion, and covered, at his particular desire, with numerous carvings in wood. A great many persons, and not a few illustrious persons, have come into this parlour; and before we quit it you may perhaps think it worth while to notice a memorial left by one of them. It is there, on the door, and consists of a few illegible chalk marks. That is the signature of Peter the Great, Emperor of Russia; and so valuable has it been thought as a memorial of him, that it has been protected by being framed and glazed.—*Leisure Hour.*

LUTHER AS A HYMN WRITER.

His opinion of his own poetical powers was the humblest and most modest. He long sought to induce others to compose hymns, and only addressed himself to the task as a matter of necessity. Passionately fond of music, gifted with a strong, sweet voice, he mostly added tunes to his hymns, and in general revised, with Walther, all those which were to be sung in the churches of Protestant Germany. The life of Luther is full of anecdotes showing how sensitive he was to the influence of music, recurring to it whenever he was in sorrow or trouble, and on one occasion being restored by it to consciousness after a long and deadly faint. His prefaces to the various editions of his hymn-books, as well as that 'to all good hymn-books,' and his poem in honour of music, show in what high esteem he held 'the noble art,' which, indeed, he placed next to theology. His hymns are all terse, manly, and yet childlike, full of the deep faith of a strong man's soul, the form being always subservient, corresponding to the substance. Thus there is often a single unrhymed line at the end of each stanza to express in simple language the leading thought. Like all true compositions, the music of Luther singularly corresponds to his poetry. Of the latter it may be said that if the object of every good hymn is praise, and its characteristics that it is Scriptural in contents, popular in form, experimental in cast, then Luther's hymns may be regarded as the very model, and Germany itself has never superseded or excelled them. Yet they are comparatively few in number—altogether only thirty-six; some translations from the Latin, some emendations of old German hymns, some metrical renderings of the 'Belief,' the Lord's Prayer, the Ten Commandments, etc.; only a small proportion being hymns proper, partly renderings of psalms, like 'Ein feste Burg,' and a few wholly original compositions, like the Christmas Hymns. Yet in the day when all secrets of a Christian life shall be laid open, how many of its deepest and strongest impulses during the last three centuries shall be traced up to the psalmody of him whose watchword in ong and in word was the pure and simple truth of the Gospel!—*Leisure Hour.*

ERASMUS.

This celebrated scholar has been variously represented by persons of both sides; but the fact is that he was neither a theologian nor a partisan in our sense of the word. 'When by study of his writings we come to know Erasmus intimately, there is revealed to us one of those natures to which partisanship is an impossibility,' says the Rev. M. Pattison in the *Encyclopædia Britannica.* 'It was not timidity or weakness which kept Erasmus neutral, but the reasonableness of his nature. It was not only that his intellect revolted against the narrowness of party, his whole being repudiated its clamorous and vulgar excesses. As he loathed fish, so he loathed clerical fanaticism. Himself a Catholic priest—" the glory of the priesthood and the shame".—the tone of the orthodox clergy was distasteful to him; the ignorant hostility to classical learning which reigned in their colleges and convents disgusted him; in common with all the learned men of his age, he wished to see the power of the clergy broken, as that of an obscurantist army arrayed against light. He had employed all his resources of wit and satire against the priests and monks, and the superstitions in which they traded, long before Luther's name was heard of. The motto, which was already current in his lifetime, that Erasmus laid the egg and Luther hatched it,' is so far true and no more.

LUTHER, MELANCTHON, AND ERASMUS.

In *The Gentleman's Magazine* for 1973, Clericus thus narrates a conversation which took place on board of the packet between Harwich and Holland during a holiday trip:—

Several of the passengers were men of sense and knowledge; and, soon after the vessel sailed, a conversation took place upon deck respecting the reformation of religion in the 16th century, and the comparative merits of the three great luminaries of that age, Luther, Melancthon, and Erasmus. One gentleman observed that the revival of polite literature in Germany was chiefly owing to the exertions of Melancthon. 'True,' said another; 'but had the revival of evangelical truth depended upon his exertions, it is to be feared that the Reformation would have been strangled in its infancy.' 'Yes, yes,' said a lively young gentleman, 'had Luther been such a man as Melancthon, we should have had no Reformation.' This seemed to be the general sense of the company, who were of opinion that he frequently displayed a timidity which was unworthy the character of a great man; that his concessions to the adverse party were unwarrantable; and that it was happy for the cause of truth that Luther was always at hand to control him. I ventured to stand up as the apologist of that amiable and mild reformer by remarking that I did not recollect any transaction in the history of his life which would warrant the charge of his having shown a disposition to sacrifice the cause of truth to any consideration whatever; but it was well known that he never laid so great a stress upon the abolition of external rites and ceremonies as Luther and others; and that he thought great concessions ought to be made upon that score for the sake of peace. At the same time I was very ready to allow that, in some instances, he showed too much condescension to the fierce and intolerant bigots with whom he had to deal at diets and public conferences; but, notwithstanding, I made no scruple of giving my decided opinion that Melancthon's temper and conduct ought to be held out as a model to modern ecclesiastical reformers in preference to the rough and unaccommodating spirit of Luther. We all agreed in condemning Erasmus as a trimmer in the affair of the Reformation, although it was allowed that he paved the way for the favourable reception of Luther's opinions by his humorous and satirical writings against the monks.

EXCESS OF BOOKS AN EVIL.

The multitude of books is a great evil. There is no measure or limit to this fever for writing; every one must be an author; some out of vanity, to acquire celebrity and raise up a name; others for the sake of lucre and gain. The Bible is now buried under so many commentaries, that the text is nothing regarded. I could wish all my books were buried nine ells deep in the ground, by reason of the ill example they will give, every one seeking to imitate me in writing many books, with the hope of procuring fame. But Christ died not to favour our ambition and vain-glory, but that His name might be glorified.

The aggregation of large libraries tends to divert men's thoughts from the one great book, the Bible, which ought, day and night, to be in every one's hand. My object, my hope, in translating the Scriptures, was to check the so prevalent production of new works, and so to direct men's study and thoughts more closely to the Divine Word. Never will the writings of mortal man in any respect equal the sentences inspired by God. We must yield the place of honour to the prophets and the apostles, keeping ourselves prostrate at their feet as we listen to their teaching. I would not have those who read my books, in these stormy times, devote one moment to them which they would otherwise have consecrated to the Bible.—*Table-Talk*.

THE JEWS.

The Jews are the most miserable people on earth. They are plagued everywhere, and scattered about all countries, having no certain resting-place. They sit as on a wheelbarrow, without a country, people, or government; yet they wait on with earnest confidence; they cheer up themselves and say, It will soon be better with us. Thus hardened are they; but let them know assuredly, that there is none other Lord or God, but only He that already sits at the right hand of God the Father. The Jews are not permitted to trade or to keep cattle; they are only usurers and brokers; they eat nothing the Christians kill or touch; they drink no wine; they have many superstitions; they wash the flesh most diligently, whereas they cannot be cleansed through the flesh. They drink not milk, because God said, 'Thou shalt not boil the young kid in his mother's milk.' Such superstitions proceed out of God's anger. They that are without faith have laws without end, as we see in the papists and Turks; but they are rightly served, for seeing they refused to have Christ and His Gospel, instead of freedom they must have servitude.

If I were a Jew, the Pope should never persuade me to his doctrine; I would rather be ten times racked. Popedom, with its abomination and profanities, has given to the Jews infinite offence. I am persuaded if the Jews heard our preaching, and how we handle the Old Testament, many of them might be won, but, through disputing, they have become more and more stiff-necked, haughty, and presumptuous. Yet if but a few of the rabbis fell off, we might see them come to us, one after another, for they are almost weary of waiting.

At Frankfort-on-the-Maine there are very many Jews; they have a whole street to themselves, of which every house is filled with them. They are compelled to wear yellow rings on their coats, thereby to be known; they have no houses or grounds of their own, only furniture; and, indeed, they can only lend money upon houses or grounds at great hazard.—*Ibid.*

BOOKS AND GIRLS.

Luther advised all who proposed to study, in what art soever, to read some sure and certain books over and over again; for to read many sorts of books produces rather confusion than any distinct result; just as those that dwell everywhere, and remain in no place, dwell nowhere, and have no home. As we use not daily the community of all our friends, but of a select few, even so we ought to accustom ourselves to the best books, and to make them familiar unto us, so as to have them, as we say, at our fingers' end. A fine talented student fell into a frenzy; the cause of his disease was that he laid himself out too much upon books, and was in love with a girl. Luther dealt very mildly and friendly with him, expecting amendment, and said, Love is the cause of his sickness; study brought upon him but little of his disorder. In the beginning of the gospel it went so with myself.—*Ibid.*

THE REFORMATION PROMOTED BY TRACTS.

It has often been remarked that the Reformation could not have been carried through so triumphantly as it was had it not been for the invention of printing, but few are probably aware of how large a number of small publications were put in circulation by the Reformers, and written by themselves. 'As the only original and authentic records of the Reformation,' remarks an anonymous writer early in the present century, 'these little productions have always been held in the highest reverence and esteem by the theologian as well as the historian, and have been collected with avidity and at a considerable expense. Owing, however, to the remoteness of the time of their publication, and to the persecution that some of them experienced, it was always a very difficult task to bring together these scattered productions; and, except in some ancient towns in Germany that were the first to adopt the principles of the Reformation, it was almost impossible to meet with any considerable number of them.'

The most successful collectors were Professor Will of Nuremburg, the bibliographer G. W. Panzer, and Dr. May of Augsburg, the latter having devoted about thirty years to the business of procuring copies of the once popular little messengers. His collection was exhibited in London in 1818, having then consisted of 1676 separate tracts in quarto, all published between 1517 and 1550; and no less than 644 were written by Luther himself. Others were by Melancthon and other comrades in the great work, while some were by adversaries such as Eck, Erasmus, and others.

LUTHER'S LOVE OF MUSIC.

Such was the Reformer's love of music that he not only composed several pieces which became popular in Germany, he was wont to find a solace in music when depressed or weary. 'Whoever despises music I am displeased with,' he once remarked. 'Next to theology I give a place to music; for thereby all anger is forgotten, the devil is driven away, and melancholy, and many tribulations, and evil thoughts are expelled. It is the best solace for a desponding mind.'

ANTI-LUTHERANS.

Felix, Earl of Wirtemberg, one of the captains of the Emperor Charles V., being at supper at Augsburg with many of his companions, they breathed out horrid threatenings of what cruelty they intended to exercise upon the poor Protestants; and the Earl swore before them all that before he died he would ride up to his spurs in the blood of the Lutherans; but it happened the same night that vengeance overtook him, for he was strangled and choked in his own blood before morning; and so he did not ride, yet bathed himself, not up to the spurs, but up to the throat, not in the blood of the Lutherans, but in his own blood, and so miserably ended his life.

John Martin of Piedmont continually boasted how he would root out the Protestants, and in much gallantry cut off a minister's nose of Augrogne; but immediately after he himself was set upon by a wolf, which bit off his nose, as he had abused the minister, whereupon he grew mad, and died miserably; which strange judgment was much discoursed of by all the country round about, because it was never known that this wolf had done any hurt to any man before.

Albertus Pighius (a great enemy to the Gospel, insomuch that he was called The Lutherans' scourge) being at Bulloign at the coronation of the Emperor, to behold the pomp and glory thereof, it happened that the scaffold whereupon he stood fell down with the weight of the people, and Pighius came tumbling headlong amongst the guards that stood below, and fell upon the points of their halberts, which ran quite through his body; the rest of the company escaping without any great hurt.—*Prodigies of Judgment.*

A LUTHERAN COLPORTEUR.

In his *Acts and Monuments*, Foxe tells of a council of French bishops which met at Avignon in 1540 for the purpose of devising the best means of encompassing the ruin of the Lutherans of Merindol.

After they had dined, says the martyrologist, they fell to dancing, playing at dice, and such other pastimes as are commonly wont to be frequented at the banquets and feasts of these holy prelates. After this they walked abroad to solace themselves, and to pass the time till supper.

As they passed through the streets, every one leading his minion upon his arm, they saw a man who sold base images and pictures, with filthy rhymes and ballads annexed to the same, to move and stir up the people to whoredom and knavery. All these goodly pictures were bought up by the bishops, which were as many as a mule could well carry; and if there were any obscure sentence, or hard to understand in those rhymes or ballads, the same these learned prelates did readily expound, and laughed pleasantly thereat. In the same place, as they walked along, there was a foreign bookseller, who had set out to sale certain Bibles in French and Latin, with divers other books; which, when the prelates beheld, they were greatly moved thereat, and said unto him, 'Darest thou be so hardy to set out such merchandise to sell here in this town? Dost thou not know that such books are forbidden?' The bookseller answered, 'Is not the Holy Bible as good as these goodly pictures which you have bought for these gentlewomen?' He had scarce spoken these words but the Bishop of Aix said, 'I renounce my part of Paradise if this fellow be not a Lutheran! Let him be taken,' said he, 'and examined what he is.' And incontinently the bookseller was taken and carried unto prison, and spitefully handled, for a company of knaves and ruffians who waited upon the prelates began to cry out, 'A Lutheran! a Lutheran!' 'To the fire with him!' And one gave him a blow with his fist, another pulled him by the hair, and others by the beard, in such sort that the poor man was all imbrued with blood before he came to prison.

The morrow after he was brought before the judges in the presence of the bishops, where he was examined in this form as followeth: 'Hast thou not set forth to sale the Bible and the New Testament in French?' The prisoner answered that he had so done. And being demanded whether he understood or knew not that it was forbidden throughout all Christendom to print or sell the Bible in any other language than in Latin, he answered that he knew the contrary, and that he had sold many Bibles in the French tongue, with the Emperor's privilege, and many others printed at Lyons; also New Testaments imprinted by the King's privilege.

Foxe gives the bookseller's address to the people of Avignon, and his impeachment of the bishops because they 'maintained filthy books and abominable pictures,' while 'refusing the holy books of God.' He was speedily condemned and burned on the same day.

A LUTHERAN AT MEAUX.

Among the martyrs of France in the days when the Reformed doctrines promised to make complete headway in the provinces, the name of the poor wool carder Jean Leclerc must be honoured by posterity. The reading of the New Testament brought light and liberty to his soul, and taught him to regard the Pope as Antichrist, and worshippers of the virgin and images as veritable idolaters. A bull of Clement VII. offering indulgences and enjoining certain fastings was secretly torn down from the cathedral door, and a paper substituted in its place in which the Pope was depicted in his true colours. The rage of the ecclesiastics knew no bounds; and on Leclerc being discovered as the offender, he was sentenced to receive a number of whippings, and to be branded with a red-hot iron. This happened in the spring of 1525. 'A superstitious multitude flocked together to see and gloat over the condign punishment of a heretic, and gave no word of encouragement or support,' remarks Prof. Baird. 'But as the iron was leaving on Leclerc's brow the ignominious imprint of the *fleur-de-lis*, a single voice suddenly broke in upon the silence. It was that of his aged mother, who, after an involuntary cry of anguish, quickly recovered herself and shouted, "Hail Jesus Christ and His standard-bearer!" Although many heard her words, so deep was the impression that no attempt was made to lay hands upon her.'

With a heroism such as faith in Christ alone could have imparted, Leclerc went on his way teaching the doctrines of grace to all those with whom he came in contact; and he did all that lay in his power to protest against the prevalent image worship. When a grand procession was to be made to a certain shrine without the city, he went in the darkness and threw the images down; and it was this final blow at the papacy which cost him his life. Though horribly tortured before he was finally burned, he died without uttering any cry of anguish; but, on the contrary, calmly uttered the Psalmist's words, 'Their idols are silver and gold, the work of men's hands,' etc. until the flames stopped his repetition of the inspired denunciation.

LEFEVRE, FAREL, AND LUTHER.

One of the most distinguished men of letters in France in the earlier part of the sixteenth century was Lefevre, who in a commentary on Paul's Epistles published in 1508 clearly taught the Reformation doctrine of Justification by Faith. Farel became Lefevre's pupil; and the latter was eventually indebted to his younger friend for clearer views of Scriptural truth than he had hitherto enjoyed; for it is remarkable that even while he caught sight of the Pauline doctrine of salvation by grace, Lefevre was still addicted to the worship of pictures and images. From having been a papist of the papists, Farel groped his way into the Gospel daylight; and one day seizing his friend's hand, Lefevre cried with enthusiasm, 'William, the world is going to be renewed, and you will behold it.' The old scholar had caught the Lutheran 'heresy' years before the monk of Wittenberg exposed the impostures of Tetzel.

LUTHER AND CHARLES V.

No one will find fault with the kindly policy of the Elector of Saxony which confined Luther in the Wartburg to save him from the vindictiveness of the Emperor, who had no sympathy with the new awakening. The edict sent forth prescribed heavy penalties on those who should ever accord the Reformer shelter or countenance; and thus without consulting either friend or foe the good Elector became the secret host and protector of his *protégé*. People were not only not to give the heretic shelter or food, they were not to tolerate his books; they were rather to collect them in order that they might be burned. Printers who should produce, or dealers who should sell, publications inimical to the Pope were threatened; but although 'the faculty of theology at the nearest university' were commanded to examine all religious writings before publication, the stream could not be stopped. A great fire of Luther's books was made in the square at Worms; but on the very day after the booksellers hawked other copies about the city, and are said to have even called with their wares at the imperial residence itself.

LUTHER'S PRINTERS AND PUBLISHERS.

Michelet tells us that 'nothing lent more powerful assistance to Luther than the zeal manifested by the printers and booksellers in the favour of the new ideas.' He then quotes the testimony of Cochlæus, *e.g.*, 'The books in support of Luther were printed by the typographers with minute care, often at their own expense, and vast numbers of copies were thrown off. There was a complete body of ex-monks, who, returned to the world, lived by vending the works of Luther throughout Germany. On the other hand, it was solely by dint of money that the Catholics could get their productions printed, and they were sent forth with such a host of faults, that they seemed the work of ignorant barbarians. If any printer, more or less conscientious than the rest, gave himself any trouble with any Catholic work, he was tormented to death by all his fellows, and by the people in the public streets, as a papist and as a slave of the priests.' Michelet adds, 'The Confession of Augsburg was printed and diffused all over Germany even before the Diet was concluded; the Refutation by the Catholics, which the Emperor had ordered to be printed, was given to the printers, but did not appear. Luther reproached the Catholics that they dared not publish it, and called it a night-bird, a bat, an owl.' *

Though extremely poor all his life, Luther did not write for money. His income is said to have been never more than two hundred florins; and he speaks of having had to sell or pawn goblets to meet current expenses. Speaking of his publishers, he says, 'I get no money from them for my labour, nor any other return, except that of now and then a copy or two of my productions.'

ENGLISH AND FOREIGN PRINTERS.

We may repeat what has been said before, that the Reformation could never have been consummated but for the aid rendered by the printing-press and the booksellers. Even the dissemination of the Latin Bible in large numbers must have soon proved obnoxious to the Papacy; but the rapid multiplication of copies in the vulgar tongue was the most fatal blow at the Pope's ascendency that could possibly be given. Probably the first sellers of these printed books entertained very humble notions concerning

---

* 'The Life of Luther, Written by Himself,' collected and arranged by M. Michelet, is a work of exceptional value and interest. It is one of the series in Bohn's Standard Library, and is published by Messrs. George Bell and Sons.

the importance of the innovations they had introduced into the world, although they may have lived long enough for their art to become detested by the ecclesiastics, or to find themselves suspected of magic.

It is now about forty years since the citizens of Mentz unveiled a statue of Gutenberg, their fifteenth-century printer-bookseller, a copy of whose Latin Bible, produced in 1455, would now realize sufficient to purchase a small family estate. This active genius, who was really the inventor of printing, found a comparatively safe asylum at Strasburg in times which were frequently dangerous through civil commotion. He remained in the city of his adoption about twenty years, afterwards returning to his native place. Being a man far in advance of his time, and the discoverer of a valuable art, the value of which would not be all at once acknowledged by the world, he was naturally troubled with poverty and its attendant trials. While in this condition he had the good sense to form an alliance with John Faust, a goldsmith of the city, whose capital was thus made to serve one of the best of enterprises. The son-in-law of Faust was Schoeffer, who is supposed to have advanced printing from wooden blocks to separate types similar to those now in use. These accomplished men not only inherited genius for their work, but would almost appear to have been raised up by Providence for a special purpose. Referring to their labours in his exhaustive work on the English Bible, Dr. Eadie says, 'When one looks at the form of the letters, the strength of the paper, and the lustre of the ink in these earliest volumes, he is inclined to conclude that printing has for the last four centuries made little improvement save in quickness and cheapness, and that the art was perfect at its birth, like Athene springing at once in full armour from the brain of Zeus.'

What we should now call the accidents of war had the effect of dispersing the compositors and press-men; and thus the knowledge was carried to other countries. Perhaps the vulgar eyes of the world never looked on more striking novelties than the wares which stocked the earliest booksellers' shops; for when told that the volumes were not written with a quill, according to the ancient fashion, it was not always certain that intelligent persons would credit their informants. It has even been affirmed, but perhaps without sufficient foundation, that when Faust was on his travels, for the purpose of selling the copies of the second edition of the Bible, printed in 1462, he was actually arrested as a magician who multiplied books by some secret supernatural process.

The printers were thus a race of pioneers who were unconsciously preparing the way for better days in the future. When the Reformation was actually in progress, the excitement of controversy created a taste for reading, and the result of that reading was the breaking away from the slavery of Antichrist of a mighty section of the human race. It is curious to note how our English Reformers, either at home or in exile, associated themselves with the leading printers. In the middle of the 16th century, Basle was the most renowned seat of typography in the world; and, as correctors of the press, the English refugees were preferred above all rivals.

As an incorporated company with new privileges, the stationers of London date from 1556; and as their charter was granted by Mary, just before her death, the booksellers were expected to aid the Government in checking the inroad of those winged messengers of Luther, Calvin, and other Reformers, which the papacy dreaded as mortal enemies. During the ascendency of Elizabeth the press appears to have enjoyed greater liberty than in the succeeding reigns of the Stuarts; for restrictions on printing constituted a part of that celebrated policy of Thorough which ended in the ruin of its authors.

When books were sufficiently scarce to command fabulous prices, there was no fear of their not being duly prized and well thumbed; and, accordingly, the martyrologist affords us additional entertainment by the vivid glimpse he allows us to enjoy into English every-day life during the early years of the reign of Henry VIII. People who were able to procure them read assiduously their precious books, and then went abroad to converse about the truths they had learned at the firesides of less favoured neighbours. If Popery had to be maintained at any price, well might Henry's daughter Mary aim her royal thunderbolts against booksellers and their dangerous wares. On the other hand, when he realized how thoroughly the good seed had been scattered, the captive John Huss could hopefully write: 'Beloved, I thought it needful to warn you that you should not fear or be discouraged because the adversaries have decreed that my books shall be burnt.' Scattered through his ample volumes, old Foxe has very many references to the book trade of three and four centuries ago; and he abruptly leaps from grave to gay like a veteran author whose art consisted in not sparing words and in telling the whole truth. Thus, as a contrast to the heroic Bohemian confessor, pining in prison and encouraging his followers, we might bring forward Sir Thomas More, sitting before a vast pile of volumes, which he was licensed to read while the booksellers were warned against importing them. Nor was Sir Thomas to rest content with reading alone; he was strongly urged to 'show his cunning, and play the pretty man, like a Demosthenes, in expunging the doctrine of these books.' The art of writing and the practice of selling the best literature, not excepting the Bible, were about equally dangerous in those rough old transition times.

The bookseller of the sixteenth century was not always a man who served volumes to inquiring customers from behind a counter in a comfortable shop. In order to thrive, those who dealt in the good, and those who vended what was corrupt, had to take to travelling, much after the manner of our hardy colporteurs in the present day. The risk and general discomfort of the road were of course immense; and not seldom the men who braved these and endured the toil must have been animated by the most genuine philanthropy. The martyr bookseller who fell at Avignon is a telling example in point.

JOHN DAYE AT ALDERSGATE.

When we emerge into the daylight of the Reformation in England, the leading printer and bookseller of this great era was John Daye, who occupied the apartments of Aldersgate. Having secured the countenance of Elizabeth and of the leading Protestants, Daye, in London, is with great propriety regarded as the printer of the English Reformation. He not only published several editions of Foxe's 'Acts and Monuments,' but employed the martyrologist in his office, and found him a home. With such companionship we are not surprised that Daye showed an extraordinary zeal in the promulgation of anti-Romish works. During the reign of Edward VI., his press had been busy in printing the Bible; and after the accession of Elizabeth it worked like an unfettered giant, whose mission was to enlighten the nation. Among the books here printed were Latimer's Sermons, and the works of

Tyndale, Frith, and Barnes. It is curious to note, that although a very limited number of compositors were required, Master Daye sometimes experienced no small difficulty in making up the complement, foreigners also having to be employed. In one of the scarcest of his books there is a pictorial illustration of Mr. Daye at home, which affords us such an insight into an Elizabethan printing-office as might at first sight lead us to infer that the old printers were exacting taskmasters. In the picture the press-men and compositors are represented as being asleep, with the rays of the rising sun streaming in at the casement. Calling out, 'Arise, for it is day,' and carrying a whip in his hand, the master printer enters the work-room to rouse the sleepers. It is easy to see that the whole thing looks like a pun on a name; and the meaning may have been more apparent in those times than in our own. The picture is truth in allegory, and cannot be literally characteristic of either Daye or his times. In an era when a score of competent compositors could not have been collected throughout the whole of London, it is hardly to be supposed that the men would have answered to the whip of an Egyptian taskmaster.

LIFE IN THE WARTBURG.

'At times the chatelain sent secretly for some of Luther's acquaintance,' we are told in a passage quoted by Michelet, 'the nearest at hand, who repaired to Wartburg at night, and, rising early in the morning, assembled around the monk in one of the castle halls, and heard from his lips the words of the doctrine, returning to their homes at nightfall. Luther's table was well served, daily provided with game and with plenty of the glorious Rhine wine the monk was always so fond of. The chatelain was courteous, attentive, respectful to his *prisoner*, who at one time felt a mistrust that he was living at the worthy man's expense. "But after all," he writes to Spalatin, "I am satisfied it is the prince who is paymaster; I would not remain here another hour if I really thought upon reflection that I was living at my guardian's cost. At the cost of the prince, with all my heart; for if one must be a charge to somebody, it is well to be a charge upon princes; princes and thieves, you know, are pretty well synonymous terms. But I wish you to ascertain the precise state of the case and let me know."'

The record of his personal experience, as related by himself, shows that the superstitions of the age clung fast to the Reformer. He speaks of having been disturbed by violent commotions on the stairs when it was quite certain that no mortal could possibly have passed the chained iron door. He shows that he was not peculiar in regard to these notions, for a visitor who occupied the same quarters while Luther was accommodated in another part of the castle heard such an uproar that at least a thousand demons were supposed to be in the place. Thus the Wartburg was regarded as a haunted house by its old residents.

LUTHER AND THE PLAGUE.

The people who lived in the sixteenth century were accustomed to hear of ravages committed by the plague. The pestilence was raging at Wittenberg in 1527, and two visitors at Luther's house were seized with the disease. Then again he writes that the wife of their chaplain died of the distemper; and because all the town appeared to be afraid to approach the afflicted man, Luther took him and his children beneath his own roof, although Catherine, the Reformer's wife, was on the eve of her confinement. In another place as quoted by Michelet, Luther thus refers to the plague which had broken out at Madeburg: —

'The intelligence you send respecting the apprehensions of the plague which prevail with you quite corresponds with the experience which former events of a like nature afforded me. I am astonished, I own, to observe that the more widely the Word of life through Jesus Christ is spread, the greater becomes the fear of death amongst the people. Thus, whilst in former years, under the Pope's domination, a false and illusory hope of eternal life diminished in men's estimation the fear of death, it seems as if, when the well-founded and certain expectation of the life to come is placed before them, it brought with it a sense of the weakness of our nature, and thereby permits Satan to acquire more strength and boldness? So long as we held by the papal faith, we were like drunken men, stupid and asleep, mistaking death for life; that is to say, utterly ignorant of death and of the wrath of God. Now that the light has manifested itself, and that the wrath of God is better understood by us, human nature has extricated itself from the trammels of folly and of indolence. Hence it results that some have greater apprehensions than they formerly entertained.'

LUTHER AND THE EUROPEAN STATES.

'I have got some cloth for breeches, but I have not as yet determined upon giving it out to be made up. Those I have have been mended four times, and shall be mended once more. The tailors here are very bad and very dear. Things in this respect are much better in Italy. There one particular class of tailors makes nothing else but breeches.'

'In Italy and France the ministers are for the most part

mere asses. . . In France, the people are so sunk in superstition that all the serfs and peasants wanted to turn monks. The king was absolutely obliged to forbid this monkerizing. France, in fact, is a perfect abyss of superstition. The Italians are either sunk in superstition or daring free-thinkers. It is a common saying there when they are going to church, "We must humour the popular prejudice." '

' Dr. Staupitz heard at Rome in 1511, that, according to an old prophecy, a hermit would arise under Pope Leo X. and attack papacy. Now the Augustines were also called hermits.'

' There was in Italy a particular order calling themselves *Brothers of Ignorance*. They all took an oath to know nothing, and to learn nothing. All the monks in reality belong to this order.'

One evening there was at Luther's table an old priest, who related a great many things about Rome. He had been there four times, and had officiated there two years. On being asked why he had gone there so often, he replied, ' The first time I went in search of a knave ; the second time I found him ; the third time I brought him away with me ; the fourth time I took him back again, and placed him behind the altar of St. Peter.'

' The Scotch are a very proud people ; a great many of them have taken refuge in Germany, and more particularly at Erfurt and Wurtzburg. They admit none but their own countrymen into their convents. The Scotch are looked down upon by other countries as the Samaritans were by the Jews.'

' The plague still rages in England. England is a piece of Germany. The Danish and English languages are Saxon, that is to say, true German, but the language of Upper Germany is not true German. . . The German language is superior to all others of modern times.'

'In France every one has a glass of his own at table. The French are very chary of exposing themselves to the air; if they happen to perspire, they cover themselves all up, creep up to the fire, or go on bed for fear of fever. At their balls, the people dance together, the rest looking on. It is different in Germany. The priests of France and Italy do not know their own language.'

'The old Elector of Brandenburg, Joachim, once said to the Duke of Saxony, Frederick, "How do you manage to coin so much money, you princes of Saxony?" "Oh," replied the other, "we make money by it!" And so they did, by the quantity of alloy they put into their coin.'

Luther entertained in his house for some time a Hungarian named Mathias von Vai. When the latter returned to his own country, he preached the new doctrine, and was forthwith denounced to the monk George, brother of the Waywode, and who was at this time governing at Buda as regent. George had two barrels of gunpowder brought into the market-place, and said to the papist who had denounced Mathias, and to Mathias himself, 'Each of you say that your particular doctrine is the right one; stand upon these bands, I will fire the train, and we shall see which of the two remains alive.' The papist refused the test, but Mathias at once took his stand on one of the barrels; whereupon the papist and his people were condemned to pay four hundred Hungarian florins to the State, and to keep, moreover, two hundred soldiers for a certain time, while Mathias was allowed to preach the Gospel.—*Translated by Michelet.*

LUTHER AT MELANCTHON'S SICK-BED.

Not long after the unhappy marriage of his daughter Anna in 1536, Melancthon was brought to the verge of the grave, and the Elector despatched a messenger to Wittenberg for his son and for Luther, who rode night and day till he reached Weimar. Melancthon lay apparently at the point of death. His eyes were already dim, reason and speech, sight and hearing gone; his countenance shrunk and fallen, he lay without taking notice of any one, and could take no nourishment. Luther was terribly shocked as he gazed upon him unrecognized, and exclaimed, 'God forbid.' He then withdrew to the window, and betook himself to earnest pleading with God for the life of his friend. 'I cast my burden (he says) down before His door, and besieged His ear with every promise He has made to prayer, which I recalled from the Holy Scripture.'

He then went up to the bed and took his friend by the hand, saying, 'Be of good cheer, my Philip; thou shalt not die.' While Luther was giving vent to the fulness of his heart, Melancthon began to recover consciousness and breathe again, but for a long time he was unable to utter a word. At last he turned his face to Luther and began to entreat him, for God's sake, not to seek to detain him longer here. 'I am now (he said) on a good journey. I beseech thee, suffer me to go on; nothing better than this can happen to me.' 'It cannot be, Philip,' answered Luther; 'thou must serve our God yet a little longer.'

Melancthon continued to revive, and Luther ordered some food to be prepared, and himself brought it to him. Melancthon refused to eat. Then Luther said, 'Hear me, Philip; thou must eat, or I must excommunicate thee.' With these words, uttered half threateningly, half jestingly, he prevailed; the sick man began to eat, and strength slowly returned. Melancthon declared afterwards, that if Luther had not come then, he must have died. He said also, that as he lay, as he thought, in the last death anguish, the words came before him as if written on the wall, 'I shall not die, but live, and shall declare the works of the Lord,' and brought with them powerful consolation. On his recovery it was not permitted him to return to his wife and home; he was sent for, with Luther, by the Elector, to Eisenach, and from thence he was summoned to attend the convention at Worms. While at Eisenach he wrote thus to Bugenhagen, in Wittenberg, 'I thank you heartily, my best and dearest pastor, that during my absence you have comforted me in so Christian a manner and that in my home my wife has been aided by your counsels. I have been restored from death to life by the power of God. This is the testimony of all who were with me. Oh that I might thank God aright and live to His glory. I commend myself and the Church of Christ to your prayers.'—*Christian Witness.*

LUTHER'S DOMESTIC LIFE.

A contemporary writer once described Luther and Melancthon: 'Melancthon is a small, insignificant personage; by the side of Martin Luther he looks like a boy of eighteen. They are always together, and as they walk along, Martin rises a head and shoulders higher than his companion. When I saw him in his forty-first year he was somewhat stout, but so upright that he rather inclined backwards than forwards, while his dark-brown eyes were directed heavenwards, sparkling and flashing like stars, so that their gaze was hard to bear.' There seems to have been a united testimony in regard to Luther's eyes 'flashing like stars;' for Cajetan, who spoke with all the prejudice of a cardinal, however said that he had no desire to speak a second time with so uncouth a man —' He has strange thoughts in his head,' added the churchman, 'and his eyes are too deep and fiery for me.' The

Emperor Maximilian I. held more flattering notions regarding Luther's presence, having thought it to be a pity for a man to be a monk who was evidently endowed by nature to do great things as a soldier.

Luther appears to have taken pleasure in bearding his chief enemies, or, at all events, in proving to them that neither their frowns nor their caresses would suffice to turn him aside from his allotted work. Thus, on a certain morning the Reformer applied to his barber unusually early, and on the man's inquiring the reason, it transpired that Vergerius, the Pope's representative, wished for an interview, and Luther wished to appear at his best so that his opponents might be correctly informed as regarded his capacity for further labour in the world. It was remarked by the barber that the nuncio would be vexed, when Luther replied that such had vexed the Church more than enough, and needed to be dealt with as with foxes.

The Reformer's parents were greatly pleased at his taking a wife; but having been accustomed to a different kind of experience, his Catherine did not always find things go as smoothly as she desired in the house. Her husband was wont to show her that in any case much depended on the wife. The way to have a thing well done was to do it herself; and beside, the old-fashioned custom of 'early to bed and early to rise' was confidently inculcated as a prescription likely to bring contentment. One day, when his wife was speaking rather sharply to her maids, he asked if she had begun her sermon with the Lord's Prayer. At another time when she rather petulantly interfered with his reading of the Scriptures, he bade her beware lest the love of new books should displace the Bible. Their discourse was often of the most serious kind; and how greatly he valued his wife, who was more to him than a kingdom, is shown by his letters sent to her during his frequent absences from home. He was devotedly fond of his children, hospitable to a fault, and ever careful about not wounding the feelings of the poor, who sometimes called him the right pope. A waggoner was once introduced to him in his house at Wittenberg, whose one desire had been to see the great doctor. 'Let him come in,' cried Luther; and on the peasant coming forward, the Reformer held out his hand, telling the man to assure his friends on his return that he had shaken hands with the arch-heretic. The waggoner's health was then drunk, and, being dismissed, he ever afterwards told of his adventure with great glee.

AN EXAMPLE OF REMORSE.

Arnold Bonelius was a student in the university of Lovain, a man much commended for an exceeding ripeness of learning and for favouring the Protestant religion, but afterwards apostatizing to Popery; he began to be much troubled in mind, and then fell into despair, against which he wrestled a great while. At length being wholly overcome by it, as he went out to walk in the fields with some scholars and a few friends, he pretended himself weary, and sat down by a spring's side, and his friends being gone a little before, he drew out a dagger, and stabbed himself into the breast. His friends observing him to shrink down, and the water discoloured with his blood, ran to him, took him up, carried him to the next house, and searched his wounds; but whilst they were busy about him, he espied a knife by one of their sides; whereupon he plucked it forth, and suddenly stabbed himself into the heart, whereby he miserably died.
—*Acts and Monuments.*

LUTHER AND HENRY VIII.

The Reformer's pen was extremely busy in the Wartburg, and among the things he composed there was the reply to Henry VIII., who had undertaken to write down that treatise of Luther's which had greatly vexed the papists, *The Captivity of the Church at Babylon*. Michelet quotes some passages from the Reformer's treatise which give us a view of the way in which controversy was carried on at that time, *e.g.*, 'He who lies is a liar; and I fear him not be he who he may.' He then deals out to the English king some plain-speaking such as can hardly be read without astonishment even after the lapse of 360 years:—

'Ah! ah! my worthy Henry, you've reckoned without your host in this matter; you've had your say, and I'll have mine; you shall hear truths that won't amuse you at all; I'll make you smart for your tricks. This excellent Henry accuses me of having written against the Pope out of personal hatred and ill-will; of being snarlish, quarrelsome, back-biting, proud, and so conceited that I think myself the only man of sense in the world. I ask you, my worthy Hal, what has my being conceited, snappish, cross-grained—supposing I am so—to do with the question? Is the papacy free from blame because I am open to it? Is the King of England a wise man because I take him to be a fool? Answer me that. The best of it is, that this worthy monarch, who has such a horror of lying and calumny, has assuredly gathered together more lies and more slanders in this little book than can be charged upon me, by my worst enemies, in the whole extent of my writings.'

This, and much more of the same kind which follows, shows that the era of the Reformation was not a time of gentle controversy.

LUTHERAN WORKS IN FOREIGN LANDS.

It was hardly to be expected that while Luther was exercising so vast an influence in his own country by his works, they should not penetrate into other countries, in spite of restrictive laws. Frobenius of Bâle, one of the most celebrated of Continental printers, collected the Reformer's writings at an early date, and even dignitaries of the Church read them with admiration. Writing from Rotterdam, Erasmus declared that it was quite out of his power to describe the emotions and tragic scenes which the reading of the imported books produced. At Paris even the doctors of the Sorbonne were captivated; and perhaps because some of them had hardly seen the Scriptures from childhood to middle-age, they thought it was time that a commentator of Luther's calibre should arise. We are told how the Spanish merchants of Antwerp sent them into their native land; and happy had it been for the ruined Spain of to-day if the seed thus scattered had been allowed to bear fruit. It is even more curious to find that the proscribed books of the German Reformers were translated into Italian, and openly sold even in Rome under other titles. M'Crie tells us how the *Common Places* of Melancthon were thus printed at Venice, to be sold at Rome during a whole year, or until a friar in the city detected the trick and complained to the authorities. 'A similar anecdote is told of Luther's preface to the Epistle to the Romans and his treatise on Justification, which were eagerly read for some time as the productions of "Cardinal Fregoso,"' remarks M'Crie. 'The works of Zwingli were circulated under the name of "Coricius Cogelius;" and several editions of Martin Bucer's Commentary on the Psalms were sold in Italy and France as the work of "Aretius." In this last instance, the learned stratagem was used with the consent of the author.' The historian then quotes from a remarkable letter of Bucer to Zwingli: 'I am employed in an exposition of the Psalms, which, at the urgent request of our brethren in France and Lower Germany, I propose to publish under a foreign name, that the work may be bought by their booksellers; for it is a capital crime to import into these countries books which bear our names. I therefore pretend that I am a Frenchman, and if I do not change my mind, shall send forth the book as the production of Aretius Felinus, which, indeed, is my name and surname, the former in Greek, and the latter in Latin.'

MARTYR BOOKSELLERS.

The Reformation could not have spread so rapidly as it did if it had not been for a devoted host of hardy colporteurs who spread themselves over the country and seconded the efforts of the booksellers in the towns. Some of these indefatigable men were monks, who having hitherto wasted their time and talents, made the best atonement in their power for past mistakes. Stimulated by printers and merchants, they worked on in spite of imperial edicts for the suppression of their wares, the people reading what was offered them all the more eagerly on account of the Government opposition. According to D'Aubigné, only thirty-five publications had appeared in Germany up to 1517; but in the year 1523, about 498 separate publications appeared, nearly all of which were published at Wittenberg, and a large proportion of which were written by Luther.

Among the martyrs who fell in this holy war was Gaspard Tauber, of Venice, who was himself also an author. He was detected in the act of disseminating Lutheran literature;

and, after being imprisoned, Tauber's judges supposed that they had persuaded him to recant. A vast assembly gathered in one of the churches to hear him do so; but instead of denying his Lord, the Reformer appealed to the holy Roman empire. He stood like a pillar of the truth before the astonished multitude; and after he was beheaded and his body burned, the Venetians remembered what Tauber had said about faith and judgment.

Another bookseller was committed to the flames at Bude in Hungary, the fire being fed by piles of his own books. Instead of flinching in any degree, the martyr declared that he was happy in thus yielding up his life for the sake of Christ and the Gospel. Luther said that the blood thus shed would in time suffocate the pope and his abettors. As early as 1524 there existed at Bâle a Bible and Tract Hawking Society, whose agents traversed France, so that Luther's prediction had some promise of being fulfilled.

PATIENCE.

A certain honest and God-forbearing man at Wittenberg told me, that though he lived peaceably with every one, hurt no man, was ever quiet, yet many people were enemies unto him. I comforted him in this manner: 'Arm thyself with patience, and be not angry though they hate thee; what offence, I pray, do we give the devil? What ails him to be so great an enemy unto us? only because he has not that which God has; I know no other cause of his vehement hatred towards us. If God give thee to eat, eat; if He cause thee to fast, be resigned thereto; gives He thee honours? take them; hurt or shame? endure it; casts He thee into prison? murmur not; will He make thee a king? obey Him; casts He thee down again? heed it not.'—*Table-Talk.*

LUTHER ON TEMPTATION.

All heaviness of mind and melancholy come of the devil; especially these thoughts, that God is not gracious unto him; that God will have no mercy upon him, etc. Whosoever thou art possessed with such heavy thoughts, know for certain that they are a work of the devil. God sent His Son into the world, not to affright, but to comfort.

Therefore be of good courage, and think, that henceforward thou art not the child of a human creature, but of God, through faith in Christ, in whose Name thou art baptized; therefore the spear of death cannot enter into thee; he has no right unto thee, much less can he hurt or prejudice thee, for he is everlastingly swallowed up through Christ.

The devil often casts this into my breast: How if thy doctrine be false and erroneous, wherewith the pope, the mass, friars and nuns are thus dejected and startled? at which the sour sweat has drizzled from me. But at last, when I saw he would not leave, I gave him this answer: Avoid, Satan; address thyself to my God, and talk with Him about it, for the doctrine is not mine, but His; He has commanded me to hearken unto this Christ.

It is better for a Christian to be sorrowful than secure, as the people of the world are. Well is it for him that stands always in fear, yet knows he has in heaven a gracious God, for Christ's sake, as the psalm says, 'The Lord's delight is in them that fear Him, and put their trust in His mercy.'

There are two sorts of tribulations—one, of the spirit; another, of the flesh. Satan torments the conscience with lies, perverting that which is done uprightly, and according to God's Word; but the body, or flesh, he plagues in another kind.

No man ought to lay a cross upon himself, or to adopt tribulation, as is done in Popedom; but if a cross or tribulation come upon him, then let him suffer it patiently, and know that it is good and profitable for him.—*Table-Talk.*

LUTHER ON ANTICHRIST.

Antichrist is the Pope and the Turk together; a beast full of life must have a body and soul; the spirit or soul of antichrist is the Pope, his flesh or body the Turk. The latter waits and assails and prevents God's Church corporally; the former spiritually and corporally too, with hanging, burning, murdering, etc. But, as in the apostle's time, the Church had the victory over the Jews and Romans, so now will she keep the field firm and solid against the hypocrisy and idolatry of the Pope, and the tyranny and devastations of the Turk and her other enemies.

'And the king shall do according to his will, and he shall exalt himself, and magnify himself above every god, and shall speak marvellous things against the God of gods, and shall prosper until the indignation be accomplished: for that that is determined shall be done. Neither shall he regard the God of his fathers, nor the desire of women, nor regard any god, for he shall magnify himself above all.'

This prophecy, as all the teachers agree, points directly at the Antichrist, under the name of Antiochus; for Antichrist will regard neither God nor the love of women—that is, the state of matrimony. These two, Antichrist contemns on earth—God, that is religion, and mankind. He will not regard women, that is, he will contemn temporal and house-government, laws, jurisdiction, emperors and kings: for through women children are born, and brought up, to the perpetuation of mankind and replenishing of the world;

where women are not regarded, of necessity temporal and house government is also contemned, and laws, and ordinances, and rulers.

Daniel was an exceeding high and excellent prophet, whom Christ loved, and touching whom he said: Whoso readeth, let him understand. He spoke of that Antichrist persecutor as clearly as if he had been an eye-witness thereof. Read the eleventh chapter throughout. It applies to the time when the Emperor Caligula and other tyrants ruled; it distinctly says: 'He shall plant the tabernacles of his palace between the seas, in the glorious holy mountain,' that is, at Rome, in Italy. The Turk rules also between two seas, at Constantinople, but that is not the holy mountain. He does not honour or advance the worship of *Maosim*, nor does he prohibit matrimony. Therefore Daniel points directly at the Pope, who does both, with great fierceness. The prophet says further: 'He shall also be forsaken of his king.' It is come to that pass already, for we see kings and princes leave him. As to the forms of religion under the Pope and Turk, there is no difference, but in a few ceremonies; the Turk observes the Mosaical, the Pope the Christian ceremonies—both sophisticate and falsify them; for as the Turk corrupts the Mosaic bathings and washings, so the Pope corrupts the sacrament of Baptism and of the Lord's Supper.

The kingdom of Antichrist is described also in the Revelation of John, where it is said: 'And it was given unto him to make war with the saints and to overcome them.' This might seem prophesied of the Turk and not of the Pope, but we must, on investigation, understand it of the Pope's abominations and tyranny in temporal respects. It is further said in the Apocalypse: 'It shall be for a time, and times and half a time.' Here is the question; what is a time?

If time be understood a year, the passage signifies three years and a half, and hits Antiochus, who for such a period persecuted the people of Israel, but at length died in his own filth and corruption. In like manner will the Pope also be destroyed; for he began his kingdom, not through power of the divine authority, but through superstition and a forced interpretation of some passages of Scripture. Popedom is built on a foundation which will bring about its fall. Daniel prophesies thus: 'And through his policy he shall cause craft to prosper in his hand; but he shall be broken without hand.' This refers specially to the Pope, for all other tyrants and monarchs fall by temporal power and strength. However, it may hit both Pope and Turk. Both began to reign almost at one time, under the Emperor Phocas, who murdered his own master, the Emperor Maurice, with his empress and young princes, well-nigh nine hundred years since. The Pope began to govern the Church spiritually at the same time that Mohammed founded his power; the Pope's temporal kingdom stood scarce three hundred years, for he plagued and harassed kings and emperors. I cannot well define or comprehend this prophecy, 'A time, and times, and half a time.' I do not know whether it refers to the Turk, who began to rule when Constantinople was taken, in the year 1453, eighty-five years ago. If I calculate a *time* to be the age of Christ (thirty years), this expression would mean one hundred and five years, and the Turk would still have twenty years' swing to come. Well, God knows how it stands, and how He will deliver those that are His. Let us not vex ourselves with seeking over-knowledge. Let us repent and pray.

Seeing the Pope is Antichrist,* I believe him to be a devil

---

* The identity of Antichrist with the Pope had already been asserted by John Huss, in his *De Anatomia Antichristi*.

incarnate. Like as Christ is true and natural God and man, so is Antichrist a living devil. It is true, too, what they say of the Pope, that he is a terrestrial god—for he is neither a real god nor a real man, but of the two natures mingled together.

He names himself an earthly god, as though the only true and almighty God were not God on earth! Truly, the Pope's kingdom is a horrible outrage against the power of God and against mankind, an abomination of desolation, which stands in the holy place. 'Tis a monstrous blasphemy for a human creature to presume, now Christ is come, to exalt himself in the Church above God. If it had been done amongst the Gentiles before the coming of Christ, it would not have been so great a wonder. But though Daniel, Christ Himself, and His apostles, Paul and Peter, have given us warning of that poisoned beast and pestilence, yet we Christians have been, and still are, so doltish and mad, as to adore and worship all his idols, and to believe that he is lord over the universal world, as heir to St. Peter; whereas neither Christ nor St. Peter left any succession upon earth.

The Pope is the last blaze in the lamp, which will go out and ere long be extinguished, the last instrument of the devil, that thunders and lightens with sword and bull, making war through the power and strength of others, as Daniel says, 'He is powerful, but not by his own strength.' It has been affirmed that the Pope has more power in one finger than all the princes in Germany; but the spirit of God's mouth has seized upon that shameless strumpet, and startled many hearts, so that they regard him no more; a thing no emperor, with sword and power, had been able to accomplish: the devil scorns these weapons; but when he is struck with God's Word, then the Pope is turned to a poppy and a frothy flower.

Some one, speaking of the signs and marvels which are to herald the coming of Antichrist, when he shall present himself previous to the last judgment, said he was to be armed with a breath of fire, which would overthrow all who might seek to oppose him. Dr. Luther observed, These are parables, but they agree in a measure with the prophecies of Daniel; for the throne of the Pope is a throne of flame, and fire is his arm, as the scymetar is the Turk's. Antichrist attacks with fire, and shall be punished with fire. The villain is now full of fear, crouching behind his mountains, and submitting to things against which heretofore he would have hurled his lightning and his thunder.—*Ibid.*

LUTHER'S ADVICE TO PREACHERS.

God often lays upon the necks of haughty divines all manner of crosses and plagues to humble them; and therein they are well and rightly served; for they will have honour, whereas this only belongs to our Lord God. When we are found true in our vocations and calling, then we have reaped honour sufficient, though not in this life, yet in that to come; there we shall be crowned with the unchangeable crown of honour, 'which is laid up for us.' Here on earth we must seek for no honour, for it is written, Woe unto you when men shall bless you. We belong not to this life, but to another far better. The world loves that which is its own; we must content ourselves with that which it bestows upon us, scoffing, flouting, and contempt. I am sometimes glad that my scholars and friends are pleased to give me such wages; I desire neither honour nor crown here on earth, but I will have compensation from God, the just Judge, in heaven.

From the year of our Lord 1518, to the present time, every Maunday Thursday, at Rome, I have been by the Pope excommunicated and cast into hell; yet I still live. For every year, on Maunday Thursday, all heretics are excommunicated at Rome, among whom I am always put first and chief. This do they on that blessed, sanctified day, whereas they ought rather to render thanks to God for the great benefit of His Holy Supper, and for His bitter death and passion. This is the honour and crown we must expect and have in this world. God sometimes can endure honour in lawyers and physicians; but in divines He will no way suffer it; for a boasting and an ambitious preacher soon contemns Christ, who with His blood has redeemed poor sinners.

A preacher should needs know how to make a right difference between sinners, between the impenitent and confident and the sorrowful and penitent; otherwise the whole Scripture is locked up. When Amsdorf began to preach before the princes at Schmalcalden, with great earnestness he said, The Gospel belongs to the poor and sorrowful, and not to you princes, great persons and courtiers that live in continual joy and delight, in secureness, void of all tribulation.

A continual hatred is between the clergy and laity, and not without cause; for the unbridled people, citizens, gentry, nobility, yea, and great princes also, refuse to be reproved. But the office of a preacher is to reprove such sinners as lie in open sin, and offend against both the first and second table of God's commandments; yet reproof is grievous for them to hear, wherefore they look upon the preachers with sharp eyes.

To speak deliberately and slowly best becomes a preacher; for thereby he may the more effectually and impressively deliver his sermon. Seneca writes of Cicero, that he spake deliberately from the heart.

God in the Old Testament made the priests rich; Annas and Caiaphas had great revenues. But the ministers of the

Word, in which is offered everlasting life and salvation by grace, are suffered to die of hunger and poverty, yea, are driven and hunted away.

We ought to direct ourselves in preaching according to the condition of the hearers, but most preachers commonly fail herein; they preach that which little edifies the poor simple people. To preach plain and simply is a great art; Christ Himself talks of tilling ground, of mustard-seed, etc.; He used altogether homely and simple similitudes.

When a man first comes into the pulpit, he is much perplexed to see so many heads before him. When I stand there I look upon none, but imagine they are all blocks that are before me.

I would not have preachers in their sermons use Hebrew, Greek, or foreign languages, for in the church we ought to speak as we use to do at home, the plain mother tongue, which every one is acquainted with. It may be allowed in courtiers, lawyers, advocates, etc., to use quaint, curious words. Doctor Staupitz is a very learned man, yet he is a very irksome preacher; and the people had rather hear a plain brother preach, that delivers his words simply to their understanding, than he. In churches no praising or extolling should be sought after. St. Paul never used such high and stately words as Demosthenes and Cicero did, but he spake properly and plainly, words which signified and showed high and stately matters, and he did well.

If I should write of the heavy burthen of a godly preacher, which he must carry and endure, as I know by mine own experience, I should scare every man from the office of preaching. But I assure myself that Christ at the last day will speak friendly unto me, though He speaks very unkindly now. I bear upon me the malice of the whole world, the hatred of the Emperor, of the Pope, and of all their retinue.

Well, on in God's name; seeing I am come into the lists, I will fight it out; I know my quarrel and cause are upright and just.—*Table Talk.*

STUDENTS' ADVANTAGES.

The student of theology has now far greater advantages than students ever before had; first, he has the Bible, which I have translated from Hebrew into German, so clearly and distinctly, that any one may readily comprehend it; next, he has Melancthon's *Common-place Book* (Loci Communes), which he should read over and over again, until he has it by heart. Once master of these two volumes, he may be regarded as a theologian whom neither devil nor heretic can overcome; for he has all divinity at his fingers' ends, and may read, understandingly, whatsoever else he pleases. Afterwards he may study Melancthon's Commentary on Romans, and mine on Deuteronomy and on the Galatians, and practise eloquence.

We possess no work wherein the whole body of theology, wherein religion is more completely summed up, than in Melancthon's *Common-place Book;* all the Fathers, all the compilers of sentences, put together, are not to be compared with this book. 'Tis, after the Scriptures, the most perfect of works. Melancthon is a better logician than myself; he argues better. My superiority lies rather in the rhetorical way. If the printers would take my advice, they would print those of my books which set forth doctrine—as my commentaries on Deuteronomy, on Galatians, and the Sermons on the four books of St. John. My other writings scarce serve better purpose than to mark the progress of the revelation of the Gospel.—*Table Talk.*

LUTHER ON THE BIBLE.

I admonish every pious Christian that he take not offence at the plain, unvarnished manner of speech of the Bible. Let him reflect that what may seem trivial and vulgar to him emanates from the high majesty, power, and wisdom of God. The Bible is the book that makes fools of the wise of this world; it is understood only of the plain and simple-hearted. Esteem this book as the precious fountain that can never be exhausted. In it thou findest the swaddling-clothes and the manger whither the angels directed the poor simple shepherds; they seem poor and mean, but dear and precious is the treasure that lies therein.

In times past, as in part of our own, 'twas dangerous work to study, when divinity and all good arts were contemned, and fine, expert, and prompt wits were plagued with sophistry. Aristotle, the heathen, was held in such repute and honour, that whoso undervalued or contradicted him was held, at Cologne, for a heretic; whereas they themselves understood not Aristotle.

In the apostles' time, and in our own, the Gospel was and is preached more powerfully and spread further than it was in the time of Christ; for Christ had not such repute, nor so many hearers as the apostles had, and as now we have. Christ Himself says to His disciples: Ye shall do greater works than I; I am but a little grain of mustard-seed; but ye shall be like the vine-tree, and as the arms and boughs wherein the birds shall build their nests.

All men now presume to criticise the Gospel. Almost every old doting fool or prating sophist must, forsooth, be a Doctor in Divinity. All other arts and sciences have masters, of whom people must learn, and rules and regulations which must be observed and obeyed; the Holy Scriptures only,

God's Word, must be subject to each man's pride and presumption; hence so many sects, seducers, and offences.

I did not learn my divinity at once, but was constrained by my temptations to search deeper and deeper; for no man, without trials and temptations, can attain a true understanding of the Holy Scriptures. St. Paul had a devil that beat him with fists, and with temptations drove him diligently to study the Holy Scripture. I had hanging on my neck the Pope, the universities, all the deep-learned, and the devil; these hunted me into the Bible, wherein I sedulously read, and thereby, God be praised! at length attained a true understanding of it. Without such a devil, we are but only speculators of divinity, and according to our vain reasoning dream that so-and-so it must be, as the monks and friars in monasteries do. The Holy Scripture of itself is certain and true; God grant me grace to catch hold of its just use.—*Table Talk.*

GOD'S PROVIDENCE.

When God contemplates some great work, He begins it by the hand of some poor, weak, human creature, to whom He afterwards gives aid, so that the enemies who seek to obstruct it are overcome. As when He delivered the children of Israel out of the long, wearisome, and heavy captivity in Egypt, and led them into the land of promise, He called Moses, to whom He afterwards gave his brother Aaron as an assistant. And though Pharaoh at first set himself hard against them, and plagued the people worse than before, yet he was forced in the end to let Israel go. And when he hunted after them with all his host, the Lord drowned Pharaoh with all his power in the Red Sea, and so delivered His people.

Again, in the time of Eli the priest, when matters stood very evil in Israel, the Philistines pressing hard upon them, and taking away the Ark of God into their land, and when Eli, in great sorrow of heart, fell backwards from his chair and broke his neck, and it seemed as if Israel were utterly undone, God raised up Samuel the prophet, and through him restored Israel, and the Philistines were overthrown.

Afterwards, when Saul was sore pressed by the Philistines, so that for anguish of heart he despaired and thrust himself through, three of his sons and many people dying with him, every man thought that now there was an end of Israel. But shortly after, when David was chosen king over all Israel, then came the golden time. For David, the chosen of God, not only saved Israel out of the enemies' hands, but also forced to obedience all kings and people that set themselves against him, and helped the kingdom up again in such manner, that in his and Solomon's time it was in full flourish, power, and glory.

Even so, when Judah was carried captive to Babylon, then God selected the prophets Ezekiel, Haggai, and Zechariah, who comforted men in their distress and captivity; making not only promise of their return into the land of Judah, but also that Christ should come in His due time.

Hence we may see that God never forsakes His people, not even the wicked, though by reason of their sins He suffer them a long time to be severely punished and plagued. As also, in this our time, He has graciously delivered us from the long, wearisome, heavy, and horrible captivity of the wicked pope. God of His mercy grant we may thankfully acknowledge this.—*Table Talk.*

LUTHER ON THE WORLD.

"Tis inexpressible how ungodly and wicked the world is. We may easily perceive it from this, that God has not only suffered punishments to increase, but also has appointed so many executioners and hangmen to punish His subjects, as evil spirits, tyrants, disobedient children, knaves, and wicked women, wild beasts, vermin, sickness, etc., yet all this can make us neither bend nor bow.

Better it were that God should be angry with us, than that we be angry with God, for He can soon be at an union with us again, because He is merciful; but when we are angry with Him, then the case is not to be helped.

God could be exceeding rich in temporal wealth, if He so pleased, but He will not. If He would but come to the pope, the emperor, a king, a prince, a bishop, a rich merchant, a citizen, a farmer, and say, Unless you give me a hundred thousand crowns, you shall die on the spot, every one would say, I will give it, with all my heart, if I may but live. But now we are such unthankful slovens, that we give Him not so much as a *Deo gratias*, though we receive of Him, to rich overflowing, such great benefits, merely out of His goodness and mercy. Is not this a shame? Yet, notwithstanding such unthankfulness, our Lord God and merciful Father suffers not Himself to be scared away, but continually shows us all manner of goodness. If in His gifts and benefits He were more sparing and close-handed, we should learn to be thankful. If He caused every human creature to be born but with one leg or foot, and seven years afterwards gave him the other; or in the fourteenth year gave one hand, and afterwards, in the twentieth year, the other, then we should better acknowledge God's gifts and benefits, and value them at a higher rate, and be thankful. He has given unto us a whole seaful of His Word, all manner of languages and liberal arts. We buy at this time, cheaply, all manner of good books. He gives us learned people, that teach well and regularly, so that a youth, if he be not altogether a dunce, may learn more in one year now than formerly in many years. Arts are now so cheap, that almost they go about begging for bread; woe be to us that we are so lazy, improvident, negligent, and unthankful.

We are nothing worth with all our gifts and qualities, how great soever they be, unless God continually hold His hand over us: if He forsake us, then are our wisdom, art, sense, and understanding futile. If He do not constantly aid us, then our highest knowledge and experience in divinity, or what else we attain unto, will nothing serve; for when the hour of trial and temptation comes, we shall be despatched in a moment, the devil, through his craft and subtilty, tearing away from us even those texts in Holy Scripture wherewith we should comfort ourselves, and setting before our eyes, instead, only sentences of fearful threatening.

Wherefore, let no man proudly boast and brag of his own righteousness, wisdom, or other gifts and qualities, but humble himself, and pray with the holy apostles, and say, 'Ah, Lord! strengthen and increase the faith in us!'—*Table Talk.*

LUTHER ON GIVING.

Give, and it shall be given unto you: this is a fine maxim, and makes people poor and rich; it is that which maintains my house. I would not boast, but I well know what I give away in the year. If my gracious lord and master, the Prince Elector, should give a gentleman two thousand florins, this should hardly answer to the cost of my housekeeping for one year; and yet I have but three hundred florins a year, but God blesses these, and makes them suffice.

There is in Austria a monastery which, in former times, was very rich, and remained rich so long as it was charitable to the poor; but when it ceased to give, then it became indigent, and is so to this day. Not long since, a poor man went there and solicited alms, which was denied him; he demanded the cause why they refused to give for God's sake? The porter of the monastery answered, 'We are become poor;' whereupon the mendicant said, 'The cause of your poverty is this: ye had formerly in this monastery two brethren, the one named *Date* (give), and the other *Dabitur* (it shall be given you). The former ye thrust out; the other went away of himself.'

We are bound to help one's neighbour three manner of ways—with giving, lending, and selling. But no man gives; every one scrapes and claws all to himself; each would willingly steal, but give nothing, and lend but upon usury. No man sells unless he can over-reach his neighbour therefore is *Dabitur* gone, and our Lord God will bless us no more so richly. Beloved, he that desires to have anything must also give: a liberal hand was never in want or empty.—*Ibid.*

THE HOLY GHOST.

The Holy Ghost has two offices: first, He is a Spirit of grace, that makes God gracious unto us, and receive us as His acceptable children, for Christ's sake. Secondly, He is a Spirit of prayer, that prays for us, and for the whole world, to the end that all evil may be turned from us, and that all good may happen to us. The Spirit of grace teaches people; the Spirit of prayer prays. It is a wonder how one thing is accomplished various ways. It is one thing to have the Holy Spirit as a Spirit of prophecy, and another to have the revealing of the same; for many have had the Holy Spirit before the birth of Christ, and yet He was not revealed unto them.

We do not separate the Holy Ghost from faith; neither do we teach that He is against faith: for He is the certainty itself in the world, that makes us sure and certain of the Word; so that, without all wavering or doubting, we certainly believe that it is even so and no otherwise than as God's Word says and is delivered unto us. But the Holy Ghost is given to none without the Word.

Mohammed, the Pope, Papists, Antinomians, and other sectaries, have no certainty at all, neither can they be sure of these things; for they depend not on God's Word, but on their own righteousness. And when they have done many and great works, yet they always stand in doubt, and say: Who knows whether this which we have done be pleasing to God or no? or, whether we have done works enough or no? They must continually think with themselves, We are still unworthy.

But a true and godly Christian, between these two doubts, is sure and certain, and says, I nothing regard these doubtings; I neither look upon my holiness nor upon my unworthiness, but I believe in Jesus Christ, who is both holy and worthy; and whether I be holy or unholy, yet I am sure and certain that Christ gives Himself, with all His holiness, worthiness, and what He is and has, to be mine own. For my part, I am a poor sinner, and that I am sure of out of God's Word. Therefore, the Holy Ghost only and alone is able to say, Jesus Christ is the Lord; the Holy Ghost teaches, preaches, and declares Christ.

The Holy Ghost goes first and before in what pertains to

teaching; but in what concerns hearing, the Word goes first and before, and then the Holy Ghost follows after. For we must first hear the Word, and then afterwards the Holy Ghost works in our hearts; He works in the hearts of whom He will, and how He will, but never without the Word.—*Ibid.*

THE PAINTER OF WITTENBERG.

Lucas Cranach—1472-1553—has had great distinction accorded to him, and not without good reason. He resided at Wittenberg, where his name appears among the records as early as 1504. In his earlier days he followed more than one branch of his calling, now using the pencil of the artist with characteristic skill, or, if need arose, using the brush of the house-painter without complaint. He was the friend of Luther in early life, and several times delineated the Reformer's features. Cranach was known and honoured by the Emperor Maximilian and his successor Charles V. In addition to his art, however, the painter followed several other occupations; for as the *protégé* of the Elector, he held a monopoly of medicine-vending in the town besides another monopoly of Bible-selling. He was a printer also; and Luther's works were multiplied by his presses. The shop in which the artist thus sold drugs and books, and accepted orders for pictures, remained as a chemist's shop until about twelve years ago, when it was destroyed by fire. Cranach was equally expert as an engraver; and this gift also was made to redound to the furtherance of the Reformation. He produced a large number of portraits of Reformers and royal personages; and thus we are indebted to him for the lifelike portrayals of the busy actors of those stirring times which we now possess. In 1877, General von

Cranach, commander of the fortress of Cologne, was recognised as 'one of the last descendants of the painter of Wittenberg.'

CHRIST AND HIS ENEMIES.

All heretics have set themselves against Christ. Manicheus opposed Christ's humanity, for he alleged, Christ was a spirit. 'Even,' says he, 'as the sun shines through a painted glass, and the sunbeams go through on the other side, and yet the sun takes nothing away from the substance of the glass, even so Christ took nothing from the substance and nature of Mary.' Arius assaulted the Godhead of Christ. Nestorius held there were two persons. Eutychius taught there was but one person; 'for,' said he, 'the person of the Deity was swallowed up.' Helvidius affirmed, the mother of Christ was not a virgin, so that, according to his wicked allegation, Christ was born in original sin. Macedonius opposed only the article of the Holy Ghost, but he soon fell, and was confounded. If this article of Christ remain, then all blasphemous spirits must vanish and be overthrown. The Turks and Jews acknowledge God the Father; it is the Son they shoot at. About this article much blood has been shed. I verily believe that at Rome more than twenty hundred thousands of martyrs have been put to death. It began with the beginning of the world— with Cain and Abel, Ishmael and Isaac, Esau and Jacob; and I am persuaded that 'twas about it the devil was cast from heaven down to hell; he was a fair creature of God, and, doubtless, strove to be the Son.

Next, after the Holy Scripture, we have no stronger argument for the confirmation of that article than the sweet and loving cross. For all kingdoms, all the powerful, have striven against Christ and this article, but they could not prevail.—*Table-Talk.*

THE GOSPEL FEAST.

Dr. Justus Jonas told Dr. Martin Luther of a noble and powerful Misnian, who above all things occupied himself in amassing gold and silver, and was so buried in darkness that he gave no heed to the five books of Moses, and had even said to Duke John Frederic, who was discoursing with him upon the Gospel: 'Sir, the Gospel pays no interest.' 'Have you no grains?' interposed Luther; and then told this fable:—'A lion making a great feast, invited all the beasts, and with them some swine. When all manner of dainties were set before the guests, the swine asked, "Have you no grains?" Even so,' continued the doctor, 'even so, in these days, it is with our epicureans: we preachers set before them, in our churches, the most dainty and costly dishes, as everlasting salvation, the remission of sins, and God's grace; but they, like swine, turn up their snouts, and ask for guilders: offer a cow nutmeg, and she will reject it for old hay. This reminds me of the answer of certain parishioners to their minister, Ambrose R. He had been earnestly exhorting them to come and listen to the Word of God. "Well," said they, "if you will tap a good barrel of beer for us, we'll come with all our hearts and hear you." The Gospel at Wittenberg is like unto the rain which, falling upon a river, produces little effect; but, descending upon a dry, thirsty soil, renders it fertile.'—*Ibid.*

LUTHER A SHARP REPROVER.

I was once sharply reprimanded by a popish priest because with such passion and vehemence I reproved the people. I answered him, Our Lord God must first send a sharp, pouring shower, with thunder and lightning, and afterwards cause it mildly to rain, as then it wets finely through. I can easily cut a willow or a hazel wand with my trencher-knife; but for a hard oak, a man must use the axe, and little enough, to fell and cleave it.

A comet is a star that runs, not being fixed like a planet, but a bastard among planets. It is a haughty and proud star, engrossing the whole element, and carrying itself as if it were there alone. 'Tis of the nature of heretics, who also will be singular and alone, bragging and boasting above others, and thinking they are the only people endued with understanding.

Here, to-day, have I been pestered with the knaveries and lies of a baker, brought before me for using false weights, though such matters concern the magistrate rather than the divine. Yet if no one were to check the thefts of these bakers, we should have a fine state of things.

There is not a more dangerous evil than a flattering, dissembling counsellor. While he talks, his advice has hands and feet, but when it should be put in practice, it stands like a mule, which will not be spurred forward.—*Ibid.*

LUTHER'S STYLE AND INFLUENCE ON LITERATURE.

It was Luther who gave that impulse towards spiritual philosophy, that thirst for education, that soundness of logic, which have made of the Germans one of the most generally instructed, most rational and moral, and most intellectual nations of Europe. Being convinced that education is the natural ally of religion and morality, Luther pleaded, unceasingly, for that of the laborious classes, boldly telling the princes and rulers how dangerous as well as unjust it was to keep their subjects in ignorance and mental degradation. His catechisms for children are masterpieces in their simplicity; the moral precepts which they contain are exactly adapted to the tender capacities of the readers. His explanations of the Psalms, and of passages taken from the Old and New Testaments, his sermons and other works, are all full of useful moral precepts; they all bear testimony to the profound religious conviction of the author; they all exhibit his admiration for the works of the creation, and his deep sense of the perfection of the Creator. His penetrating eye dives into the abyss of the human heart, and discovers its darkest recesses. But he is no gloomy ascetic, no contemplative visionary satisfied with deploring evil, or seeing no remedy but in extremes; his precepts are all practicable, his morality is social, and his faith is cheered by hope and charity.

To Luther the German language is indebted for much of its improvement, for its clearness and loftiness, and for that flexibility which distinguishes the works of later writers. The style of Luther is vigorous, straightforward, and comprehensive; it is not the style of a conceited sceptic, who doubts because he is ignorant, and who renders us as weak and undecided as himself; it is the style of a sacred orator who affirms because he himself believes, and who believes in obedience to the inspiration of his conscience, and to that divine light which the Gospel displays before him. He employs, at the same time, all the resources of polemical rhetoric to move and to convince; he appeals to the heart as well as to reason; he mixes passion with dialectics; sometimes even he descends to a vulgar jocularity of manner; he mixes bad taste with genius; and the German idiom, which was still cramped and unmanageable, comes from his pen more ductile and fashioned, though not disfigured, by his genius. Luther's version of the Scriptures, an imperishable monument of his learning and patience, a master-piece of precision, fidelity, and elegance, constitutes his best title to the gratitude and veneration of Germany, for having rendered the Bible popular and intelligible to all classes, and made it the domestic book of the people.—*Foreign Review*.

LUTHER'S ACHIEVEMENTS.

He emancipated half Europe (I trust for ever) from the curse of great errors on matters of greatest importance to man's eternal interests, and diffused through the same the light of the knowledge of the way of access to God through Jesus Christ alone. He restored to men a true exhibition of their peculiar relation to God through Christ, which had been obscured for a thousand years. He so proclaimed the distinguishing and life-giving doctrines of the Gospel as that they took effect upon the hearts of men then, and have lived in them till now. He saw with a clearness such as none for centuries before him had seen the importance of such truths as these—that we can learn little of God's purposes towards man anywhere but from Christ; that the desire to justify ourselves, and to depend upon our own strength in getting to heaven, is the misery and destruction of man; that by the most earnest striving to fulfil the moral law, we cannot attain peace of heart; that faith in Christ and obedience to Him, flowing from that love which such faith must inspire, is the only permanent source of peace of heart and purity of life; that the principle from which anything is done can alone give it worth in God's sight, and that therefore we do not become good by doing good works, but when we are good we do good works. God's sympathy with man, and man's responsibility to God; the necessity of the Holy Spirit's influence, and the efficacy of prayer; the entire absence of merit on the part of man, and the thorough freeness of remission of sin; how strong and happy we may be if united to Christ through faith, and how apart from Him we can be neither,—these things Luther saw and taught when no man about him did so. Now it was the proclamation of such truths as these that gave Luther his power over the hearts of his fellows. The faithful preaching of the Gospel of God; the earnest, bold, free assertion of the remission of sins through the blood of Christ, and through it alone; his knowing and stating the true answer to the question which every man must answer somehow, 'What must I do to be saved?' his having taught the true doctrine about things which all men are most interested in—repentance and regeneration, belief and duty, faith, hope, and love—this was what gave Luther the lever whereby he moved Europe from its old foundations. He had the truth in him, and other men had not, and herein was the secret of his strength; thus men were to him but as Philistines to Samson, as a forest to fire, as innumerable birds of darkness to light.—*Myer, 'Lectures on Great Men.'*

WHY LUTHER SUCCEEDED.

The success which Luther experienced is chiefly to be attributed to two circumstances, of which he availed himself with uncommon dexterity, to increase the number of his adherents and to give respectability to his cause. He was himself a man of considerable learning; and although his chief proficiency was in ecclesiastical and scholastic studies, yet he was not destitute of some acquaintance with polite literature, and was perfectly aware of the advantages which he should obtain by combining his own cause with that of the advancement of learning, and thereby securing the favour and assistance of the most eminent scholars of the time. In the letter . . . written by him to Melancthon, on his leaving Wittenberg to repair to Augsburg, this object is apparent; and many other indications of it appear in his works. His friends are always represented by him as the friends and patrons of liberal studies; and his adversaries are stigmatised, in the most unqualified terms, as stupid, illiterate, and contemptible. Notwithstanding the gravity of his cause, he is at some times sarcastically jocular; and his parody on the first lines of the Æneid, whilst it shows that he was not unacquainted with profane writers, contains an additional proof of his endeavours to mark his enemies as the enemies of all improvement. On this account he sought with great earnestness, in the commencement of his undertaking, to attach Erasmus to his cause, as he had already done Melancthon. And although, by the violence of his proceedings, and the overbearing manner in which he enforced his own peculiar opinions, he afterwards lost, in a great degree, the support of that eminent scholar, yet he has himself acknowledged that the credit and learning of Erasmus were of no inconsiderable service to him. This attempt to unite the cause of literature with that of reform is also frequently noticed by Erasmus. 'I know not how it has happened,' says he, ' but it is certain that they who first opposed themselves to Luther were also the enemies of learning, and hence its friends were less averse to him, lest by assisting his adversaries they should injure their own cause.' Erasmus could, however, have been at no loss to know how this was effected, for certainly no one contributed to it in so eminent a degree as himself, as may sufficiently appear from numerous passages in his letters, in which he has most forcibly inculcated these sentiments.* Afterwards, indeed, when the inflexible temper of Luther had given offence to Erasmus, and when, perhaps, the danger of adhering to him had increased, Erasmus endeavoured to frustrate the effects of his former labours, and to convince his friends that the cause of learning, of which he considered himself and Reuchlin as the patrons in Germany, had no connection whatever with that of Luther. But the opinion was now too deeply impressed on the public mind, and all his efforts served rather to establish than to obliterate it. The advantages which Luther derived from this circumstance are incalculable. His adversaries were treated with derision and contempt; and the public opinion was so strongly in his favour that his opponents could scarcely find a printer in Germany who would publish their works. Nor is it improbable that the same reasons which attached the most eminent scholars in Germany to the cause of Luther operated also in Italy to prevent that opposition which might otherwise have defeated his success, or at least retarded his progress. For Sadoletti, Bembo, and the rest of the Italian scholars kept aloof from the contest, unwilling to betray the interests of literature by defending the dogmas of religion; and left the vindication of the Church to scholastic disputants, exasperated bigots, and illiterate monks, whose writings for the most part injured the cause which they were intended to defend.—*Roscoe,* 'Leo the Tenth.'

THE DEATH OF LUTHER.

Luther had arrived at Eisleben on 28th of January, and, although very ill, he took part in the conferences which en-

* Erasmus was accused of having laid the egg which Luther hatched. This appears in his letter to Joannes Cæsarius, 7 Kal. Jan. 1524.

sued, up to 17th of February. He also preached four times, and revised the ecclesiastical regulations for the territory of Mansfeldt. On the 17th he was so ill that the counts entreated him not to quit his house. At supper, on the same day, he spoke a great deal about his approaching death; and some one having asked him whether we should recognize one another in the next world, he said he thought we should. On retiring to his chamber, accompanied by Maître Caelius and his two sons, he went to the window, and remained there for a considerable time, engaged in silent prayer. Aurifaber then entered the chamber, to whom he said, 'I feel very weak, and my pains are worse than ever.' They gave him a soothing draught, and endeavoured to increase the circulation by friction. He then addressed a few words to Count Albert, who had joined him, and laid down on the bed, saying, 'If I could manage to sleep for a half-hour, I think it would do me good.' He did fall asleep, and remained in gentle slumber for an hour and a half. On awaking about eleven, he said to those present, 'What! are you still there? will you not go, dear friends, and rest yourselves?' On their replying that they would remain with him, he began to pray, saying with fervour, 'Into Thy hand I commend my spirit; Thou hast redeemed me, O Lord God of Truth.' He then said to those present, 'Pray, all of you, dear friends, for the Gospel of our Lord; pray that its reign may extend, for the Council of Trent and the Pope menace it round about.' He then fell asleep again for about an hour. When he awoke, Dr. Jonas asked him how he felt. 'O my God!' he replied, 'I feel very ill. My dear Jonas, I think I shall remain here at Eisleben, here, where I was born.' He took a turn or two in the room, and then lay down again, and had a number of cloths and cushions placed upon him to produce perspiration.

Two physicians, with the count and his wife, entered the chamber. Luther said to them feebly, 'Friends, I am dying; I shall remain with you here at Eisleben.' Doctor Jonas expressing a hope that perspiration would, perhaps, supervene and relieve him, 'No, dear Jonas,' he replied, 'I feel no wholesome perspiration, but a cold, dry sweat; I get worse and worse every instant.' He then began praying again, 'O my Father, Thou the God of our Lord Jesus Christ, Thou the source of all consolation, I thank Thee for having revealed unto me Thy well-beloved Son, in whom I believe, whom I have preached, and acknowledged, and made known; whom I have loved and celebrated, and whom the Pope and the impious persecute. I commend my soul to Thee, O my Lord Jesus Christ! I am about to quit this terrestrial body, I am about to be removed from this life, but I know that I shall abide eternally with Thee.' He then thrice repeated, 'Into Thy hands I commend my spirit; Thou hast redeemed me, O Lord God of Truth!' All at once his eyes closed, and he fell back in a swoon. Count Albert and his wife and the physicians made every effort to restore him to life, but for some time altogether in vain. When he was somewhat revived, Dr. Jonas said to him, 'Reverend father, do you die firm in the faith you have taught?' He opened his eyes, which were half closed, looked fixedly at Jonas, and replied, firmly and distinctly, '*Yes*.' He then fell asleep; soon after those nearest him saw him grow paler and paler; he became cold, his breathing was more and more faint, at length he sent forth one deep sigh, and the great Reformer was dead.—*Michelet.*

LUTHER NOT PERFECT.

Was Luther, then, a perfect character? No; a very imperfect one. He was a sincere Christian, but not a mature one.

He was given to see some truths and to attain to some virtues in such degree as few others have been; but the completeness of the Christian character, its symmetry, certainly was not his. A good many fruits of the Spirit were wanting in him. Meekness, long-suffering, gentleness,—these were not his; and without these a man cannot be a model man. Luther was an instrument fitted for his work, but not a pattern for all time. He had, too, considerable mental weakness, as I think. His writings are not altogether possessions for posterity; they are truly straightforward and emphatically practical; but they, for the most part, aspire to only immediate usefulness, and they attain to little more than they aspire to. They are not consistent one with another, and they are not safe guides for this age, though they were the best for his own. Luther was not a patient man, and none but a patient man can be a good theologian. Wherever Luther goes beyond the plain letter of Scripture, it appears to me that he goes astray; wherever he theorises, he had better be silent; when he is betrayed into Philistine ground— that is, into philosophical—he loses his strength, and becomes much as other men. The scientific intellect and philosophic temper did not shine out in him at all. He was an admirable advocate, but the judicial element (which is the highest) was not his. His views of great questions have all that compactness and manageableness which is the consequence and the convenience of narrowness; but the significance of the Gospel as a whole was not clear to him. The mysteries of the universe pressed but lightly upon him. He cut every knot. A rough, strong, practical grasp of things contented him. He had few scruples and no fears. He would dogmatise more than he had need to do, and thus was obliged to accept consequences which he might have avoided. He saw some things far off vividly, and others close by, through eagerness not at all. The shortest practicable way to a point he had in view, that he saw, and with his gigantic mode of striding, it little mattered what kind of ground lay between it and him; firm or boggy, turnpike or trespass, over it he would go, and went. Such an one I will not blame; but I dare not follow.—*Myer's ' Lectures on Great Men.'*

LUTHER STILL POPULAR—ANOTHER REFORMER WANTED.

It is an anomaly that Luther should still be so popular as he is in a country where his evangelical teachings have for so long been superseded by the ultra-Rationalism which appears to be indigenous to Germany. The explanation is found in the fact that human nature *will* estimate at something like its proper worth such heroism as was exemplified in the lowly-born monk's self-denial and self-sacrifice. Though they may no longer live up to the standard Luther set up, or may even maintain that his teachings have been abrogated by the advances of science, Germans are still proud of the man who broke the shackles of a degrading sacerdotalism, and delivered the nation from a slavery all the more galling because its task-masters were priests. We are glad that it should be so, while regetting that a great population, for whom better things were anticipated, should have come down to ignoring the old landmarks which the Reformation itself set up on their favoured soil. Delivered from one error, the people of their own accord have gone off into the opposite extreme, and unhappily they have strayed into a region rife with speculations and negations from which it is not easy to win them back. At the same time the country is in a very different condition from what would have been the case had Romanism retained its hold on the Church and Government. The intellectual activity of the people, as indicated by the condition of the book market, is entirely characteristic of a community who have once and for all severed their connection with the Vatican, and who, in theory at least, declare for spiritual freedom. They, at all events, profess to be searching after truth; they are not in the hopelessly dead condition of those who breathe an atmosphere of apathy and indifference through supposing that all truth is deposited with their ecclesiastical guides. Then, beyond all this, we gratefully acknowledge that very much of what is Scripturally pure is still to be found within the pale of the Lutheran Church. To mention a few names of men who have stood forth as evangelical leaders would be invidious when so many suggest themselves—preachers and theologians whose literary works are valued by students of more than one continent. Such men belong to the Catholic Church at large, and as the embodiment of Protestantism themselves first, and then their works after them, are a standing protest against that pretentious, paganised sacerdotalism which would usurp the functions of Christ Himself. However widely we may be divided from, perhaps, the majority of Lutherans, the fact may not be overlooked, that we are still united by strong Protestant sympathies. This alone is a comfortable reflection in such times as these, when a revolution may, as it were, be born in a day; and when the political atmosphere of Europe is subject to sudden and violent changes. We do not, it is true, fight for and argue about the old bugbear called 'Balance of power;' but a balance of opinion against the Pope in Germany and America is something to be prized. Hence the Luther celebration has deepest meaning for us in the British Isles as well as for our cousins in the German fatherland.

It would be a blessing indeed if the revival of Luther's memory were directly or indirectly to lead to a revival of evangelical religion in the country which was the cradle of the Reformation. 'Would to God there were a second Luther,' wrote the late Dr. Macleod during a visit to Weimar in his younger days. 'Germany is in a most extraordinary state. The clergyman here is the head of the Rationalist school; of religion there is none, and most of the clergy merely follow it as a power in the hands of the State. I am credibly informed by competent judges that ninety-nine out of a hundred are infidels.' Though written nearly half a century ago, that description still retains a good deal of truth. Perhaps some improvement has taken place, but the great want of the people is the Gospel still; and it might be said with justice to-day, as it was in 1834, 'If you wish to *adore* your own church, country, and profession, come abroad.' The work of Luther has become obscured until in some Continental communities Protestant has become synonymous with Unbeliever. May a revival be inaugurated such as the Reformers would have been glad to have witnessed. The Fatherland could enjoy no greater blessing.

LUTHER'S HOUSE PRESERVED.

Though unable to be present at the recent festivities at Wittenberg in connection with the Luther celebration, the venerable Emperor wrote as follows while commissioning the Crown Prince to take his place:—

'But, as an Evangelical Christian, and head of the ecclesiastical *régime*, I feel the most cordial sympathy with every festival of this kind, in which the Evangelical faith finds unrestrained expression. I also fully appreciate the great boon it is to our dear Evangelical Church that her members should everywhere be reminded of their great inheritance, and the noble benefits which the Almighty bestowed upon us through the Reformation. As Wittenberg was the chief scene of Luther's powerful and divinely blessed labours, I would not willingly be unrepresented at such a festival, the less so as it is a festival of more than merely local import. I therefore charge you to represent me on this occasion. At the same time I beseech the Almighty that the approaching Luther Festival may tend to awaken and deepen true Evangelical piety, and contribute to preserve the good morals and maintain the peace of our Church.'

The Crown Prince accordingly attended the celebration in the town, and laid a magnificent wreath on the Reformer's grave, a great procession, headed by Luther's descendants—the latter including some English people—taking part in the ceremonies. In Luther's house the Crown Prince spoke as follows:—

'May this festival serve as a holy exhortation to us to uphold the great benefits of the Reformation with the same courage as was displayed in acquiring them for us. May it above all strengthen us in the resolution to be ready at all times to defend the Evangelical creed, and with it liberty of conscience and religious toleration. The strength and essence of Protestantism do not rest upon any stiff form of written words, but in the striving after the knowledge of Christian truth. May Luther's anniversary help to strengthen Protestant feeling, preserve the German Evangelical Church from disunion, and lay for her the foundation of lasting peace.'

According to *The Standard's* account, the hall was once an Augustinian monastery, which was presented by the Elector Frederick the Wise to Luther, who lived there with his wife, Katherine Bora, and it was there that their six children were born. The rooms inhabited by Luther, consisting of the saloon and six other apartments, are now transformed into the so-called Luther Hall. In it there is exhibited a large collection of interesting pictures and drawings by Cranach, Albrecht Dürer, and others. There are also many of Luther's polemical writings, and other documents, including a copy of the Papal Bull of Excommunication which was burnt by Luther; also numerous mementoes not only of Luther, but of all the other leaders of the Reformation period. The Municipality of Wittenberg wanted to call the rooms the Reformation Hall, but the Minister of Worship altered the title to the Luther Hall. Henceforth this building and museum will form the chief attraction to visitors to Wittenberg. The exhibition contains, besides the things above mentioned, a remarkable signature of the Czar, Peter the Great, written by himself in chalk, and now protected by glass above Cranach's picture of Luther.

POPE ALEXANDER VI.

The character of the Church which Luther reformed may be judged of by this portrait of Alexander VI. as drawn by Mr. Roscoe :—

The historians of this period, eager to represent both Alexander and his son in the most odious colours, have asserted that the death of the one and the disorder of the other were occasioned by poison prepared by them for the destruction of several cardinals of whose wealth they intended to possess themselves; but which, by the error of an attendant, was incautiously administered to themselves. That the horrid and detestable practice of destroying persons by poison was frequently resorted to in these profligate times is certain; and that Alexander and his son had employed these measures for the gratification of their avarice, their ambition, or their revenge, is positively asserted by many historians; but it by no means accords with the acknowledged ability, caution, and penetration of these men, that they would risk their lives upon the negligence or fidelity of a servant, or place them in the power of accident to render them the victims of their own crime. If, therefore, the death of Alexander is to be attributed to poison, it was most probably administered to him by some of those numerous enemies whom his rapacity and violence had incited to this deed of revenge; but documents recently produced, and a more dispassionate inquiry, afford sufficient reason to conclude that the death of the pontiff was not occasioned by poison, but was the effect of a fever, which in a few days hurried him to the grave.

Were we to place implicit confidence in the Italian historians, no period of society has exhibited a character of darker deformity than that of Alexander VI. Inordinate in his ambition, insatiable in his avarice and his lust, inexorable in his cruelty, and boundless in his rapacity, almost every crime that can disgrace humanity is attributed to him without hesitation by writers whose works are published under the sanction of the Roman Church. He is also accused of having introduced into his territories the detestable practice of searching for state offences by means of secret informers,— a system fatal to the liberty and happiness of every country that has submitted to such a degradation. As a pontiff he perverted his high office by making his spiritual power on every occasion subservient to his temporal interests; and he might have adopted as his emblem that of the ancient Jupiter, which exhibits the lightning in the grasp of a ferocious eagle. His vices as an individual, although not so injurious to the world, are represented as yet more dis-

gusting; and the records of his court afford repeated instances of a depravity of morals, inexcusable in any station, but abominable in one of his high rank and sacred office. Yet with all these lamentable defects, justice requires that two particulars in his favour should be noticed. In the first place, whatever have been his crimes, there can be no doubt but they have been highly overcharged. That he was devoted to the aggrandizement of his family, and that he employed the authority of his elevated station to establish a permanent dominion in Italy in the person of his son, cannot be doubted; but when almost all the sovereigns of Europe were attempting to gratify their ambition by means equally criminal, it seems unjust to brand the character of Alexander with any peculiar and extraordinary share of infamy in this respect. Whilst Louis of France and Ferdinand of Spain conspired together to seize upon and divide the kingdom of Naples, by an example of treachery that never can be sufficiently execrated, Alexander might surely think himself justified in suppressing the turbulent barons, who had for ages rent the dominions of the Church with intestine wars, and in subjugating the petty sovereigns of Romagna, over whom he had an acknowledged supremacy, and who had in general acquired their dominions by means as unjustifiable as those which he adopted against them.
—*Life of Leo X.*

WHY THE REFORMATION SUCCEEDED.

Had the whole Christian world, at the time when Luther began to preach against indulgences, been devoted to the Roman faith, however absurd the doctrines of the clergy, and however profligate their lives, he could not possibly have met with any considerable success. Such is the power of established authority and universally received opinion. But the never-ceasing contest between the popes on the one part, and the emperor with other sovereign princes on the other, diminished of themselves the reverence for the papal jurisdiction, and roused an inquiry into the grounds on which it was established,—an inquiry which was facilitated by the revival of literature. The discoveries of grave theologians and antiquarians were followed by the ridicule of wit and humour. Savonarola and Wickliff were aided by Dante, Petrarch, and Erasmus. In the beginning of the sixteenth century, the primitive doctrine of Christianity had taken root in most countries of Europe. The materials for reformation were collected and the foundations laid deep before Luther and Calvin raised and completed the superstructure. The minds of men being thus prepared, the doctrines of the reformers spread far and wide. The reformed religion was adopted and protected by sovereign, states, and princes; and after a war, continued with little interruption for more than a century, was finally established as the national worship of near the half of Europe, together with the balance of political power by the Peace of Westphalia in 1648. This Peace, which terminated the disputes, religious and civil, between the Catholic powers on the one hand and the Protestant powers on the other, was the greatest event, and that which was most characteristic of the seventeenth century. From the Treaty of Westphalia to the middle of the eighteenth century and upwards, the spirit that still presided in the great councils of Europe was a jealousy of religious interests and views of political aggrandizement. Politicians talked of the Catholic and Protestant interests; and so late as 1755-6, the great King of Prussia, Frederic II., was called the Protestant Hero.—*Anon.*

SCOTLAND BEFORE THE REFORMATION.

The vast benefits derived from Scotland by the Reformation may be inferred from the following description by a contemporary writer of the condition of the country in the fourteenth century:—

In Scotland a man of gentle manners or honourable sentiments is not easily to be found. Those of their country are like wild and savage people, shunning acquaintance with strangers, envious of the honour or profit of every one besides themselves, and perpetually jealous of losing the mean things they have; that hardly any of the nobility kept intercourse with the French, except the Earls of Douglas and Murray; that Edinburgh, although by this time the first city n Scotland, could not accommodate the French, many of whom were obliged to seek lodgings at Dunfermlin and other towns at still greater distances; that the French knights complained grievously of their wretched accommodation, no comfortable houses, no soft beds, no walls hung with tapestry, and that it required all the prudence of the French commander to restrain their impatience to leave so miserable a country. That when they wanted to purchase horses from the Scots, they were charged six, nay, even ten times the price for which these horses would have been sold to their own countrymen; that when the French sent forth their servants a-foraging, the Scots would lie in wait for them, plunder them of what they had gathered, beat, nay, even murder them; that they could not find saddles nor bridles, leather to make harnesses, nor iron to shoe their horses, for that the Scots got all such articles ready made from Flanders; that, in their military excursions, they carried along with them no provisions of bread nor wine, no pots nor pans, for that they boiled the cattle in their hides; that upon their precipitantly quitting their camp on the borders, the English found in it the carcases of 500 beasts, mostly deer, and 300 cauldrons made of their skins, with the hair still on them, stretched on stakes, filled with water, and the flesh put in them, ready to be boiled ; that they found also a thousand spits, with flesh for roasting, and 5,000 pair of shoes, made of raw leather, with the hair still on them.

CHAUCER'S PICTURES OF CHURCH LIFE.

In his own manner the poet introduces us to the Tabard Inn, where the apartments are spacious, and where a genial host dispenses a liberal hospitality. When the pilgrims arrive, nine-and-twenty in a company, the ecclesiastical personages are so clearly drawn that they stand out in charming distinctness.

First, look at the mediæval *nun*, one who as a prioress belongs to the aristocracy of her order. She is a maiden both coy and meek, who swears daintily, and who, while ignorant of the French of Paris, speaks in the fashionable Norman-French jargon of the day. At repast her demeanour is that of a well-bred lady, who never allows either drop or morsel to stain her spotless lappet. Reserved as becomes her sex and supposed sacred calling, she is naturally cheerful—she will not descend to the meanness of counterfeiting any grace. A prioress must be ingenuous, and, as we infer, must carry her heart on her sleeve. Then what woman ever before inherited so tender a heart? She has no disposition to inflict pain or to look on suffering. The sight of a mouse in a trap suffices to draw tears from her eyes; and she is equally pained if a gentleman beats one of her favourite dogs. Her open features and expansive brow bear abundant traces of breeding and intellectual force;

while the guiding motto of her life is *Amor vincit omnia*. In looking at this fascinating character we have only to remember that Chaucer wrote in the age of chivalry, and that he was speaking about a woman.

The *monk* presents an unfavourable contrast; but then he is only a don, a mere man, is not even an abbot, though ambitious of becoming one. Being a good rider, he loves hunting, hates books with corresponding intensity, and scarcely deems those texts of canonical authority which condemn the worldly lives of churchmen. Every man to his taste would evidently seem to have been the language of monkery in the fourteenth century. Did Augustine verily prescribe hard study and other duties? The monk acts as though he had mighty little respect for the old saint's authority; at any rate, he will have his dogs, brown palfreys, supple riding boots, rich furs, and fine broad-cloths. While his shaved head shines like a looking-glass, his eyes gleam merrily in his fat, round face. Since Chaucer has left us materials for drawing this portrait of a mediæval cloister-lounger, we need not go out of our way to doubt its correctness. Such holiness as our friend cultivated well agreed with his constitution; for the poet expressly says that while a fat swan was the monk's favourite dish, he did not show the paleness of a wasted ghost.

Socially, the *mendicant friar* is of a still lower genus. He united in one person the impudence of a conscious impostor and the wantonness of a merry-andrew. As a licensed beggar he is privileged, and if he once enter a house, he is not disposed to recross the threshold without his farthing. Yet the man's circle of acquaintance is large, and in its way influential, though certain of his circle of friends are not professors of common morality. Being wise in his generation, the friar is master of those arts which earn popular favour. He marries young aspirants without taking fees; in the confessional he avoids the assumption of a stern countenance; gross sinners get off easily with a light penance; and, by a still more masterly stroke of policy, he substitutes money gifts for sorer inflictions, the cash of course going to his own order.

We also have some revelations of life at the universities five hundred years ago. The *Oxford scholar* who makes one of the Canterbury pilgrim-band is a representative man, and to look at him is to become aware of the fact that in mediæval times scholarship and worldly gear were but seldom allied. Looked at from a worldly standpoint, the Oxford scholar of Old England is a sorry character, though not without his points of interest. His coat is threadbare, his features tell of scanty repasts, while his horse, through sharing the fortunes of an unlucky master, might fitly be compared, for leanness, with a garden rake. Yet the man knows how to maintain a certain amount of scholarly dignity in spite of his grinding poverty. His natural habit tends towards taciturnity; but while willing to learn, he is always ready to teach. Though his stomach may be stinted, his head is always stuffed full of Aristotle. He reads in bed, worries his friends for loans, and when unable to repay them in cash, he undertakes to pray for their souls. A grave place, indeed, must the world have proved to a scholar of mediæval Oxford. He again lives before us in the numbers of the poet as vividly as if he were a creature of to-day. Too learned to smile, he is still a self-satisfied creature; and while possessing a world in Aristotle, he is content with short commons and a bony hack.

Now turn to the *sompnour*, who, when the papacy was at the height of its power, was the summoning officer of the bishop's court, a kind of inspector-general of ecclesiastical nuisances. This office was naturally unpopular in a loose, unsettled age; it would have been so had the sompnour been a man of probity and sanctity; but when he was known to be unscrupulously corrupt, he was regarded as a mere ecclesiastical tormentor. This inspector of other people's morals is a man whose crimes in our own day would ensure him the penalty of penal servitude for life. His tastes are grovelling, his connections are low—too bad, indeed, for particular description. The friar who undertakes to depict character calls the sompnour a false thief. We shall of course remember that the poor fellow is painted by a bitter enemy; but even though the pot calls the kettle black-sides, we may still suspect that the libel is true. Abandoned and unprincipled, the sompnour is ready to soil his hands with any roguery which promises to replenish his pocket. How he procures his iniquitous pelf is to him a matter of supreme indifference; and hence his income is augmented by first threatening innocent individuals, and then by taking a bribe to let them off. By the aid of a parable the friar exposes the ecclesiastical villainy of the age. On a certain day a sompnour rides forth intent on evil business. Lacking richer prey, he purposes to arraign by false accusation an 'old rebeck,'—*i.e.*, a shrill-tongued woman—in expectation of taking a bribe. Ere he has advanced very far along the road, he overtakes one who appears to be a gay yeoman, and, after passing the word of honour as brethren, the stranger makes the rather unwelcome confession that he is a fiend in human shape. Though he may be somewhat startled, the sompnour will not retreat while there is money to be made, not even though his partner 'were the devil Satanas.' As brethren the two ride forward as partners on the look-out for any spoil that may come into their net. They come up to a cart laden with hay, and, in consequence of certain language used by the carter, the sompnour eagerly calls on his ally to claim the booty as a rightful possession. This, however, cannot be; for while he spake one thing the peasant thought another; in other words, the expressions of his lips were worse than the thoughts of his heart. Proceeding on their way, the church man undertakes to defraud a certain widow by threatening her with a false accusation. The story culminates when the sompnour is forcibly carried away to the dark regions by the fiend and claimed as rightful prey, having arrived at that state of badness in which every word and action are only so many sparks from the evil fires within. When the sompnour of the Canterbury band had listened to a recital of the sins of his order he did 'quake for ire,' and at once proceeded to retaliate. The accusing friar is a false self-seeker, who preaches for gain—is always seeking to impose on the unwary and the sick, while he gives forth the praises of himself and of his own order. Looking back through the mists of five centuries, we are able to judge between the rivals, well knowing that there was more than a little truth in their mutual accusations.

No less odious than the sompnour is *the pardon-monger*, and, indeed, the two appear as friends of a similiar calling who could sing a jovial song together. As he guides his steed along the Southwark High Street, and turns into the court-yard of the *Tabard*, it is well known to the company that the pardoner has newly arrived from Rome. 'The Eternal City' is the central market whence he draws fresh supplies of the wares in which he trafficks, the Pope being chief sales-man. He is not ashamed of his calling; he regards his business as a legitimate one; he has wares to sell, and, when buyers come upon the scene, he is able to pocket his receipts with the complacency of a man who gives value for money. Nor has fortune dealt unkindly with him—he is not underfed;

on the contrary, while his ample yellow ringlets cover his shoulders, he strikes us as being a man who for a roast capon and a tankard of ale would any day barter both Aristotle and all the learning in Christendom. Eager to take advantage of every opportunity, the searching glance of his eye resembles in keenness that of a hare on the watch. Naturally, his voice is powerful; when singing a convivial song, he can compete with the loudest; but on ordinary occasions policy demands that he speak in the low key of a cleric who understands his business and knows that he is conferring a favour. He is no half-and-half man, for so greatly does he excel in his craft that from end to end of Britain there is no such pardon-monger as he. The rarity and virtue of the relics he carries are calculated to command the awe and envy of the rural populace. In his cap he wears an image of Christ; in his wallet there are pardons new from Rome. He can show a tattered remnant of the Virgin's veil; he has a piece of the sail from St. Peter's ship; and not least among his treasures is a glass of 'pigges bones.' With so ample a stock-in-trade, and possessing besides a stock of assurance and a good horse, he is able to bag more gains in a day than an honest priest can do in a month. With words of guile and flattery, with a due allowance of lies, he is always ready to command an audience. Alas! he is able to engage at any time the admiration of simple peasants and credulous villagers, and, what is worse, the people crowd around his trumpery knick-knacks, having little notion that they are being befooled.

The picture is relieved by more cheerful colourings. The mediæval clergy were not universally corrupt; in the darkest times of history the Lord reserved a remnant to call upon His Holy Name. Chaucer's portraiture of *the good town parson* might almost pass for the picture of a God-fearing pastor of our own day. He is a man who meditates deeply on divine things, and he is zealous in good works. He is a constant preacher of the Word, and a teacher of his parishioners; while, as patient as he is diligent, he distributes to the poor with no niggardly hand. Staff in hand, he perambulates his broad and wild parish, as even the outskirts of a town would then be, hindered by no kind of weather. Were we to ask him, he himself would tell us,

> ' Well ought a priest ensample you to give
> By his own cleanness how his sheep would live.'

He seems to work like a man who has a call from God, and who is in love with his work. He is no self-seeker; he hankers after no preferment; he does not seek his own pleasure abroad while the wolf worries the flock at home. His example is pure, his charity abundant, so that when need arises he can with the more authority 'snib' a parishioner when detected in a fault. Better than all, we do not find that he falls down before an image of the Virgin or loses sight of Christ.

> ' But Christë's love and His apostles twelve
> He taught, and first he followed it himself.'

A GREAT PIONEER.

Robert Grossetête, the good Bishop of Lincoln in the fourteenth century, was a reformer in his day, and if opposition to the arrogance of the Pope and the claims of the papacy constitute a valid claim to the title, he was a Protestant. During his long life of nearly eighty years the country passed through many vicissitudes, and especially the crisis of Magna Charta. He lived in the reigns of four kings, Henry II., Richard I., John, and the long, feeble government of Henry III. During the rule of the latter monarch the papacy was at the height of its power, and while England licked the dust at the feet of the supreme Roman Pontiff, our kings were regarded as vassals whom the Bishop of Rome could at any time deprive of their crowns and shut up in prison. Henry was unsuccessful in war; he encouraged the insolent exactions of the Pope; and he made enemies of those who should have been his friends by striving after that absolute power which our forefathers from very early times have been loth to tolerate. This was the reign under which Robert Grossetête spent the greatest portion of his life, and the darkness and the troubles of the age exhibit to advantage the greatness of his character.

According to contemporary testimony, he was acquainted with all the sciences; but, according to Lechler, the chief aim and moving-spring of the bishop's life was 'his godly solicitude and care for souls.' Though born of humble parentage at Stradbrook, in Suffolk, he attained to the noblest of characters through studying the holy lives of Bible saints, and prayerfully endeavouring to conform to their standard.

In those days those who were educated were really learned, and among the learned none were more illustrious than Grossetête. He studied both at Oxford and Paris, and besides becoming eminent as a theologian, he mastered medicine and the canon law. From the close of the thirteenth century till the year 1335, when he became Bishop of Lincoln, he resided at Oxford, working hard as a lecturer and author. Some three or four years prior to his acceptance of the see of Lincoln, he was laid low by severe illness, when he 'experienced something of the nature of a religious awakening.' It may have been what we should call conversion; but, at all events, Grossetête was ever after a changed man. The ecclesiastical sinecures which he then held lay heavy on his conscience, and he determined on surrendering the flocks to those who could exercise the functions of shepherds. He sought counsel's opinion at Rome, and as Lechler remarks, 'The answer which was orally communicated to him was thoroughly Roman—by no means could he retain such a plurality *without a dispensation.*' That advice, as completely characteristic of Romanism to-day as it was six hundred years ago, failed to satisfy the burdened heart, and lucre was relinquished for the Gospel's sake.

In those days Lincoln diocese occupied a broader area, and contained a larger population than any other in the country. 'The cathedral,' says the German historian. 'built at the commencement of the Norman period, stands, with the older portion of the city, upon a height, while the newer portion of the city descends the hill to the plain watered by the river Witham. None of the English cathedrals has so splendid a site as that of Lincoln; with its three towers, it is seen at a distance of fifty miles to the north and thirty to the south, and is considered one of the most beautiful cathedrals in the kingdom.' The elevation of Grossetête to this high station must have created some consternation in the camp of the loose-living clergy; for the first business to which he gave attention was the checking of abuses, and the dismissal of unworthy abbots and priors. He urged his archdeacons to check immoral customs which tended to the desecration of the Sabbath and religious festivals, and was even bold enough to attempt a reformation of his own cathedral. This led to a quarrel not only with the chapter, but with the ecclesiastical forces of the day. In a word, Grossetête, both in his principles and in his zeal, was in advance of his age; and on this account he was regarded as a man of war while he was a lover of peace—

'the true peace, not the false.' His chief characteristic is said to have been 'an earnest solicitude for souls.' When Innocent IV., by a special brief, conferred a canonry in Lincoln on a youthful non-resident nephew of his own, Grossetête resisted the Pope to his face, and actually thwarted the designs of his holiness. The bishop even wrote to the Pope, quoting chapter and verse in self-vindication, a procedure which under such circumstances in the thirteenth century would savour strongly of amazing impudence. 'Who is that crazy, foolish, silly old man who has the effrontery to sit in judgment upon my doings?' cried the insolent pontiff, wild with passion. 'Is not the King of England our vassal, yea slave, who at a wink from us can shut him up in prison, and send him to ruin?' Such a speech reveals, in a short sentence, the arrogant pretensions of the popes in that age; and the God-fearing fortitude of the man who, with the Pope and his legions for enemies, could still fight and win.

It is shown by Foxe that, in the time of Innocent IV., the money taken in England by foreign ecclesiastics was seventy thousand marks, or three times as much as the crown revenues. After the death of Grossetête the vindictive pope purposed to have the bishop's ashes cast out of the cathedral of Lincoln, but was hindered by a terrible dream. In his uneasy sleep Innocent saw his great enemy and heard him speak: 'Sirribald, thou most wretched pope.... Woe to thee that despisest; shalt not thou also be despised?'

PRE-REFORMATION 'DONS' AND 'SIRS.'

In the fourteenth century at least one-and-a-half per cent. of the entire populace were ecclesiastics of some degree;

and a large proportion of official posts were occupied by priests. They eagerly sought the most lucrative offices under the crown, while energetic farmers and pushing traders were frequently of the same order. Men of all grades were eager for priestly honours on account of the advantages arising from connection with the Church; and thorough-going men of the world made no secret of their design in taking holy orders. When Wycliffe entered on the scene, it was not thought singular that worldly adventurers, young and profligate, allied themselves with the Church for the sake of the tithes of parishes in which they were seldom seen, and over which they exercised no sort of spiritual oversight. The absentees were the clerical fops of mediæval England. They donned gay clothing, strutted hither and thither in academical cloaks, ornamented themselves with jewels, and squandered in town the revenues of their country livings. Clerical society included many grades, each with its separate sympathies and prejudices. The *dons*, who were the monks, and the *sirs*, who were the curates, represent the factions which most frequently came into collision. Of the plump-featured, jovial mediæval monk art has helped us to form an opinion, correct or otherwise. His time is supposed to have passed lightly, while his fare was good and his lodging not indifferent. Worldly care pressed much more severely on the curate in charge of a parish. He was of a lower caste, and his stipend corresponded with his station no less than with his tastes. The village hostelry was his common haunt, where he lounged or talked away the hours, and emptied a tankard with those who thought with himself that good ale was the nectar of life. These old-fashioned *sirs* were a convivial class; and though it would not be right to say that more than a small percentage were addicted to excess, Wycliffe has shown us how curates occasionally brawled in the streets, and wended their homeward way raving a drunkard's ditty. A portion of the inferior clergy continued to indulge their abandoned tastes until late in the sixteenth century. Henry the Eighth, with a zeal which all will commend, ordered the whole of the clergy, the bishops excepted, to spend in Scriptural and holy exercises the time hitherto given to cards and to tavern pastimes. The reaction in the Church set in with Wycliffe and the Lollards when corruption among the clerical orders had reached its height. While rich absentees were enjoying a luxurious life in the towns, while begging friars were spreading themselves over the country, and curates, both drunken and lewd, were frequently a scandal to their order, professors of a purer doctrine arose to rebuke the excesses of the times. Like the Friends of our own day, the Lollards adopted a plain costume, and also refused to take any kind of oath. Still the doctrines of these Gospellers, who were cautiously groping their way from the darkness engendered by centuries of heresy, were not identical with those of the Reformers of two centuries later. In the matters of purgatory, image worship, and shrine miracles they went more or less astray; but they merely showed the fallibility of men who were incompetent at one stride to arrive at the whole truth.

MINOR PIONEERS.

Celebrated men, who in the fourteenth century served the cause of liberty by resisting the encroachments of the papacy, were the eminent jurists, *Henry Bacton* and *William Occam*. The latter, as a Franciscan, was a pupil of Duns Scotus, at Oxford; and after relinquishing the philosophy of his tutors, Occam gained such an ascendency in controversy that he was called 'the invincible.' According to Lechler, he dared to be independent. ' His philosophical nominalism had a prophetic and national signification, inasmuch as it prepared the way for that induction method of philosophising which was put forward several centuries later by able countrymen of his own, such as Francis Bacon, Thomas Hobbes, and John Locke.'

Richard Fitzralph, Archbishop of Armagh, became celebrated as an opponent of the shameless mendicant orders in the fourteenth century. During one of his visits to London he found the ecclesiastics warmly discussing the subject of the poverty of Jesus; and being asked to preach on the subject, he taught as follows: ' Jesus Christ, during His sojourn upon earth, was always a poor man; but He never practised begging as His own spontaneous choice. He never taught any one to beg. On the contrary, Jesus taught that no man should practise voluntary begging.'

A writer to whom Wycliffe himself was indebted, and a reviver of the doctrine that salvation is by grace from above, was *Thomas Bradwardine*, who died Archbishop of Canterbury in 1349, after holding the office for a few weeks only. He was a great favourite with Edward III., and without being suspected of heresy, he was celebrated both at court and in the army as a man of holy walk and conversation. While the most illustrious Christians of those most distant times are well-nigh forgotten, we may safely conclude that there must have been many others in the ranks of ordinary life.

Robert Longland, the reported author of ' The Visions of Piers Plowman,' also deserves honourable mention in this category as one of the disciples of Wycliffe. Longland was a native of Mortimer's Cleobury, Shropshire; he was educated at Oxford; and his poem is made up of a series of visions supposed to have been witnessed on the Malvern Hills. The poet exposes, without mercy, the corruptions of the age, and especially the delinquencies of the clerical orders. 'The whole drift of the poem is to recommend practical Christianity,' we are told. 'The kernel of its moral teaching is the pure Christian love of our neighbour—love especially to the poor and lowly; a love of our neighbour, reaching its highest point in patient forbearance and love towards enemies—a love inspired by the voluntary passion of Christ for us.' Piers Plowman exercised a vast influence for good in his age.

THE BAPTISM OF BELLS.

We suppose that the pre-Reformation custom of baptizing new bells still survives in Romish countries, although certain of the grosser observances may have been allowed to fall into abeyance. In the darkest times the bells were not only christened according to prescribed order, but regular sponsors were provided just as though the baptism of a child were taking place; and these, while holding a rope, replied to sundry questions after the manner of an ordinary service. This pagan-like custom is said to have been invented by John XIII., who flourished as pope in the tenth century; and the ceremony is thus described by an anonymous writer of fifty years ago: 'The bell is so placed that it can be easily got at; and then water, a whisk for sprinkling, salt, white linen clothes, holy oil, chrism, an incensoir with hot coals, etc., and a seat for the bishop are put by it. The bishop comes in state, sits on his faldistorium, and goes through various evolutions of putting on and off his headgear, while he exorcises the salt and the water, and the salt and water together as before. He washes the bell with the salt and water, and after it has been dried he dips his thumb in holy oil and makes the sign of the cross on the outside of the bell, and says, " We beseech Thee, O Lord, who hast commanded Moses to make silver trumpets, that this machine may be consecrated by the Holy Ghost, so that all the snares of the evil one, hail, and tempest may be driven away." Next he washes away the cross made with oil, and says, " The voice of the Lord is over the waters," which is repeated by the choir. Then after certain psalms he makes seven crosses outside with holy oil, and four inside with chrism, and consecrates the bell to the honour of some saint.' The service concludes with prayer, incense, and gospel kissings, and 'sundry evolutions with the head-gear;' but the form was not always precisely the same. The godfathers and godmothers of bells were usually persons of high rank; and a few years prior to the Revolution the ill-fated king and queen of France are said to have allowed their names to be associated with this superstitious folly.

Thus the more we look at the tree of popery the more shall we become convinced that it is a pagan branch grafted on to the Christian stock. By going low enough we may still find some of the old Gospel truths; but still, in spite of all, the pagan graft sucks up the sap intended by divine beneficence to be life to the soul; and, flourishing like a vampire tree, brings forth the fruits of death.

MEDIÆVAL BELLS.

The Church of Rome has long shown an almost superstitious affection for church bells. Though, according to Southey, bell-ringing is one of the most harmless methods of making a noise in the world, he was not able to tell us anything about the origin of the custom. An authority on the subject says that, 'In what country large bells did really originate it must be confessed is still involved in some obscurity. It has been supposed that long before bells were known in Europe, they were used in Hindoo temples for the purpose of frightening away evil spirits; but the architecture of their sacred edifices does not seem adapted to the suspension of large bells; and our utmost inquiry leads us to the conviction that church bells were invented by the Christian Church herself, and not at a very early period of her existence.' Thus bells were unknown in the primitive Church, when Christians went softly and unobserved to their secluded house of prayer; they came into existence as ecclesiastical appendages, in a prouder era of liberty. In the hands of the hierarchy of the middle ages bells were made to serve a number of purposes, the majority of which are now obsolete in Protestant countries. The Ave Maria bell called on all to offer prayers to the Virgin Mary; but in the most benighted times there appears to have been a remnant who knew enough about the Scriptures to prompt their disobeying the summons. 'Whilst others direct their prayers to her,' says Sir Thomas Brown, 'I offer mine to God, and rectify the errors of their prayers by rightly ordering my own.' The vesper bell was the signal for leaving off work to assemble at evening prayers. The Sanctus was rung when the priests came to certain words in the service; and the curfew, as everybody knows, was the summons to rest. The most solemnly touching of all must have been the passing bell, which, in mediæval times, told the parishioners that one at least in their midst was passing through the valley of the shadow of death to the eternal world. The solemn appeal which rang out loud and clear over fields, home, and workshop, was 'Pray for the passing soul;' and if Romanism had done nothing less scriptural than that, we should not have known whither to turn with any prospect of finding our present illustration.

BISHOPS BEFORE THE REFORMATION.

At the end of the thirteenth century Richard de Swinfield was Bishop of Hereford, and happily the prelate's household roll of expenses is extant. Whether or not his lordship of Hereford excelled his brethren in zeal for the faith and general industry it would perhaps be unfair to judge; but he was certainly a busy personage, whose train was composed of an immense retinue of servants. He possessed an episcopal castle besides seven manor houses, and he was continually travelling from one to the other of these, while further diversity in life was ensured by an occasional trip to the capital. Swinfield was not a man who could boast of any illustrious lineage. From being chaplain to his predecessor, he reached his high position through sheer merit, as merit went in those days. Each manor house was the centre of a large estate, of which the bishop was lord, and each mansion was literally a hall after the old English fashion. Petitioners, dependants, tenants, and others assembled in the great hall or common apartment, such as accepted lodging being content to sleep on the strawed floor, while the great man, as became his dignity, occupied a separate chamber. It would seem that the bishop was a good and liberal master in the old English sense. Some notion of the magnitude of his household may be gathered from the fact that at Michaelmas fifty-two beeves were slaughtered for the salting-tubs, besides large numbers of pigs, sheep, and deer. The bishop brewed his own ale, burned home-manufactured candles, and took care that ample stores of wine of the choicest vintages were duly cellared. Sugar was also an article used in the prelate's household; but it was used sparingly, the price having been eightpence, or two-thirds the cost of a sheep, for a single pound. At Christmas the feast was provided in coarse abundance. Seven quarters of beef, and veal, with pork and poultry in proportion, were brought to table to be despatched amid hilarious rejoicings. The London house was in Old Fish Street, and these premises were let to a grocer, who by agreement allowed the bishop possession whenever called upon to do so. Contrary to the custom of prelates in that age, his lordship of Hereford was a preacher, though we have no evidence to offer respecting the strength of his intellect and the quality of his doctrine.

WYCLIFFE'S BIBLE.

The translation of the Bible was the crowning work of Wycliffe's life. The idea of giving the people the *whole* Bible was in that age as novel as it was dangerous; and the magnitude of the undertaking, without the press to multiply the copies, should also be taken into account. Indeed, the extraordinary manner in which the corps of scribes got through their work constitutes one of the greatest wonders of the age, and reflects no little credit on Wycliffe's abilities in organization. In the days of the Reformation the more enlightened men, such as Sir Thomas More, appear to have been ashamed of the Romish policy of withholding the Bible from the people, and to have denied the fact. It was asserted that beautiful old manuscripts, more ancient than Wycliffe's version, existed; but the whole was nothing better than a picturesque myth. Portions of the sacred books had, during the ages, been rendered into the three old languages, Anglo-Saxon, Anglo-Norman, and Old English; but as a general translator of the Bible, Wycliffe was the first in the field. As a Middle English classic Lechler places Wycliffe before Chaucer, who has been commonly regarded as the standard of his day. 'If Luther, with his translation of the Bible, opened the epoch of the High German dialect, so Wycliffe, with his English Bible, stands side by side with Chaucer at the head of the Middle English.'

WYCLIFFE AT ST. PAUL'S.

There is some mystery enshrouding Wycliffe's celebrated appearance before his ecclesiastical superiors at St. Paul's in 1377; but it is probable that the causes were political as well as religious. John O'Gaunt, Duke of Lancaster, as a man who desired to curb the political power of the bishops, was naturally hated very heartily by the haughty Courtenay, who occupied the see of London. Obscure as the proceedings are when looked at through the haze of five centuries, it is quite understood that, in summoning Wycliffe into its presence, Convocation aimed at wounding higher game. Protected by his powerful friends, Wycliffe stood in St. Paul's, 'a tall, thin figure, covered with a thin, light gown of black colour, with a girdle about his body; the head, adorned with a full flowing beard, exhibiting features keen and sharply cut.' The proceedings in the cathedral began and ended in a violent quarrel between Lancaster and Courtenay. The affair culminated in a street riot during the evening, the citizens thinking themselves insulted in the person of their bishop. Soon after Gregory XI. signed five bulls in one day against the Reformer; but, to borrow a figurative scriptural expression, the stars in their courses fought against the papacy. The over-reaching greed of the Pope and his unprincipled favourites had produced strong resentment in England, both in the Parliament and at the universities. Wycliffe was in favour at court, so that bulls were more easily signed than carried into effect. With becoming prudence, the English wolves held back the instruments, softened their previous language into a milder dialect, and did not make themselves ridiculous by attempting impossibilities. Just at this juncture, moreover, the powerful Edward I. breathed his last; and a few months later Gregory XI. also died. After the death of Gregory, the world was entertained with the surprising spectacle of two rival popes, both gifted in the art of abuse, and this schism was an opportunity which the Reformers turned to account.

WYCLIFFE'S ITINERANTS.

The old itinerants of Wycliffe have frequently been portrayed, and their appearance and habits are better understood than the spurious preaching they sought to supersede. The ordinary sermons of the few preachers who then served in the pulpits of the church were not adapted either to enlighten or edify, and not seldom they contained more of profane buffoonery than of religion. Lechler tells us that 'even an archbishop of Canterbury, and a learned scholastic and cardinal, Stephen Langton, 1288, saw nothing offensive in taking for the text of a short Latin sermon, which still exists, a dancing song in old French, allegorically applying, indeed, "The Fair Alice," and all that is said of her, to the holy Virgin. Things of this sort, however, may have been of comparatively rare occurrence; but in the thirteenth and fourteenth centuries it had become almost a prevailing pulpit fashion, instead of opening up Bible thoughts, and applying them to life, to draw the materials of sermons from civil and natural history, from the legendary stores of the Church, and even from the fable world of the middle ages, and the mythology of the heathen gods.' In opposition to all this, Wycliffe prescribed that 'in every proclamation of the Gospel the true preacher must address himself to the heart.' The preparatory work of fitting these men for their duties occupied some years—the time, as is supposed, which the Reformer spent in comparative quietness at Oxford. The 'poor priests' who undertook this innovating toil were manifestly men of character, whose poverty was no counterfeit. They went forth, chiefly through the midland counties, in truly apostolic fashion. Their long habits were made of coarse red cloth; they wore no shoes, but each carried a staff in his hand. They were the open air preachers of Old England before the Reformation revived the Gospel which had been treasured by the ancient Church in Britain before the blight of popery cursed our island. 'Their sermons were, before everything else, full of Bible truth.'

WYCLIFFE'S TEACHING.

Wycliffe was a reviver of Bible teaching. In a corrupt age, when tradition was commonly allowed to be equal in weight to the inspired Word, he swept the cobwebs of superstition away, and with a boldness wonderful in that age, proclaimed the Scriptures to be the only rule of faith and practice. On this account he was called *Doctor Evangelicus*; but he was not so advanced as later reformers. He worked in the starlight, before the full dawn of the Reformation appeared. Familiar as he was with all parts of Scripture, he was not evangelical 'in the full sense of a decidedly Pauline theology, and of a truly evangelical doctrine of salvation.' He withstood the Pope as an anti-Christian pretender, exposed the excesses of image worship and the absurdities of transubstantiation; but he did not altogether escape from the mazes of priestly error which had grown up in the course of centuries. In a half-way manner he even denied the doctrine of salvation by human merit. 'On the other hand,' says Lechler, ' he recognised a merit bearing an improper sense, and also some co-operation of man's own moral power, partly in the matter of forgiveness of sin, and partly in reference to the hope of eternal blessedness.' The life of Wycliffe was a progress from truth to truth. He groped along, praying and working as he went, relinquishing at one stage the errors he had fondly embraced in earlier days. Had life been prolonged, he would undoubtedly have acquired more abundant light. We honour him as one who, centuries before Chillingworth wrote, proclaimed throughout England that the Bible, the Bible alone, is the religion of Christians.

DEATH OF JAMES IV.—THE EVE OF THE REFORMATION.

It is a very memorable thing which (from the mouth of a very credible person, who saw it) George Buchanan relates concerning James the Fourth, King of Scotland, who intending to make a war with England, a certain old man, of a very venerable aspect, and clad in a long blue garment, came to him at the church of St. Michael's at Linlithgow, while he was at his devotion, and leaning over the canon's seat where the king sat, said, ' I am sent unto thee, O king! to give thee warning that thou proceed not in the war thou art about, for if thou do, it will be thy ruin.' And having so said, he withdrew himself back among the multitude. The king, after service was ended, inquired earnestly for him, but he could nowhere be found, neither could any of the standers-by feel or perceive how, when, or where he passed from them, having as it were vanished in their hands; but no warning could divert his destiny, which had not been destiny if it could have been diverted. His queen also had acquainted him with the visions and affrightments of her sleep, that her chains and armlets appeared to be turned into pearl; that she had seen him fall from a great precipice; that she had lost one of her eyes. But he answered, 'These were but dreams arising from the many thoughts and cares of the day;' and therefore marched on and fought with the English, and was slain in Flodden Field, with a great number of his nobility and common soldiers, upon Sept. 9th, 1513.

Buchanan, who relates this anecdote, lived to see the Reformation triumphant, the poet and historian having died at Edinburgh in 1582.

THE ENGLISH MONASTERIES.

The notion has been too commonly entertained that Henry VIII. first looked with greedy eyes on the religious houses, and next, in a covetous spirit, planned their destruction for the sake of the spoil. The truth is, that the need for those institutions was superseded; and not only had they grown unpopular, they were a moral eyesore and a sham. While, therefore, he dealt with them as his wisdom dictated, the king in the main yielded to the pressure of public opinion. The worst about these refuges of sin is not known, for Bonner, instructed by Queen Mary, destroyed every copy of the 'Black Book' laid before Parliament by the Commission of Inspection. Much more is known about the abounding iniquity, however, than can be told with decency by modern historians. Despised in common by squire and peasant, those ignorant and indolent monks, who wasted their lives in feasting and sensuality, inherited sufficient wit to perceive that the Pope was their stoutest defender, and that Rome was the only capital whither they could safely appeal against English affronts—an important consideration, since certain yeomen were now beginning to feel aggrieved at handing over the fat of the land to incompetent pastors and useless monks, while they, the thrifty producers, were constrained to live on common fare. The days had been when the religious houses in a certain manner had served the nation. Learning had been encouraged, travellers hospitably entertained, and the needy sick carefully succoured. But mediæval night had departed, and institutions which, with all their errors, were once a partial blessing, were now an insupportable burden. Thus because the fabric was rotten, and invitingly attracted the hand of the spoiler, the agitation and threatened quarrel with Rome on the question of the divorce bred alarm and apprehension. To complete the breach with the papacy, it was seen, would seal the doom of the convents. When the dreaded rupture was actually occasioned by the Pope's declaring against the divorce, the Government had no alternative, while preserving its honour and safety, but to defend itself by collecting information respecting the interior of houses crowded with transgressors, who, to the list of crimes contained in the first of Romans, occasionally added the art of false coining. The exposure of the fraudulent sins and low sensuality of the monks contributed much towards preparing the way for the swift demolition of their sanctuaries, besides hastening the complete separation of the national heart from Rome, by revealing the true nature of monasticism.

The idea of visiting the monasteries was not altogether novel. Towards the end of the preceding century reports were murmured among the populace of the amazing wickedness to be found in the places consecrated to holy purposes, and some abortive attempts at reform were made by the reigning pope. But now everything was ripe for immediate action. England was under an interdict. Her monarch was excommunicated, and political as well as moral and religious considerations made it necessary for due surveillance to be exercised over houses which, under the hitherto impregnable shield of a holy profession, promised to become temples of treason as well as moral lazarettos. The well-timed inspection of these places greatly aided the Reformation; and the principle then acted on still remains as just and as reasonable as it did of yore. It is no encroachment on the liberty of the subject, nor does it savour of intolerance, to bring within the jurisdiction of the magistrate institutions whose nature is subversive of liberty. If the commissioners in their progress were not scattering light, they were at least exposing darkness. Nor were the written reports the only evidence given to the country of monastic abominations. Wherever the visitors halted, nuns under age, and monks not older than twenty-four, were allowed their freedom; and the numbers who accepted the boon dispersed themselves over the country, to become witnesses against an unnatural system. Many of the circumstances attendant on the visitation were sufficiently ludicrous, though painfully illustrative of a phase of the papacy which cannot with propriety be exhibited in all its enormous wickedness. A company of Waltham Abbey monks were literally caught in a strong game net on their return from a midnight debauch. At one place a phial, said to contain some of the blood of Christ, was found.

This fluid, now discovered to be the blood of a duck, renewed weekly, became visible to penitents only; and, as sorrow for sin and handsome donations were commonly blended, the bottle was conveniently constructed with a thin and thick side, the former being turned towards the sinner on the forthcoming of something substantial. At another place a crucifix with a nodding and winking figure was brought to light, and when the people realised how they had been befooled by mechanical contrivances, the bitterness manifested towards their detractors helped to widen the great breach.

ENGLAND AT THE OPENING OF THE REFORMATION.

The times in this country were times of appalling spiritual darkness; and hopes of better things in the future could not have been based on any apparent loosening in the bonds of superstition. The state was jealous of the power of the priests, and recent Acts of Parliament limited their stipends, or otherwise set bounds to their pretensions; but their dreaded power was still supreme, for priestcraft ruled the minds of the multitude. The notions of the people in regard to spiritual truth were of the most grovelling description. 'Our Lady's House at Walsingham' was a shrine which attracted hosts of pilgrims, and appears to have served as a popish substitute for the cross of Christ. 'A husband is sick in London,' remarks Charles Knight in his History of England, 'and his anxious wife writes, "My mother behested another image of wax of the weight of you to our Lady of Walsingham, and she sent four nobles to the four orders of friars at Norwich to pray for you; and I have behested to go on pilgrimage to Walsingham and St. Leonard's." These were not the mere fancies of the women of that time. William Yelverton, a judge of the King's Bench, writes to thank his cousin for his zeal "for our Lady of Walsingham;" adding, "for truly if I be drawn to any worship or welfare to discharge of mine enemies' danger, I ascribe it to Our Lady."' The wills of the period afford abundant testimony to the dominant power of the Church; for among the many bequests we find money left for all kinds of ecclesiastical purposes—requiems, paternosters, tapers, altars. A supposed saint would have it engraved on his tombstone how he had purchased a free pardon for his sins; another would in death delegate a priest to go on pilgrimage, and to say masses for the testator's soul. Candles on the high altar, images of the Virgin, and all kinds of priestly assumptions were multiplied until the Saviour Himself was lost sight of and virtually forgotten.

Tyndale himself says, 'Remember ye not how within this thirty years and far less, and yet dureth to this day, the old barking curs, Duns' disciples, and the like draff called Scotists, the children of darkness, raged in every pulpit against Greek, Latin, and Hebrew; and what sorrow the schoolmasters, that taught the true Latin tongue, had with them; some beating the pulpit with their fists for madness, and roaring out with open and foaming mouth, that if there were but one Terence or Virgil in the world, and that same in their sleeves, and a fire before them, they would burn them therein, though it should cost them their lives; affirming that all good learning decayed and was utterly lost, since men gave them unto the Latin tongue.'

TYNDALE AT ANTWERP.

Foxe thus alludes to the translator's mode of life at Antwerp. He was a man very frugal and spare of body, a great student, an earnest labourer in the setting forth of the Scriptures of God. He reserved to himself two days in the week, which he named his pastime—Monday and Saturday. On Monday he visited all such poor men and women as were fled out of England, by reason of persecution, into Antwerp; and these, once well understanding their good exercises and qualities, he did very liberally comfort and relieve, and in like manner provided for the sick and diseased persons. On the Saturday he walked round about the town, seeking every corner and hole where he suspected any poor person to dwell, and when he found any to be well occupied and yet overburdened with children, or else were aged and weak, these also he plentifully relieved. And thus he spent his two days of pastime, as he called them. And, truly, his alms were very large, and so they might well be, for his exhibition that he had yearly of the English merchants at Antwerp, when living there, was considerable; and that, for the most part, he bestowed upon the poor. The rest of the days of the week he gave wholly to his book, wherein he most diligently travailed. When the Sunday came, then went he to some one merchant's chamber or other, whither came many other merchants, and unto them would he read some particle of Scripture, the which proceeded so fruitfully, sweetly, and gently from him, much like to the writing of John the Evangelist, that it was a heavenly comfort and joy to the audience to hear him read the Scriptures; likewise, after dinner, he spent an hour in the same manner. He was a man without any spot or blemish of rancour or malice, full of mercy and compassion, so that no man living was able to reprove him of any sin or crime, although his righteousness and justification depended not thereupon before God, but only upon the blood of Christ, and his faith upon the same.

TYNDALE AND ERASMUS.

When William Tyndale, the translator of the New Testament, was at Antwerp, he was told of a remarkable conjuror who by magical arts could place upon the table dainty dishes of choice meats and the rarest wines. Whether wizard or genius, Tyndale wished to see this extraordinary gentleman, and ventured even to sit down to table when the viands were to be of his procuring. The company assembled, the juggler came, but soon found that he could do nothing, and thereupon confessed that there was some one at the table who hindered his work. This is how the story runs, and it was commonly believed that the obstacle was a man of piety in the person of William Tyndale. Probably the presence of a man of sense was as much the hindrance as Tyndale's piety.

Erasmus was fortunate beyond most men in attracting the favour of kings, for he may be said to have enjoyed the friendship of almost all the crowned heads of Europe. Our own Henry the Eighth wrote him an autograph letter, offering him a home and competency in England, while Francis, King of France, acted in a similar manner. From Charles the Fifth came an offer of a bishopric, and from other courts there came similar offers of honour and preferment. When books were few and scholars scarce, men of the calibre of Erasmus were valued according to their rarity, but after making all allowance, this celebrated philosopher was among the fortunate of the fortunate. His trimming and time-serving may account for it. Who would not far rather have the present fame of Tyndale the brave than of Erasmus the timid?

HUMPHREY MONMOUTH, TYNDALE'S FRIEND.

There was then living in the parish of All Hallows, Barking, a rich and liberal cloth merchant, well-disposed to the Reformation, and of the name of Humphrey Monmouth. This good trader was moved to become Tyndale's friend and patron. At the abundant table of his city home Monmouth entertained with his lodger a number of the best-informed of the London clergy; little suspecting, in the meantime, that his Christian kindness was serving a double purpose. Tyndale was assisted through a necessitous season, and he also learned, from his knowing town-companions, that openings and opportunities existed on the Continent for carrying out the scheme which lay nearest his heart. Here is a portrait of Monmouth taken from one of Latimer's sermons, quoted by Mr. Demaus: 'In expounding the Epistle to the Romans, Master Stafford, coming to that place where St. Paul saith that we shall overcome our enemy with well-doing, and so heap up hot coals upon his head, brought in an example, saying that he knew, in London, a great merchant, which merchant had a very poor neighbour, yet, for all his poverty, he loved him very well, and lent him money at his need, and let him come to his table whensoever he would. It was even at that time when Dr. Colet was in trouble, and should have been burnt if God had not turned the King's heart to the contrary. Now the rich man began to be a Scripture-man, he began to smell the Gospel; the poor man was a papist still. It chanced, on a time when the rich man talked of the Gospel, sitting at his table, where he reproved popery, and such kind of things, the poor man being then present, took a great displeasure against the rich man, insomuch that he would come no more to his house, he would borrow no more money of him, as he was wont to do beforetimes. Yea, and conceived such hatred and malice against him that he went and secured him before the bishops. Now the rich man, not knowing any such displeasure, offered many times to talk with him and set him at quiet; but it would not be; the poor man had such a stomach that he would not vouchsafe to speak with him; if he met the rich man in the street, he would go out of his way. One time it happened that he met him in so narrow a street that he could not avoid but come near him; yet, for all that, this poor man had such a stomach against the rich man to say that he was minded to go forward and not to speak with him. The rich man perceiving that, catcheth him by the hand, and asked him saying, "Neighbour, what is come into your heart to take such displeasure with me? What have I done against you? Tell me, and I will be ready at all times to make you amends." Finally, he spake so gently, so charitably, so lovingly and friendly, that it wrought in the poor man's heart, that by-and-by he fell down upon his knees and asked him forgiveness. The rich man forgave him, and so took him again to his favour, and they loved as well as ever they did afore.'

TYNDALE IN PRISON.

Once in safe custody, the translator was confined in the castle of Vilvorde, and the hardships of his prison life will be best described in his own words. The letter is supposed to have been addressed to the governor of the castle :—

'I believe, right worshipful, that you are not ignorant of what has been determined concerning me; therefore I entreat your lordship, and that by the Lord Jesus, that if I am to remain here during the winter, you will request the procureur to be kind enough to send me from my goods which he has in his possession a warmer cap, for I suffer extremely from cold in the head, being afflicted with a perpetual catarrh, which is considerably increased in the cell. A warmer coat also, for that which I have is very thin; also a piece of cloth to patch my leggings: my overcoat has been worn out; my shirts are also worn out. He has a woollen shirt of mine, if he will be kind enough to send it. I have also with him leggings of thicker cloth for putting on above; he also has warmer caps for wearing at night. I wish also his permission to have a candle in the evening, for it is wearisome to sit alone in the dark. But, above all, I entreat and beseech your clemency to be urgent with the procureur that he may kindly permit me to have my Hebrew Bible, Hebrew Grammar, and Hebrew Dictionary, that I may spend my time with that study. And in return, may you obtain your dearest wish, provided always that it be consistent with the salvation of your soul. But if any other resolution has been come to concerning me, that I must remain during the whole winter, I shall be patient, abiding the will of God to the glory of the grace of my Lord Jesus Christ, whose Spirit I pray may ever direct your heart.'

TYNDALE'S SUCCESSORS.

The mantle of Tyndale fell on Miles Coverdale, who was equally zealous in the cause of truth, though a man of more limited powers than was the case with his predecessor. It is quite impossible for us in our privileged condition to estimate the eager interest with which the multitude, who basked in the first sunshine of the Reformation, looked into and studied the Word of God. Very naturally their appetite was whetted by what they had already tasted from beyond the sea. If the preliminary droppings of the shower were so refreshing, what might not be expected from the copious rain? The authorities thought that it would be safe to license the circulation of the Scriptures, provided they were dispensed judiciously among those who were sufficiently wise to read circumspectly; but this naturally awakened the violent opposition of the Papal party. This was the state of affairs in England when Coverdale printed the complete Bible in 1535.

Students who are interested in the growth of our mother tongue from its crude condition in the Middle Ages to its present comparative perfection will note the rapidity with which Bibles were published in succession during the reign of Henry the Eighth. Both Tyndale and Coverdale had a friend in John Rogers, whose work in revision and compilation goes by the name of Thomas Matthew's Bible, and does so for a reason which, at this distance of time, cannot be explained. 'The origination of the volume is also hidden from us,' says Dr. Eadie, the latest and completest writer on this subject. 'What suggested the preparation of it is nowhere stated. Only it may be surmised that Rogers wished the English people to be put in possession of a complete English Bible, embodying all that the martyred Tyndale had already rendered; for he had rendered from the original texts, whereas Coverdale's was only a secondary version, professedly taken, not from Hebrew and Greek, but Douche or Latyn.' An able scholar, zealous in the cause of the Reformation, and, above all, one who laboured to give the English people the best translation which the times would afford, such a man was terribly obnoxious to the Papists, who maintained, through their mouthpiece, Gardiner, that the Scriptures were the springhead of heresy and extravagance. A noble character in every particular, Rogers did not shrink from the trial by fire when the honour was accorded him of walking first in the long procession of Marian martyrs about twenty years after the completion of his work.

The fourth decade of the sixteenth century—abounding in social changes and political revolutions—was a common harvest time of Bible versions in English. The edition of Rogers was sufficiently annotated to make it a thorough Protestant performance, such as the Papal party would look upon with disfavour. In a revised form, and with its Reformation notes omitted, this went forth as the Great Bible, a work which has been associated with the name of Archbishop Cranmer without sufficient reason. The printing of this edition, published in the spring of 1539, was begun at Paris, and, strange to say, the notorious Bonner, the future persecutor, was among those English residents who countenanced the work. Before the workmen had half completed their task, however, the agents of the Inquisition scented what was in progress, so that the superintendents fled to London, only with difficulty saving a remnant of their plant and printed paper.

On the accession of 'Bloody Mary,' the illustrious band of English exiles who sought refuge in Geneva turned their leisure to good account by translating the Bible; and this Genevan version was the one best loved by the Puritans during the century following. Among the translators were Coverdale and John Knox. In the dusky recesses of old mansion libraries this goodly volume may often be discovered. Its obsolete terms are both quaint and valuable to philological inquirers. Among the common people, and second-hand furniture dealers, who may sometimes have a copy to dispose of, the book passes as the Breeches Bible, because of its well-known rendering of the seventh verse of the third chapter of Genesis. This important undertaking was not completed until Elizabeth had been some one or two years on the throne; and it was not superseded in public favour by the more pretentious Bishops' Bible, the version which, in the opinion of many sound Protestants, shed lustre on the great Queen's auspicious reign.

This activity on the part of our forefathers to attain perfection in the great business of Bible translation may be said to have culminated in the Authorised Version; and in what degree they succeeded may be inferred from the fact that the version is still the acknowledged standard of the English tongue. While these monuments of piety and industry were being raised in rapid succession one after the other, the Romish party were sensible that their system was being undermined. If the English nation would insist on reading Scripture in the vernacular, which they half believed the Word itself disallowed, it was indispensable that the faithful should have a version cast in a Romish mould. Hence the origin of the Douai Bible, a translation so palpably unjust in numbers of passages, and so wilfully obscured by Latinised terms in others, that even an honourable Romanist in an age like this can hardly appeal to its authority with a safe conscience.

As English citizens and as hearty Protestants, we cannot look into the history of the English Bible without becoming increasingly interested in the present. The Authorised Version has maintained its place in the people's affection for more than two hundred and sixty years; and, without disparaging the Revised Version, it is hard to believe that it will ever be entirely superseded. Indeed, the work of the committee who have given us that work has been no more than the revision of a version beloved of our fathers, and too excellent to be wholly laid aside by their Bible-reading children.

THE ROYAL EXCHANGE A MEMENTO OF THE REFORMATION.

Sir Thomas Gresham, one of the most familiar of names among the long list of merchant benefactors of London, was born in 1519, just when the Reformation was beginning to relight the torch of truth among the nations of Europe; and he died at the age of sixty, in 1579. Those sixty years were crowded with momentous events, one seemingly over-towering the others, until at last, nine years further on, there came that astonishing and crowning providence the destruction of the Spanish Armada. We sometimes speak of a man's leaving the world better than he found it; but the world into which this celebrated trading adventurer was born was so different from that in which he died, that it seems as though a complete transformation had occurred. In 1519 the darkness of Popery seemed to be unbroken; but in 1579 Protestant episcopacy was established in England and Presbyterianism in Scotland, while the Bible, having been several times revised, was printed in the vulgar tongue for even village folk to read. The world in the early years of the reign of Henry VIII. had some of the dark clouds of mediævalism still hanging over it; the middle of the reign of Elizabeth was a time of comparative light.

The family came originally from Norfolk, some time in those dim and distant ages when adventurers coming to the capital were named by their neighbours after the place of nativity. In the time of Thomas's youth, his father, Sir Richard, and his uncle, Sir John Gresham, were both opulent merchants in the old city, and in favour with that uncertain monarch whose smile sometimes foreboded more evil than his frown. Thomas was from the first intended for a merchant; but intending also that he should be a scholar, his father placed him at the University of Cambridge; and doubtless the advantages there received helped to make young Gresham the friend of learning he afterwards became. Like all youths of that age, he was obliged to go through a long apprenticeship before he was able to appropriate the honours belonging to a free man of London and a member of the Mercers' Guild. At the age of twenty-four he married, and settling in Antwerp, he acted an important part in that quaint city as the agent of his family, and also, when required, of the English Government. These services, which were both of a commercial and diplomatic character, were continued through the reigns of Edward VI. and Mary, and also after the accession of Elizabeth, until the outbreak of war in the Low Countries obliged Gresham to seek refuge in his native city of London. As a Protestant, indeed, the young merchant was not in very high favour with Queen Mary and her advisers; but as his services were too valuable to be lightly esteemed, he was not only allowed to retain his office, but was rewarded with ecclesiastical lands of the value of £200 a year in addition to his regular salary of a pound a day.

It is more than probable that Gresham was more disposed to accommodate himself to the changing times and to the various tempers of those he successfully served, than would now be judged to be consistent with diplomatic honour; and the tactics he sometimes employed to gain his end were certainly open to serious comment. Still, we must remember the standard of honour was then low. Men are not usually superior to their times; and we should at least be wanting in common-sense if we expected a man who had only just emerged with his country from the last lingering mists of the

Dark Ages to exemplify the virtues of a nineteenth-century moralist. Gresham was at all events a lover of London; and realizing with some wounded pride that his native city was inferior to antique Antwerp in some modern commercial contrivances and conveniences, he devised liberal things in his heart, as we shall presently see. Then, while he was revered by his fellow-citizens, he was a very trusted servant of the Queen; and to be a favourite of royalty in those days was an honour carrying with it some very eccentric penalties. Thus, for more than three years, he was required to accommodate a state prisoner: the high-born Lady Mary Grey, who had presumed to marry Thomas Keys, a sergeant porter,—an act of injudicious folly which so chagrined the Queen that Her Majesty handed over the offender to Sir Thomas Gresham, who kept her a prisoner in his house until the offence was sufficiently expiated.

It is generally understood that there is no truth in the tradition that Sir Thomas Gresham was a foundling, and adopted a grasshopper as the crest of his family because he was discovered by a woman through the loud chirping of a number of grasshoppers in the turf. It would appear to be far more likely that the crest was merely borrowed from the sign used in trade, the Grasshopper in Lombard Street having been the chief seat of Sir Thomas Gresham's commercial operations. Though a leading member of the Mercers' Company, it was there, according to Burgon, that he thrived as 'usurer, a pawnbroker, a money scrivener, a goldsmith, and a dealer in bullion.' The house of business was in the close, murky atmosphere of Lombard Street; the knight's dwelling was in the rather semi-rural precincts of Bishopsgate, which then overlooked the meadows of Shoreditch and the Spital Fields. The shop in Lombard Street occupied the site of the present No. 18, so that the reader may, if he chooses, make a pilgrimage to the celebrated spot. When in middle life he became what was called the king's factor, a large portion of his time was passed in travelling to and fro between London and Antwerp, forty journeys having been made in the course of two years.

Antwerp and London were then the two principal trading centres of Europe; and while the first sent to England a large number of luxuries as well as necessaries, vast quantities of cloth—200,000 pieces in a single year—were sent in return. Wool was then one of our staple products. Gresham at Antwerp, however, was a Government news-agent and general adventurer, as well as a trader on his own account; and contriving by ingenious manœuvres to raise the rate of exchange in favour of London, he made large sums for the Government. When he could not do what he wanted openly, he resorted to secret stratagems.

'In 1553,' says a recent historian, 'we find him writing to the Privy Council, proposing to send £280 (in heavy Spanish rials) in bags of pepper, four at a time, and the English ambassador at Brussels was to bring over with him twenty or thirty thousand pounds; but he afterwards changed his mind, and sent the money packed up in bales with suits of armour, and £3,000 in each, rewarding the searcher at Gravelines with new year's presents of black velvet and black cloth. About the time of the Queen's marriage to Philip, Gresham went to Spain, to start from Puerto Real fifty cases, each containing 22,000 Spanish ducats.'

The same authority informs us, that during the carrying out of 'these sagacious and important negotiations, he was rewarded with the paltry remuneration of £1 a day.' The trickery of these transactions is far more apparent than their importance. Regarding the 'paltry remuneration,' we must in fairness concede that, as money was then about six times its present value, the salary was not so insignificant as at first sight it might appear.

Gresham managed to live through the trying reign of Mary without coming to the stake. He even so far succeeded in becoming a royal favourite while others languished in prison or triumphed in martyr flames, that in the most terrible year of all—1555—he carried a present to the palace and accepted a piece of plate in return. At the same time he showed remarkable readiness in hastening to greet the rising sun, Elizabeth, when she succeeded to the throne in 1557. Though by no means aged at that period,—he was but thirty-eight—Gresham tells how the cheering words of Her Majesty made him feel 'a young man again.' The change was indeed a very genial one; it was like spring succeeding winter.

When Gresham was forty-five years of age, in 1564, death carried off his only son; and being thus left without any other heir, he began to think of adopting the city of London. The street in which he then traded was far too straitened for the numbers of merchants of all grades who there assembled, exposed to a variable climate while transacting business; and the question very naturally suggested itself, Why should London lag behind Antwerp in not having a Bourse? The citizens had talked about reform for thirty years, and in those slow times would have talked for thirty more had not Sir Thomas himself proceeded to find a remedy. Assisted by subscriptions from a number of citizens, three alleys in Cornhill, which were crowded with eighty families, were cleared for a site; and on a long-remembered auspicious day, June 7th, 1566, the first brick of the first London Bourse was laid by its founder. This foreign-looking building, surmounted by its great grasshopper, and having grasshoppers at every corner and on every window peak, is shown in contemporary and other pictures. Though not a triumph of architectural art, the design was much admired even by Elizabeth herself; and by the Queen's command the place was henceforth called THE ROYAL EXCHANGE. The piazzas were adorned with pillars of marble and statues of the English kings, as well as of Gresham himself; and while below were dark, damp vaults, there were above a hundred shops in which great varieties of goods were sold. The shops did not at first very readily let; but by skilful management after the royal visit, Gresham permanently raised their value. Erected to promote the interests of commerce alone in a time notorious for its cruel wars, no person frequenting the building for business purposes was allowed to wear a sword or to carry any other arms. The hour for closing the gates against all passengers was ten in summer and nine in winter.

Being wholly illiterate, the lower orders of London were then naturally very disorderly; and hence, before the Royal Exchange had stood ten years, we find that the noise, arising from the hilarious 'young rogues,' who turned the convenient edifice into a recreation ground on Sundays and holidays, became a public nuisance. Quiet-loving people, who would have used the piazzas and covered walks for gentle exercise and meditation, were scandalized; while worshippers at a neighbouring church complained of not being able to hear the sermon. Other references to matters affecting the Exchange afford the student of those times vivid glimpses into the London of Elizabeth and James I. Thus the 'cursing and swearing, to the great annoyance and grief of the inhabitants,' of the women fruit-sellers who carried on their traffic about the gates, was taken notice of in 1594. We are also told that 'in 1592 a tavern keeper, who had vaults under the Exchange, was fined for allowing tippling, and for broiling herrings, sprats, and bacon, to the vexation of worshipful merchants resorting to the Exchange.' Thirty years later, rat-catchers, bird-dealers, and vendors of plants were also a source of trouble. Nevertheless the institution grew in favour, and the hundred little shops in the gallery above became the favourite bazaar of the period whither beauty and fashion resorted. For this and other reasons, Stow, the historian, calls the building the eye of London. It is to us something more, with many memories of the Reformation clustering around.

THE BURNED TESTAMENTS.

The New Testament began first to be translated by William Tyndale, and so came forth in print about A.D. 1529 (1525?), wherewith Cuthbert Tonstal, Bishop of London, with Sir Thomas More, being sore aggrieved, devised how to destroy that false, erroneous translation, as he called it. It happened that one Augustine Packington, a mercer, was then at Antwerp, where the bishop was. This man favoured Tyndale, but showed the contrary unto the bishop. The bishop, being desirous to bring his purpose to pass, communed how that he would gladly buy the New Testaments. Packington hearing him say so, said, 'My lord, I can do more in this matter than most merchants that be here, if it be your pleasure; for I know the Dutchmen and strangers that have bought them of Tyndale, and have them here to sell; so that if it be your lordship's pleasure, I must disburse money to pay for them, or else I cannot have them: and so I will assure you to have every book of them that is printed and unsold.' The bishop, thinking he had God 'by the toe,' said, 'Do your diligence, gentle Master Packington! get them for me, and I will pay whatsoever they cost; for I intend to burn and destroy them all at Paul's Cross.' This Augustine Packington went unto William Tyndale, and declared the whole matter; and so, upon compact made between them, the Bishop of London had the books, Packington had the thanks, and Tyndale had the money. After this, Tyndale corrected the same New Testament again, and caused them to be newly imprinted, so that they came thick and threefold over into England. When the bishop perceived that, he sent for Packington, and said to him, ' How cometh this, that there are so many New Testaments abroad? you promised me that you would buy them all.' Then answered Packington, 'Surely, I bought all that were to be had; but I perceive they have printed more since. I see it will never be better so long as they have letters and stamps: wherefore you were best to buy the stamps too, and so you shall be sure;' at which answer the bishop smiled, and so the matter ended.—*Acts and Monuments.*

THE ROOD OF DOVERCOURT.

In times of popular revolution comparatively small actions may become so linked with great results, and be attended with such noble danger as to compel our classing them among deeds of heroism. To this order belongs an occurrence of 1532—a work that a few years later would have elicited popular applause instead of earning the death inflicted on the majority who were engaged in its completion. The Dovercourt of those days contained a wondrous rood. The nods, winks, frowns, or glances of approval of this image attracted an anxious and interested stream of pilgrims, who were not averse to paying liberally for any supposed blessing they carried away. Night and day the sanctuary remained open and unguarded; for, so the monks mysteriously intimated, whoever sought to close the door of the church was preternaturally opposed. Now it happened that four stout-hearted and comely youths, with souls irradiated by the light from Germany, not only doubted but resolved on testing the popular theories by putting them to a strain sufficiently severe to convince the populace of their truth or falsehood. The time chosen for the adventure was a frosty, moonlit night in February. After walking ten long miles they came to the open door, the same having been open, as tradition averred, from time immemorial. In ghostly solitude, with silvery light shining aslant through the windows, stood the dreaded object, now destined to be dreadful no longer. Entering the church, and deliberately taking down the image, these nocturnal reformers carried their burden into the open air, set it on fire, and while it blazed and cracked in the crisp atmosphere, returned to their homes and beds. We rightly give all honour to the leading spirits of any beneficent movement. There are lesser heroes—men who could do such a deed as that of burning the Dovercourt rood, 'their consciences being burdened to see the honour of Almighty God so blasphemed,' and their names are inscribed in noble prominence on the roll-list of British Reformers.

THE MAID OF KENT.

The tragical story of the Maid of Kent, an epileptic girl whose misfortune the opponents of reform sought to turn into capital, is too long to be given at length. Elizabeth Barton was just such an instrument as the corrupt clergy gloried in possessing, and had she lived a century earlier, she might have become the means of diverting considerable spoil into the ecclesiastical exchequer. In 1534, the village of Aldington witnessed an unwonted excitement, consequent on the strange doings of one who, the peasants believed, exhibited involuntary symptoms of speaking and acting under preternatural influence. The country people had scarcely begun accounting for her distorted features, unearthly writhings, and half-intelligible utterances, ere one Masters, a priest, and one Bocking, a friar, discovered in the epileptic a source of profit. The priest rejoiced in commanding a means of money-making, and the friar in possessing an agent of approved potency for obstructing the Reformation, and for hindering the divorce which especially threatened to trouble the hierarchy. The girl's wonderful doings were industriously noised abroad; and what were called miracles were plentifully exhibited, until the attention of high and low was attracted. Being well tutored, Elizabeth made her peculiar misfortune serve the Church, as desired by the ultramontane party. In her rustic simplicity, she may have imagined that she was the favoured medium between short-sighted humanity and invisible powers. For a time all progressed smoothly. Crafty and worldly, the churchmen cautiously felt their way. In order to prevent any flagging of the excitement, it was arranged that a forsaken and desolate chapel in the vicinity should become the scene of the maiden's miraculous cure by the Virgin Mary. This farce having passed off satisfactorily, the party adopted stronger measures. The King was threatened in church and cloister should he dare to marry Anne Boleyn. Yet one more step, and the pinnacle of triumph would be reached. Elizabeth must appear before Henry himself, and break his Tudor obstinacy with the terror of heaven, if commonplace entreaty failed. These manœuvres were partially successful. On being carried before His Majesty, the girl, in homely village phraseology, assured him he would 'die the death of a villain,' unless he changed his determination. Growing yet bolder with success and desperation, the party of which this girl was the nucleus, as they saw high and low—even Fisher and More—came over to believing in the inspiration of their *protegée*, contrived a conspiracy for restoring the Pope's supremacy. All this ended, as it could not but end in such troublous days, in ruin and death. Elizabeth admitted her fraud, and her confession, a few minutes before her death, was a protest against the iniquity of popery: 'I was a poor wretch without learning,' she cried to the Tyburn crowd, 'but the praises of the priests turned my brain.'

ENGLAND UNDER EDWARD VI.

What must have been the woful condition of those clergy whom the prelate recommended to provide themselves with a Bible, or at the least with a Testament, and to read a chapter a day, must be left to the reader's imagination to picture. With a priesthood thus sunk in ignorance, the condition of the people was correspondingly deplorable. Numbers of communicants were unable to repeat the Lord's Prayer. But here is a glimpse of a rural parish in the days of Henry the Eighth. (It is Latimer himself that tells the story, says Mr. Demaus, in one of his sermons before Edward VI.)

'I heard of a bishop of England that went on visitation. And as it was the custom when the bishop should come to be rung into the town, the great bell's clapper was fallen down, the tyall was broken, so that the bishop could not be rung into the town. There was a great matter made of this, and the chiefs of the parish were much blamed for it in the visitation. The bishop was somewhat quick with them, and signified that he was much offended. They made their answers, and excused themselves as well as they could. "It was a chance," said they, "that the clapper brake, and we could not get it mended by-and-by; we must tarry till we can have it done; it shall be amended as shortly as may be." Among the other there was one wiser than the rest, and he comes up to the bishop: "Why, my lord," said he, "doth your lordship make so great a matter of the bell that lacketh his clapper? Here is a bell," said he, and pointed to the pulpit, "that hath lacked a clapper this twenty years. We have a parson that fetcheth out of this benefice fifty pound (equal to £750) every year, but we never see him."'

In another place Latimer relates a piece of his own experience:—

'I once came myself to a place, riding on a journey homeward from London, and I sent word overnight into the town that I would preach there in the morning, because it was holiday; and methought it was a holiday's work. The church stood in my way, and I took my horse and my company and went thither. I thought I should have found a great company in the church, and when I came there, the church door was fast locked. I tarried there half-an-hour and more: at last the key was found, and one of the parish comes to me and says, "Sir, this is a busy day with us; we cannot hear you; it is Robin Hood's day, the parish are gone abroad to gather for Robin Hood: I pray you let them not." I was fain then to give place to Robin Hood: I thought my rochet should have been regarded, though I were not; but it would not serve, it was fain to give place to Robin Hood's men. It is no laughing matter, my friends, it is weeping matter, a heavy matter, a heavy matter, under the pretence for gathering for Robin Hood, a traitor and a thief, to put out a preacher, to have his office less esteemed, to prefer Robin Hood before the ministration of God's Word; and all this hath come of unpreaching prelates.'

LATIMER'S INFLUENCE.

Such sermons could not be like water spilt upon the ground: what comfort, and peace, and edification they ministered to many perplexed hearts cannot be estimated; but they have left a plain, broad mark on the history of England. He had denounced the superstitious regard for hallowed candles; on Candlemas-day of the year after his sermon, 'candles were left off' by proclamation of the Council. He had ridiculed the reverence for 'hallowed palms;' on Palm-Sunday it was forbidden to carry palms. He had specially laughed at the solemn ceremony of giving ashes on Ash-Wednesday; on Ash-Wednesday the ceremony was disused. He had condemned images; and the Council issued a peremptory order that all images should be removed from churches, whether they had been abused to superstitious purposes or not. He had characterized the use of an unknown Latin tongue in the service of the Church as a signal proof of the influence of the devil, and in March there was issued, by royal authority, an 'Order of the Communion' in the *English* language, retaining, it is true, the rites and ceremonies of the Mass, yet promising a future reformation even of these, and embodying the substance of those pious exhalations which still remain as the chief beauty of the English communion service. Some of these changes may have been suggested by Latimer's preaching; all of them were unquestionably prompted and facilitated by the great influence which his eloquence gave him over the people.—*Demaus*.

LATIMER'S YOUTH AND CONVERSION.

It is not exactly known when 'Stout Hugh Latimer' first saw the light; so that, amid many conflicting authorities, it will not be necessary to add to the confusion. We may, however, suppose the date to have been 1484. In regard to the locality of the Reformer's birth we are better informed, knowing it to have been Thurcastone, in Leicestershire—then more infected with the doctrines of the Reformation than any other English county. Thurcastone to this day is proud of its illustrious commoner; and with such pride we warmly sympathise, while the righteous are held in everlasting remembrance.

The period of Master Hugh's youth was surely a pleasant season. The father, as a well-to-do and loyal yeoman, educated his son with a liberality which called forth remarks on his extravagance. Each daughter received the comfortable and enviable dowry of five pounds. In those days, whatever a young Englishman left unlearned, he was well disciplined in the use of the bow. Thus we find that, as he advanced towards manhood, the weapon supplied to Hugh was always one corresponding to his strength. Health might be promoted by hunting and shooting; but Hugh, it appeared from the first, was not formed by nature to succeed his father on the farm. The fame of Wycliffe still lived in Leicestershire; and we are able in imagination to follow the thoughtful young yeoman as he visits Lutterworth to mark any traces of the early Reformer, or as he knocks at the door of Leicester Abbey to be admitted to the great library.

The whisperings about the extravagance of the elder Latimer were answered by Hugh's obtaining a fellowship at Cambridge University, where he studied hard and made corresponding progress. Still, as an enlightened son of the Papal Church, he only defended cherished abuses by declaiming against Melancthon, Latimer's conversion not having occurred until his fortieth year. The agent of that conversion was Bilney, the martyr; and it is from this date that the Reformer's life deepens in interest.

LATIMER AND THE BISHOP OF ELY.

One day in 1525, a very notable preacher was discoursing before the University of Cambridge, when there stepped into the church one who had long coveted the pleasure of hearing the much-talked-about orator. The speaker was Hugh Latimer; but the stranger was the Bishop of Ely. In those days pulpit etiquette had not attained its present perfection, and what would now be thought grotesque and unbecoming did not then appear singular. Latimer possessed the rare, and, if not used judiciously, the dangerous, gift of the ability suddenly to change his discourse and adapt his speech to the circumstances of his audience. On this occasion, he stopped ominously as the prelate entered, gave his lordship time to become comfortably seated, and then with that graphic power which rendered Latimer famous among his contemporaries, he dilated on the qualities of a faithful pastoral overseer. A bishop, according to Latimer's ideal, was a very admirable personage; but, sad to say, a true bishop widely differed from the counterfeit in the person of the auditor. The prelate after the sermon affected a complimentary mood, and, judged outwardly, was pleased at what he had heard. In truth, however, being much offended, he represented the matter unfavourably to the Cardinal; but, always sagacious, and a quick judge of merit, Wolsey was at this time in high spirits at the seeming success of his policy, and consequently showed little disposition to interfere, when Latimer was summoned to appear and answer for himself. In the course of conversation the Cardinal measured the Reformer before him, and then said, 'What mean you, my masters, to bring such a man before me in accusation? I thought that he had been some light-headed fellow that never studied such kind of doctrine as the school-doctors have. . . . If the Bishop of Ely cannot abide such doctrine as you have here repeated, you shall have my license, and shall preach it unto his beard, let him say what he will.'

LATIMER AND THE MONKS.

But even if so disposed, we could not supply any worthy details of Latimer's youth. It is as the greatest preacher of the English Reformation that we have to deal with him. In estimating his character, or in judging of his influence, we are to remember that he lived in days of few books, when the pulpit was the great medium of religious, or even of political, discussion. They were also days of violent invective, and of coarse abuse, no matter whether the preacher leaned towards Rome or defended Geneva. Led away by strong feeling, the speedy recantation of some preachers was as humiliating as their sermons had been intemperate and unguarded. Even Latimer himself but imperfectly understood the times; and while still clinging to the errors of Rome, he only partially comprehended the great work in which he was destined to go forth as a pioneer. His preaching was eminently practical, largely abounding in homely but striking illustrations, and from a very early date he advocated circulating the Gospel in the vulgar tongue. Those were days when such telling denunciations of irregularities of life as Latimer dealt in fell like explosives among the thousands who hung upon the preacher's lips, causing corresponding irritation among the clerical transgressors, at whose vices the rebukes of the preacher were aimed. Sometimes the monks braced themselves up to reply, but only to become more furious at having the laugh turned against them. It is not unprofitable, and it is very amusing, to mark the working of the monkish geniuses who defended the Old Learning. There arose one Buckenham, for example, whose ambition being superior to his talents, aimed at defeating the great preacher's innovations by affecting to answer him in his own change. The monk portrayed the evils likely to arise from an unrestricted circulation of the Scriptures. If simple rustics were allowed to read the Bible, not only evil, but social confusion, would ensue. The ploughman would refuse to touch his plough, fearing lest, looking back, he should become unfit for the Kingdom of God. Unlettered villagers would be found plucking out the eyes that chanced to offend; while the bakers, in equal simplicity, would spoil their bread by withholding the leaven, because a little leaven of evil leaveneth the whole lump. Some of this zealous monk's auditors may have retired, supposing that the Reformers were sufficiently answered. It was otherwise with Latimer. His strong genius readily utilised this merry nonsense, and made it tell with resistless and ludicrous effect on the luckless friar. The common people, though unlearned, were not quite such fools as their professed friends supposed. They were not too blind to comprehend a figure, as might be shown by illustration. Thus, hand them a picture of a fox preaching in a cowl, they would doubtless perceive that not a literal fox, but a deceitful friar was intended. Repartees and illustrations of this sample produced much commotion when spoken before a university congregation, and great admiration when preached to a common audience, or the royal family. It was as the first preacher of the English pulpit that Latimer, about the time of the fall of Wolsey, settled as village minister at West Kingston, near Bristol.

LATIMER'S FALL.

The lives of great men are found to have their humiliating passages if we only look for them; and to this rule the career of Latimer is not claimed as an exception. The most unsatisfactory episode in the Reformer's life, and one over which his enemies may justly exult, was his appearance before Convocation, in 1532, the citation having been issued at the instigation of the cruel Stokesley, Bishop of London. There was both subtle argument and skilful word-fencing on both sides, as we learn from Latimer's own account of that prolonged examination and its frequent remands. Enemies tried to catch him with craftiness of speech; and while speaking his answers he heard a pen scratching behind a curtain drawn before a chimney. In that contest the foes of truth surely triumphed, although the King, to whom Latimer appealed, interfered to protect the Reformer. Crushed for the moment, his brave heart yielded; he subscribed the articles, and apologised for his alleged errors. If this was all done in opposition to conscience, as we are afraid it must have been, Master Hugh was not long ere he met with faithful rebuke. Before returning to his cure, he visited the martyr Bainham, then lying under condemnation in Newgate; and we imagine, that while contrasting the prisoner's brave front with his own wavering, Latimer must have winced under those words : 'I do exhort *you* to stand to the defence of the truth, the world being so dangerous as it is.'

LATIMER'S CAUTION.

But while thus sitting in judgment on his failings, let us not mistake the character of Latimer. Let us remember that in the Reformer, prior to his appointment to the diocese of Worcester, in his fiftieth year, or in 1535, England did not possess in the great preacher an uncompromising advocate of the unadulterated Gospel. He felt his way, trod with cautious steps, and, in the first place, provoked the opposition of men in high places, by pleading for the free circulation of the Bible in the vernacular, and by exposing the loose living of the clergy. Probably the truth is, that Latimer, while naturally bold, was at one time too cautious, though it would not become us to be hard upon him as we sit secure in our comfortable homes, enjoying the freedom which he laboured and battled for even unto fire and death. He grew with his work, becoming bolder as the times favoured his innovations, if that may be called innovation which superseded time-crusted corruptions with the purity of primitive ages. Circumstances certainly did favour him. The divorce controversy which led to the break with Rome, and indirectly to the humiliation of the arrogant English clergy—the death of Wareham, and the promotion of Cranmer to Canterbury—to say nothing of the partiality of Henry, and the countenance of his great minister, Cromwell,—all favoured the advancement in power and usefulness of the great English preacher.

LATIMER THE BISHOP.

When we proceed to regard Latimer as a bishop, we look for the first time on the full-grown man. As Bishop of Worcester we see him preaching before Convocation in words which were as eagerly scanned and debated as are the utterances of prime ministers or popular monarchs in our day. Cromwell, who meditated divers religious reforms, to be introduced at a convenient season, was glad to countenance, and to have the countenance in return of so moderate, and yet so unflinching, an advocate of the pure Gospel. We see the bishop and the minister sitting side by side in the first Convocation of the Reformed Church of England; and their authority stoutly opposed the fanaticism of the vindictive Stokesley, who argued for tradition and the legends of the Church, as for 'the unwritten word of God.' The debate on the Sacraments was long and tumultuous, though amid the chaff some grains of gold occasionally appeared. Said the Bishop of Hereford: 'Truth is the daughter of time, and time is the mother of truth, and whatsoever is besieged by truth cannot long continue.'

The oversight of a vast diocese like that of Worcester before its modern division entailed heavy labour. Since the closing years of the preceding century there had been no resident bishop, and the revenues had simply enriched an Italian absentee, who had never seen his cathedral. The see in those days embraced the present diocese of Gloucester and Bristol. Master Latimer had his hands full of work indeed; for the confusion and abuses which abounded on all sides were sufficient to tax the wisdom and energy of a committee of sages. To add to the perplexity of a wise overseer, men were itinerating as preachers of sedition, having a cause of complaint as members of monasteries too rudely dissolved. Besides these there were other causes of disquietude. There were the rising in Lincolnshire and another in the North—the Pilgrimage of Grace. At Court the first was the occasion of more surprise than alarm, Lincolnshire having been regarded by Henry the Eighth as 'the most brute and beastly' county of the realm.

THE LAST DAYS OF LATIMER.

For the better portion of the people the signs of coming storms were appearing, even while the bells of London were ringing, and while the citizens were cheering and feasting. Many sought safety in flight, but it was otherwise with Latimer. He would neither court death nor seek to evade his approach. The bishop was staying with his friend John Glover, in Warwickshire, when the fatal news arrived of Lady Jane Grey's discomfiture and of Mary's triumphant accession. Of course Gardiner was released from the Tower, and true to the presentiment of many, he began to encompass the ruin of the great preacher. But there is yet time for escape. True; but Master Latimer will not fly; he will rather, if need be, testify unto death to the truths he has taught. Smithfield, he said, had long groaned for him. 'My friend, you be a welcome messenger,' he cried to the man who carried the summons to appear in London. Next we see him in the Tower, with Cranmer and Ridley, the three conferring together over the New Testament, strengthening themselves for the coming ordeal. Then followed a mock conference at Oxford—one of the most disgraceful and humiliating scenes of English history. Finally, after a delay of several months, came the crown of martyrdom; that great prophecy, in the meantime, issuing from the flames—'WE SHALL THIS DAY LIGHT SUCH A CANDLE, BY GOD'S GRACE, IN ENGLAND, AS I TRUST SHALL NEVER BE PUT OUT.'

> Then out spake aged Latimer:
>   'I tarry by the stake,
> Not trusting to my own weak heart,
>   But for the Saviour's sake.
>
> Why speak of life or death to me,
>   Whose days are but a span?
> Our crown is yonder. Ridley, see!
>   Be strong and play the man.
>
> God helping, such a torch this day
>   We'll light on English land,
> That Rome and all her cardinals
>   Shall never quench the brand!'

A SCOTCH MARTYR.

  Mr. Patrick Hamilton, of an ancient and honourable family in Scotland, left his own country, and went into Germany, where he became acquainted with Martin Luther and Philip Melancthon, then at the famous university of Wittenberg; from thence he went to the university of Marburg, which was then newly erected, where he was intimate with other learned men, and by reason of his learning and integrity of life he was had in the admiration of many: however, he could not rest till he returned into his own country, where the doctrine of the Reformation began then to break forth, as well in public as in private; which so disturbed the Popish clergy, that James Beaton, Archbishop of St. Andrews, sent for Mr. Patrick Hamilton to St. Andrews, where after divers days' conference he had his freedom and liberty; the bishop seeming to approve his doctrine, acknowledging that in many things there needed a reformation in the Church. But withal fearing that their kingdom of darkness should be endamaged, they persuaded the King, who was then young, and much led by them, to go on pilgrimage to St. Dothers in Ross, that so by reason of his absence no application might be made to him for the saving the life of this innocent gentleman; who, not suspecting their malice, remained like a lamb among wolves. The King being gone, one night Mr. Hamilton was seized upon by the bishop's officers, and carried to the castle, and the next day was brought forth into judgment, and condemned to be burnt, upon several articles about pilgrimages, purgatory, prayers to saints, etc. After dinner the fire was prepared, and being tied to the stake, he cried out with a loud voice, 'Lord Jesus, receive my spirit; how long shall darkness overwhelm this realm; and how long wilt Thou suffer the tyranny of these men?' The fire was slow, and therefore put him to the greater torment; but that which most troubled him was the clamour of some wicked men, set on by the friars, who continually cried, 'Turn, thou heretic, call upon our Lady; say *Salve Regina*,' etc. To whom he answered, 'Depart from me, and trouble me not, thou messenger of Satan.' And speaking to one Alexander Campbell, a friar, with whom he had conferred about matters of religion, and who had informed against him, and was now the ringleader who roared against him to recant, Mr. Patrick with great vehemency said to him, 'Wicked man, thou knowest the contrary, and hast confessed the contrary to me; I appeal thee before the tribunal of Jesus Christ.' After which words he resigned up his spirit unto God, in the year 1227. Campbell was troubled at these words, and from that very day was never in his right mind, but soon after died mad.—*Burton's Prodigies.*

THE SIRLOIN OF BEEF.

The abundant and goodly fare of England was proverbial among foreigners in the olden time; but of all the viands on which French and German natives feasted during visits to our island, and fondly remembered when again housed in their own leaner Continental provinces, was that proud joint knighted by Henry the Eighth. Most of our readers are capable of relishing a loin of beef, and they doubtless prize it the more for the true, though humble, part it played in the Reformation. One day—a day destined to be eventful and fruitful of events—Henry was hunting in Windsor great forest. Having the misfortune to miss his path and separate from his party, his majesty found himself at dinner-time before the gates of Reading monastery—in those days as likely a house wherein to meet with animal comforts as the Reform Club would be in our own. Preserving his disguise, Henry knocked with the dignity becoming an illustrious stranger, and on entering the hall found the table crowded with dishes for a sumptuous mid-day repast. Seating himself, the guest and his Tudor appetite did justice, or, as a poorer host would have thought, more than justice, to what was before him. But my lord Abbot, being a man given to hospitality, rejoiced at entertaining a stranger so competent to enjoy a dinner. Every delicacy procurable by the revenue of a wealthy monastery was at the service of the august visitor, who, however, prompted by a simpler than an ecclesiastical taste, observed, 'I will stick to this Sir-loin.' Quoth the 'holy' man, unable to restrain his envious astonishment, 'I would give £100 to be able to eat with corresponding gusto; but, alas! my weak and qualmish stomach can hardly digest the wing of a fowl.' Probably a frown shaded Henry's brow, while in thought only he answered, *I know how to cure your qualms.* A few days subsequently some officers arrested the abbot, and, without any explanation, summarily imprisoned him. As week by week he languished away the weary hours, he must have vainly sought the origin of his trouble; but no clue to the mystery enlightened his den, and no omen of liberty cheered his solitude. Sunrise and sunset came and went, each bringing a spare meal of bread and water. Then at length, at a convenient season, the King visited the prison. Shielding himself from observation, Henry ordered the prisoner from his cell, and directed that a sirloin of beef should be set before him. When the famished wretch, with greedy appetite, had eaten till the bones were bare, Henry stood forth and cried, 'Sir Abbot, I have cured you of your qualms; give me my £100.' The fine was taken, and the fatal seed-thought sown, which spread its empire until the tide of public opinion told against the luxurious iniquity of monasticism.

ANNE BOLEYN'S CHARITY.

Anne Boleyn was accounted by the Reformers to possess a model charitable disposition. It was her custom to relieve the indigent from a purse she carried for that purpose; and she was not satisfied with any day during which this was not well used. She also formed her ladies into a working corps, a species of Dorcas society, which made garments for the needy. Idleness and foolish recreation were equally abhorrent to her nature. It will be long before the majority in the nation look upon her otherwise than a martyr. When Earl Russell, in his last years, invited six hundred artizans to his picturesque park at Richmond, it will be remembered that Lady Russell pointed out to the party the tree beneath which Henry VIII.

was standing when a rocket from the tower announced the welcome news of his wife's death.

The charity of the second Earl of Bedford was so generally talked about as extravagant, that Queen Elizabeth ventured to offer her royal remonstrance; but the good man answered, "It's more honourable for men to make beggars by their liberality than by their oppression." The house of Bedford has since the sixteenth century been renowned for its many-sided liberalism.

THOMAS CROMWELL'S ADVENTURES.

In his young days, according to the current report of the time, Thomas Cromwell, the Chancellor of Henry VIII., met with some adventures in Italy of a romantic kind, and characteristic of the age and perhaps of the man. The son of a cloth-worker in London, young Thomas, moved probably by a love of foreign adventure, went abroad as page to an adventurer older than himself; but on coming to grief in a fight, he was reduced to rags and the sorest straits of hunger. Having strayed as far as Florence, and not knowing what else to do, young Cromwell called on a rich merchant named Frescobald, and appealed for aid. After hearing the doleful story of the English lad, the rich merchant did even more than he was desired to do. He received the famished foreigner into his house, entertained him as a guest, and, when he left for England, gave him a horse, suitable clothes for the journey, and put gold in his purse. Time passed, Cromwell reached England in safety, prospered until he became Lord Chancellor; but the generous merchant sustained many losses and became comparatively poor. Frescobald came to London to recover some debts of which he stood in great need, and one day he chanced to meet the Chancellor on the way to court, when the great man at once dismounted to eagerly inquire if Francis were not Frescobald the Florentine. Not recognising the needy page in the chief statesman of England, the now impoverished merchant was not a little surprised at the attentions he received, the more so when he was invited to dine with the Chancellor on that day. Frescobald soon saw through the whole business, and heard his friend confess, 'This is he by whose means I have achieved this my present degree.' On that day he sat next to Cromwell at dinner, received back the gold he had put into the purse of the poor page at Florence, a hundred pieces being allowed as interest for each piece then given. More than this, Cromwell sent round to all of the Florentine's debtors, calling on them to pay their dues under pain of the Government's displeasure. Frescobald was in the meantime lodged sumptuously beneath the roof of Cromwell, who desired his friend to settle in London. Declining to forsake home and country, the traveller soon returned to Florence comparatively rich, though in a few months after he died; thus, as it appears, being spared the pain of witnessing the unhappy end of Cromwell himself.

END OF AN APOSTATE.

A smith in King Edward the Sixth's time, called Richard Denon, was a zealous professor of religion, and by his Christian instructions the happy instrument of converting a young man to the faith. Afterwards, in the reign of Queen Mary, this young man was cast into prison for his religion, who remembering his old friend the smith, to whom he always carried a reverent respect for the good that he had received by him, sent to know whether he was not imprisoned also;

and finding that he was not, desired to speak with him; and when he came, asked his advice, whether he thought it comfortable for him to remain in prison? and whether he would encourage him to burn at a stake for his religion? To whom the smith answered, that his cause was good, and he might with comfort suffer for it; 'but for my part (saith he) I cannot burn.' But he that could not burn for his religion, by God's just judgment, was burned for his apostacy; for shortly after, his shop and house being set on fire, whilst he over-earnestly endeavoured to save his goods, himself was burnt.—*Burton.*

JOHN CRAIG'S ESCAPE FROM ROME.

Persons who have passed along the Edinburgh Cowgate will probably have been interested in the old Magdalen Chapel, in which John Craig, the compeer of Knox, promulgated the principles of the Reformation. Craig was a man of travel, of enlarged experience, and of romantic adventure. Condemned at Rome to be burned at the stake, he was released from prison on the eve before the day fixed for his martyrdom in a wonderfully providential manner. News spread through the city that Paul the Fourth was dead, on which a tumult arose, the people opened the prisons, and Craig escaped. A robber on the road some distance from Rome gave him money in acknowledgment of a former kindness; but this being exhausted, he might have died of want in the wilderness but for the circumstance that he was met by a dog with a purse of money in its mouth—a boon which the animal voluntarily surrendered with signs of pleasure. After reaching Vienna, the Reformer preached before Maximilian the Second, who was asked by the succeeding pope to send Craig back a prisoner to Rome. This was refused, and with letters of safe conduct he reached Edinburgh in safety, where he laboured effectively during many years, and died at his post in the year 1600. The story of the dog is no doubt authentic; John Craig was not a man to invent a story, and he could not have been deceived.

DR. ROWLAND TAYLOR.

Of all places in England where the Reformation struck its roots and flourished none were more favoured than Hadleigh in Suffolk, the parish in which Dr. Rowland Taylor, the ancestor of Jeremy Taylor, ministered. In the middle of the sixteenth century the place was a prosperous seat of cloth manufacture; and such was the admirable way in which the people had been taught by their pastor, that common merchants and artificers were as though they had been trained in a school of divinity. The preaching of Bilney had taken effect; and, seeing how assiduously the work was being continued, Bishop Gardiner accused the vicar, and, after being condemned in London, Dr. Taylor was taken down to be burned on Oldham Common, hard by the town, and where a stone marks the site and commemorates the scene. The church was rebuilt about thirty-five years ago, but the vicarage, dated 1490, in which Taylor resided, in part survives. The wonderfully realistic account of Foxe is as touchingly graphic as anything to be found in the *Acts and Monuments*, e.g.:—

'On the next morrow, after that Dr. Taylor had supped with his wife in the Compter, as is before expressed, which was the 5th day of February, the sheriff of London, with his officers, came to the Compter by two o'clock in the morning, and so brought forth Dr. Taylor, and without any light led him to the Woolsack, an inn without Aldgate. Dr. Taylor's wife, suspecting that her husband should that night be carried away, watched all night in St. Botolph's church porch beside Aldgate, having with her two children, the one named Elizabeth, of thirteen years of age (whom, being left without father or mother, Dr. Taylor had brought up of alms from three years old), the other named Mary, Dr. Taylor's own daughter.

'Now when the sheriff and his company came against St. Botolph's church, Elizabeth cried, saying, "Oh, my dear father! mother, mother, here is my father led away!" Then cried his wife, "Rowland, Rowland, where art thou?"—for it was a very dark morning, that the one could not well see the other. Dr. Taylor answered, "Dear wife, I am here;" and stayed. The sheriff's men would have led him forth, but the sheriff said, "Stay a little, masters, I pray you, and let him speak to his wife;" and so they stayed.

"Then came she to him, and he took his daughter Mary in his arms; and he, his wife, and Elizabeth kneeled down and said the Lord's Prayer. At which sight the sheriff wept apace, and so did divers others of the company. After they had prayed, he rose up and kissed his wife, and shook her by the hand, and said, "Farewell, my dear wife; be of good comfort, for I am quiet in my conscience. God shall stir up a father for my children." And then he kissed his daughter Mary, and said, "God bless thee, and make thee His servant;" and kissing Elizabeth, he said, "God bless thee. I pray you all stand strong and steadfast unto Christ and His Word, and keep you from idolatry." Then said his wife, "God be with thee, dear Rowland; I will, with God's grace, meet thee at Hadley."

'And so was he led forth to the Woolsack, and his wife followed him. As soon as they came to the Woolsack, he was put into a chamber, wherein he was kept with four yeomen of the guard, and the sheriff's men. Dr. Taylor, as soon as he was come into the chamber, fell down on his knees and gave himself wholly to prayer. The sheriff then seeing Dr. Taylor's wife there, would in no case grant her to speak any more with her husband, but gently desired her to go to his house, and take it as her own, and promised her she should lack nothing, and sent two officers to conduct her thither. Notwithstanding, she desired to go to her mother's, whither the officers led her, and charged her mother to keep her there till they came again.

'Thus remained Dr. Taylor in the Woolsack, kept by the sheriff and his company, till eleven o'clock; at which time the sheriff of Essex was ready to receive him; and so they set him on horseback within the inn, the gates being shut.

'At the coming out of the gates, John Hull, before spoken of, stood at the rails with Thomas, Dr. Taylor's son. When Dr. Taylor saw them, he called them, saying "Come hither, my son Thomas." And John Hull lifted the child up, and set him on the horse before his father; and Dr. Taylor put off his hat, and said to the people that stood there looking on him, "Good people, this is mine own son, begotten of my body in lawful matrimony; and God be blessed for lawful matrimony!" Then lifted he up his eyes towards heaven, and prayed for his son; laid his hat upon the child's head and blessed him; and so delivered the child to John Hull, whom he took by the hand, and said, "Farewell, John Hull, the faithfullest servant that ever man had." And so they rode forth, the sheriff of Essex, with four yeomen of the guard, and the sheriff's men leading him.

'All the way Dr. Taylor was joyful and merry, as one that accounted himself going to a most pleasant banquet or bridal. He spake many notable things to the sheriff and yeomen of the guard that conducted him, and often moved them to weep, through his much earnest calling upon them to repent, and to amend their evil and wicked living. Oftentimes also he caused them to wonder and rejoice, to see him so constant and steadfast, void of all fear, joyful in heart, and glad to die. Of these yeomen of the guard, three used Dr. Taylor friendly, but the fourth (whose name was Homes) used him very homely, unkindly, and churlishly.

'When they were now come to Hadley, and came riding over the bridge, at the bridge-foot waited a poor man with five small children; who when he saw Dr. Taylor, he and his children fell down upon their knees, and held up their hands, and the man cried with a loud voice, and said, "Oh, dear father and good shepherd, Dr. Taylor! God help and succour thee, as thou hast many a time succoured me and my poor children." Such witness had the servant of God of his virtuous and charitable alms given in his lifetime, for God would now the poor should testify of his good deeds, to his singular comfort, to the example of others, and confusion of his persecutors and tyrannous adversaries. For the sheriff and others that led him to death were wonderfully astonied at this; and the sheriff sore rebuked the poor man for so crying. The streets of Hadley were beset on both sides the way with men and women of the town and country, who waited to see him; whom when they beheld so led to death, with weeping eyes and lamentable voices they cried, saying one to another, "Ah, good Lord! there goeth our good shepherd from us, that so faithfully hath taught us, so fatherly hath cared for us, and so godly hath governed us. Oh merciful God! what shall we poor scattered lambs do? What shall come of this most wicked world? Good Lord, strengthen him and comfort him;" with such other most lamentable and piteous voices. Wherefore the people were sore rebuked by the sheriff and the catchpoles, his men, that led him. And Dr. Taylor evermore said to the people, "I have preached to you God's word and truth, and am come this day to seal it with my blood."'

LUTHER'S BOOKS BURNED IN CHEAPSIDE.

Amongst Londoners troubled by the clergy was Thomas Sommers, who died in the Tower of London for confessing of the Gospel, which Thomas, being a very honest merchant and wealthy, was sent for by the lord cardinal, and committed to the Tower, for that he had Luther's books (as they termed them). After great suit made for him to the said cardinal, his judgment was, that he should ride from the Tower into Cheapside, carrying a new book in his hand, and with books hanging round about him, with three or four other merchants after the same order; which was done. And when Master Sommers should be set on a collier's nag, as the rest of his fellow-prisoners were, a friend of his, called Master Copland, brought him a very good gelding, fair dressed with bridle and saddle; and when the bishop's officers came to dress him with books, as they had trimmed the others, and would have made holes in his garments, to have thrust the strings of the books therein, 'No,' said Sommers, 'I have always loved to go handsomely in my apparel;' and taking the books and opening them, he bound them together by the strings, and cast them about his neck (the leaves being all open) like a collar; and, being on horseback, rode foremost through the streets, till they came about the Standard in Cheapside, where a great fire was made to burn their books in, and a pillory set up there for four persons, in token that they had deserved it.

In the meantime, by the way as they should come, it was appointed that one should go before them with a basin, at the noise whereof Master Sommers' horse, being a lofty gelding and fierce, was in such a rage, that he who rung the basin, being afraid of himself, was fain to go alone a great space before that any horseman followed after. At length, when they came to the fire, every one of them having a book in his hand, they were commanded to cast their books into the fire. But when Master Sommers saw that his New Testament should be burned, he threw it over the fire, which was seen by some of God's enemies, and brought to him again, commanding him to cast it into the fire, which he would not do, but cast it through the fire, which thing was done three times; but at last a stander-by took it up and saved it from burning. But not long after, the said Master Sommers was again cast into the Tower by the cardinals, through the cruelty of the bishops and their adherents, who, soon after, died in the said prison for the testimony of his faith.—*Acts and Monuments.*

THE BIRTHPLACE OF JOHN FOXE.

The Lincolnshire town of Boston—originally St. Botolph's Town, the patron of sailors—lies six miles from the sea, and anciently was of so great importance that when in the year 1204 a tax on traders of the port of London realized £836, Boston yielded no less than £780. In the days of Edward III. the town was celebrated for an immense annual fair; and was hardly second to any other English trading centre for the traffic carried on in wool, leather, and lead. Such was Boston's prosperity in these mediæval times that merchants from the Continent were attracted, and the first symptoms of decline were occasioned when, through disagreeing with the natives, those foreigners were compelled to depart. After the dissolution of the monasteries, Philip and Mary gave the town 500 acres of land; and its history was for some years a chequered one. It was afflicted by plague and inundation; and then, in the civil war time, Boston for a while became the head-quarters of the Parliamentary forces.

Boston was the native place of John Foxe; and in connection with his account of the life of Thomas Cromwell, the martyrologist gives a curious account of the pope's dear merchandise called Boston Pardons. During the first quarter of the sixteenth century the moral darkness was still dense, although the publication of Tyndale's translation of the New Testament, in 1525, may be regarded as the inauguration of the Reformation in England. At that time the Romish court drew a considerable revenue from pardons of various kinds, some affecting individuals, while others in their magnanimous comprehensiveness embraced entire towns. Boston held a couple of leases of 'his holiness'—the greater and the lesser pardons—and when these in time expired, a deputation was commissioned to visit Rome to obtain a renewal of the costly privilege.

The commissioners, one Geffery Chambers and another, appear to have set off on their difficult mission with some trepidation; but on coming to Antwerp they were sufficiently fortunate to make friends with the afterwards celebrated Thomas Cromwell, who then, as a youth, was acting as secretary to the English merchants in the port. After Cromwell had been advised with, he consented to accompany his two new friends to Rome; and even 'began to cast with himself what thing best to devise' in order to get well through with the business. 'At length,' continues Foxe in his quaint style, 'having knowledge how the Pope's holy tooth greatly delighted in new-fangled strange delicacies, and dainty dishes, it came into his mind to prepare certain fine dishes of jelly, after the best fashion, made after our country manner here in England; which to them of Rome was not known or seen before.' The pope with whom Cromwell had to deal was Julius II., the immediate predecessor of Leo X., the grand opponent of Luther. Watching his opportunity, the ingenious Cromwell approached Julius just when the Pope had returned from the hunting field; and presenting 'his jolly junkets such as only kings and princes in England are wont to feed upon,' the jellies were so well appreciated that 'the jolly pardons of the town of Boston' were at once stamped for another term of years.

THE EARLY DAYS OF JOHN FOXE.

While John Foxe was young his father died, and the widow was married again to a bigoted partisan of popery. This change boded little but ill to the youthful scholar, whom his parents designed for the old paths. He was regarded as a good Latinist, and his relish for the poetical models of antiquity was keen; but in time he relinquished the poets in favour of divinity, and this new course of reading gradually unsettled his belief in superstition, by opening his eyes to the truth of the reformed doctrines. In those days such a change of sentiment risked the loss of a man's estate, and imperilled his life; but although Foxe was reduced to poverty, he escaped with a whole skin. His father probably thought it a pious act to appropriate the portion of goods which otherwise would have fallen to the share of the renegade; and for the same reasons the convert was driven from his fellowship at Magdalen College, Oxford. Though this was a harsh discipline, the effects were so far beneficial that Foxe was once and for ever driven from that hateful, semi-pagan communion, which, to foster its own spiritual pride, would rob God of His prerogative to rule the conscience, and retain its hold on human minds by pains and penalties.

Deprived of his rightful inheritance and of his college emoluments, he now tasted the bitterness of complete poverty for Christ's sake; but relief came when the young confessor accepted a tutorship at Charlecote Hall, Warwickshire, the seat of Sir Thomas Lucy, on whose domain Shakespeare was years afterwards accused of committing depredations obnoxious to the game laws of those old times. 'Under the trees which must have been familiar to the great poet,' says Dr. Stoughton, 'the Protestant historian probably had wandered, book in hand, musing on those points which had disturbed his mind at Oxford, and gaining, as it would appear from his subsequent life, additional light upon the momentous ecclesiastical controversies of the day.' He did more at Charlecote, however, than read and meditate; he fell in love with the pretty daughter of a Coventry merchant, and their subsequent marriage proved a happy union. The time came for leaving Charlecote, and he soon found, that though married life brought additional happiness, it also had its peculiar trials. He settled at Coventry; but even in the Bible-printing era of Henry VIII., that busy town was becoming too conspicuous a residence for a well-known reformer like John Foxe, and he retired for a time to the house of his wife's father at Boston. Even there he was almost as much dreaded as a Jonah in a ship; for lynx-eyed priests, who were naturally chagrined that their prestige was on the wane, suspected the quiet observer, and would have gone a great deal further had they known that Master

Foxe, for reasons best known to himself, eagerly collected and treasured the stories of the lives and sufferings of Christian martyrs. He must have looked like a very sorry opponent of the proud hierarchy of Rome; but though poor and despised, and shunned, even by his relatives, he had truth on his side; and with the press for a sling, he had one stone in reserve which would defeat the enemy—he could write a book.

JOHN FOXE IN PROSPERITY.

While living at the mansion of the Duke of Norfolk in Aldgate, Foxe became intimately associated with the well-known citizen John Daye, printer to the Queen, and whose offices were the apartments of Alders Gate. Daye was happily something more than a printer of the old school; he was an ardent Reformer, who could second with lively zeal the anti-popish projects of his laborious literary friend. As Foxe had served the Continental printers, so now, in a similar manner, he worked for Daye; but the union was of a much closer kind. The compact they entered into was a truly patriotic one, as mere gain was not their ultimate object. For some time the martyrologist walked daily from his sumptuous retreat at the east end of the town to Daye's busy office, and finally he made the ancient gate his permanent abode. Both author and printer were sufficiently sagacious to perceive that a complete historical account of papal atrocities would do more than could be done by parliaments and armies in curtailing the power of Rome, and they were determined to see historic justice done to the noble band who had yielded up their lives in the cause of Christ. After years of toil and anxiety, the first edition of 'The Acts and Monuments' was published in 1563—a year of dread, alarm, and suffering; 'pestilence, scarcity of money, and dearth of victuals,' having pressed heavily upon the London citizens.

The affliction passed away, and Foxe was fully occupied in preparing a new and enlarged edition of his great history. So abundant were his labours, that when his old friend Grindal, Bishop of London, appointed him to preach at Paul's Cross, on Good Friday, 1570, the martyrologist would have excused himself by remarking, 'There never yet was ass or mule who was so weighted down and overdone by carrying burdens as I have long been by literary labours.' However, in that age, as is the case in our own day, multiplicity of other work was not considered a valid plea against accepting preaching engagements. While the bishop could find no better substitute, and while the people were anxious to hear an author whose book had already become popular, Foxe was obliged to preach. We seem to hear the tones of his praying words, 'Help them that are needy and afflicted. . . . And above all things continue and increase our faith,' ring forth in loud distinctness over the multitude of upturned faces. Then, with a touch of humour, he reminds his auditory that on Good Friday the Pope curses his enemies. Cursing is the natural language of blind apostates. Foxe tells his audience that he fears the blessing of 'his holiness' far more than his anathema; may he 'never bless us more as he blessed us in Queen Mary's time! God of His mercy keep away that blessing from us.'

JOHN FOXE'S WIT.

Of the martyrologist's wit, wisdom, and behaviour in private life, the following incidents, related by Samuel Foxe, and quoted by Dr. Stoughton, will afford a tolerably good notion:—' Being once asked at a friend's table what dish he desired to have to begin with, he answered the last—which word was pleasantly taken as if he had meant some choicer dish, such as are usually brought for the second course; whereas he rather signified the desire he had to see the dinner ended, that he might depart home. Going abroad by chance, he met a woman that he knew, who, pulling a book from under her arm, and saying, "See you not that I am going to a sermon?" Master Foxe replied, "But if you will be ruled by me, go home rather for to-day; you will do but little good at church." And when she asked "at what time he would counsel her to go," "Then," answered he, "when you tell nobody beforehand." It happened at his own table that a gentleman there spoke somewhat too freely against the Earl of Leicester, which, when Master Foxe heard it, he commanded a bowl, filled with wine, to be brought in; which being done, "This bowl," quoth he, "was given me by the Earl of Leicester;" so stopping the gentleman in his intemperate speeches without reprehending him. A young man, a little too forward, had in presence of many said "that he could conceive no reason, in the reading of the old authors, why men should so greatly admire them." "No marvel, indeed," quoth Master Foxe, "for if you could conceive the reason, you would then admire them yourself."'

THE MARTYROLOGIST'S ESCAPE.

During the brief and happy reign of Edward VI., Foxe resided with his patron and charge at Reigate, where he regularly preached; and when out of school hours he found a profitable recreation in cleansing the parish from the relics of popish idolatry still abounding. This Protestant activity won for him the sincere hatred of all Papists; and when the times changed with the accession of Mary, the vigilant Gardiner, like a Vatican blood-hound, scented his prey, and Foxe was compelled to escape for his life. Aided by the Duke of Norfolk, the Reformer embarked at Ipswich, and before the vessel was out of sight the Bishop of Winchester's messenger, with a warrant in his hand, stood on the quay, watching the receding sails with baffled fury. A farmer's house where the fugitive was supposed to have slept was rudely broken open and searched without avail; the bird had escaped the fowler. In the meantime a tempest arose, so that after a day of misgiving and suffering, the ship, instead of reaching the Dutch coast, put back again into Ipswich, where Foxe was more alarmed than diverted with the narrative of what had happened during his absence. Fearing to let it be known that he was stopping in the town, he rode away and secreted himself till it would be safe to attempt the voyage. Subsequently, with his anxious wife, he crossed the sea, and found the shelter which his own country denied to the faithful servants of the Lord.

AN ANTI-LUTHERAN GHOST AT ORLEANS.

The wife of the provost of the city having died, was buried, as she had requested, without any pomp and without the customary gifts to the Church. Thereupon the Franciscans conceived the scheme of making use of her example to warn others against following a course so detrimental to monastic and priestly interests. The mysterious knockings by means of which the deceased was supposed to give intimation of her miserable doom and of her desire that her body, as of one that had been tainted with heresy, should be removed from the holy ground wherein it had been interred, were listened to with amazement by the awe-stricken people. But the opportune discovery of a novice, conveniently posted above the ceiling of the convent chapel, sadly interfered with the success of the well-contrived plot, and eleven monks convicted of complicity in the fraud were banished the kingdom. They would have been even more severely punished had not fear been entertained lest the Reformers might find too much occasion for triumph.—*Baird.*

A LUTHERAN ICONOCLAST AT PARIS.

Just after the solemnities of Whit Sunday, 1528, an unheard-of act of impiety startled the inhabitants of the capital, and fully persuaded them that no object of their devotions was safe from iconoclastic violence. One of those numerous statues of the Virgin Mary, with the infant Jesus in her arms, that graced the streets of Paris, was found to be shockingly mutilated. The body had been pierced, and the head-dress trampled underfoot. The heads of the Mother and Child had been broken off and ignominiously thrown in the rubbish. A more flagrant act of contempt for the religious sentiment of the country had perhaps never been committed. The indignation it awakened must not be judged by the standard of a calmer age. In the desire to ascertain the perpetrators of the outrage, the King offered a reward of a thousand crowns. But no ingenuity could ferret them out. A vague rumour indeed prevailed that a similar excess had been witnessed in a village four or five leagues distant, and that the culprits, when detected, had confessed that they had been prompted to its commission by the promise of a paltry recompense of one hundred *sous* for every image destroyed. But since no one seems ever to have been punished, it is probable that this report was a fabrication; and the question whether the mutilation of the Virgin of the *Rue des Rosiers* was the deliberate act of a religious enthusiast, or a freak of drunken revellers, or, as some imagined, a cunning device of good Catholics to inflame the popular passions against the 'Lutherans,' must, for the present at least, remain a subject of profound doubt. —*Baird.*

PROTESTANTS AT AIX-LA-CHAPELLE.

One of Luther's first disciples, Albert van Munster, sowed the first seeds of the Reformed religion at Aix-la-Chapelle in 1524. He made few proselytes, being quickly seized, and condemned to lose his head. His body was buried ignominiously without the gate of St. James.

This instance of persecution only served to give the inhabitants a curiosity of knowing the doctrine which so greatly alarmed the clergy. Their trade with Germany augmented their inclination for these oppressed truths, and, in 1533, they secretly procured a Lutheran preacher. Their number increasing daily, their meetings could not be long kept secret. The magistrates caused the minister, with a part of his auditory, to be arrested; but he was suffered to escape out of prison, in order not to exasperate his followers. Some Anabaptists were less gently treated, being condemned to the flames, while the Lutherans were only banished, notwithstanding the concordate of religion granted to the subjects of the empire. All these severities, however, did not hinder the progress of the Reformation.

Under the government of the cruel Duke of Alva, the Low Countries were almost depopulated by the death or exile of a great multitude of Protestants. Such as escaped his fury took shelter in the neighbouring countries, and many settled at Aix-la-Chapelle, where they thought themselves the more secure, as the city was by its constitution free and imperial. Here they enjoyed repose for some time, through the indulgence of the regency, which drew others not only from the Low Countries, but from France and Germany. Nor had the city of Aix any reason to repent the shelter it gave these persecuted people. It found the advantage of their industry and trade, and if it had known rightly how to preserve these benefits, it had been one of the most flourishing cities in Germany, and its commerce would have been increased far beyond what could have been expected from its situation.

The moving example of so many families fugitive and exiled for the cause of religion had a great influence on the inhabitants of Aix. Many from admiring their constancy embraced their faith. The Reformation, by this means, gained ground insensibly, and without tumults. The priests and monks were not insulted, but they saw their churches grow thin and their offerings diminish. This was the ground of their rage against the reformed, and they employed the emperor, empire, and Spain as their instruments.—*Gentleman's Magazine.*

FRUNDSBERG.

Catholic writers are naturally zealous in pointing out the inconsistencies which marked the lives of the earliest reformers; but although such inconsistencies may furnish good grounds for impeaching their judgment, they can seldom be interpreted as proofs of insincerity. Amidst the irregular ebullition of new opinions, many of the most daring and comprehensive dogmas of innovation came first to the surface; while, on the other hand, many of those practices which to modern eyes seem most unreasonable, many which an enlightened Catholic now rejects, were among the last fully abandoned by the new believers. Hence the history of the Reformation alternately surprises us by the rapid progress made by liberal ideas and by the slow ebb of superstition. Could we look distinctly into the spirit of those confessors of our churches, as we are partially enabled to do into that of Luther by the unreserved openness of his writings on topics connected with himself, we should probably find them all exhibiting, in less striking proportions, the characteristics of his rude and gigantic intellect,—a strange mixture of the hardiest philosophy with the most vulgar prejudices. We should then be able to analyze the contradictory emotions which made Frundsberg lead armies across the Alps to humble the Pope, and yet go into battle (as he did at Pavia) with a monk's cowl drawn over his helmet in token of devotion. So that while some of his reported actions have induced the Catholics to claim him as adhering at heart to the ancient faith, Luther, who had reason to know him, mentions him 'among those heroes for whose sake God blesses a whole country;' and so shortly after his decease, as during the war of Smalkalde, he was looked back to as one of the national champions against foreign dominion, and placed in the same rank with Arminius and Fredric Barbarossa.—*Foreign Review.*

A LUTHERAN AT TOULOUSE.

At Toulouse, the seat of one of the most noted parliaments, Jean de Caturce, a lawyer of ability, was put to death by slow fire in the summer of 1532. His unpardonable offence was that he had once made a Lutheran exhortation, and that, in the merry-making on the *Fête des Rois*—Epiphany—he had recommended that the prayer, 'May Christ reign in our hearts!' be substituted for the senseless cry, 'The king drinks!' No more ample ground of accusation was needed in a city where the luckless wight who failed to take off his cap before an image, or fall on his knees when the bell rang out at *Ave Maria*, was sure to be set upon as a heretic.—*Baird*.

THE MARTYR AND THE APOSTATE.

Philibert Hamlin, a popish priest in France, was, in the year 1557, converted to the Protestant religion, and thereupon went to Geneva, where he exercised the art of printing, and published many books; after which he was made a minister of the Reformed religion, and preached with good success at the town of Alenart and other places. At last he, with his host, a priest whom he had instructed in the Protestant profession, were apprehended, and cast into prison at Burdeaux; and whilst they lay there, in came a priest with all his accoutrements, to say mass; but Philibert, inflamed with zeal against such ridiculous fopperies, went and pluckt the garments from his back, and overthrew the chalice and candlesticks, saying, 'Is it not enough for you to blaspheme God in the churches, but you must also pollute the prisons with your idolatry?' The jailor seeing this, fell upon him, and beat him with his staff, and also removed him into a dungeon, loading him with irons, which made his legs to swell, where he lay eight days. The priest, his host, terrified with the prison and fear of death, renounced his profession, and was set at liberty; whereupon Philibert said to him, 'O unhappy and more than miserable

man! is it possible that you should be so foolish as that to save your life a few days you should so start away from and deny the truth? Know you therefore, that although you have hereby avoided the corporal fire, yet your life shall be never the longer; for you shall die before me, and yet shall not have the honour to die for the cause of God; and you shall be an example to all apostates.' Having ended his speech, and the priest going out of prison, he was presently slain by two gentlemen, who formerly had a quarrel against him. Philibert hearing of it, protested seriously that he knew of no such thing before, but spoke as it pleased God to guide his tongue. Philibert being condemned, and carried to execution, they endeavoured to drown his voice by sounding of trumpets; and so, in the midst of the flames, praying and exhorting the people to constancy in the truth, he rendered up his soul unto God.
—*Prodigies of Judgment.*

QUEEN MARGARET'S PRESENTIMENT.

The night before Henry II., King of France, was slain, Queen Margaret his wife dreamed that she saw her husband's eyes put out. There were jousts and tournaments at that time, into which the Queen besought her husband not to enter, because of her dream; but he was resolved, and there did great things. When all was almost done, he would needs run at tilt with a knight, who refused him; his name was Montgomery: but the king was bent upon it; whereupon they broke their lances to pieces in the encounter, and a splinter of one of them struck the King so full in the eye, that he thereby received his deadly wound. It is observed of this king, that one Arm du Bourg, a noble councillor, and a man of singular understanding and knowledge, making a speech before him, a little before his death, in defence of the Protestant religion, and against persecuting the professors thereof, he therein rendered thanks to Almighty God for moving the King's heart to be present at the decision of so mighty a cause as that of religion was, and humbly entreated him to consider thereof; it being the cause of Christ Himself, which of good right ought to be maintained of princes, etc. But the King, instead of hearkening to his good advice, was so far incensed against him that he caused him to be apprehended by the Count of Montgomery, Constable of France, and to be carried to prison, protesting to him in these words, ' These eyes of mine shall see thee burnt ; ' and presently after he sent a commission to the judges to make his process. In the meantime great feasts were preparing in the court for joy of the marriages that should be of the King's daughter and sister. The day whereof being come, the King employed all the morning in examining the president and other councillors of the parliament against Du Bourg (and other of his companions who were charged with the same doctrines), intending to glut his eyes in seeing his execution, but that very afternoon he received that fatal blow in his right eye, which so pierced his head that his brains were perished ; which wound despising all means of cure, killed him within eleven days, whereby his hope of seeing Du Bourg burned was frustrated.—*Prodigies of Judgment and Mercy.*

FRANCE UNDER FRANCIS I.

If evidence were needed to prove that an unreformed age is necessarily an age of cruelty, we should only need to look at France as the country existed under this monarch. Though no scholar in the usually accepted sense of the term, Francis was a liberal patron of those who devoted their talents to the furtherance of literature and the arts. We do not, however, judge of a nation's prosperity by the condition of her litterateurs and artists, but by the condition of the common people. Judged of by this test, France at the opening of the Reformation period was miserable and oppressed. 'The pages of chronicles, both public and private, teem with proofs of the insignificant value set upon human life and happiness,' says Professor Baird, in his 'Rise of the Huguenots.' 'In many parts of France the peasant rarely enjoyed quiet even for a few consecutive months. Organized bands of robbers infested whole provinces, and laid towns and villages under contribution. Not unfrequently two or three hundred men were to be found in a single band, and the robberies, outrages, and murders they committed defy recital. Often the miscreants were volunteers whose employers had failed to furnish them their stipulated pay, and who avenged their losses by exactions levied upon the unfortunate peasantry. Indeed, if we may believe the almost incredible statements of one of the laws enacted for their suppression, they had been known to carry by assault even walled cities, and to exercise against the miserable inhabitants cruelty such as disgraces the very name of man.'

DEATH OF HENRY IV.

King Henry IV. of France, who had all his lifetime before been a Protestant, yet after he came to the crown of France, when he had almost subdued his enemies which opposed him therein, suddenly turned Papist. Not long after, as he was taking his walk with his nobles, to begin his progress, one John Castile, influenced by the Jesuits, intended to have stabbed him in the body with a knife; but the King, at the same time stepping down to take up one of his lords, who was on his knees before him, the blow happened upon his upper jaw, cutting out one of his teeth, and somewhat wounding his tongue. It is reported that in his progress, a Protestant minister, in private conference, said unto him, 'Sir, you have denied God with your tongue already, and have now received a wound in the same; take heed of denying with your heart, lest you receive a wound in that also;' which afterwards proved a true prophecy, for riding abroad in his coach to refresh himself as he passed through a narrow street, one Ravillack watched his opportunity, and with a dagger stabbed him first in the left side, and with a second blow struck him between the fifth and sixth rib, cutting asunder the vein which leads to the heart, of which wound he immediately died.—*Prodigies of Judgment.*

CATHERINE DE MEDICIS IN 1569.

Giovanni Correro, who was Venetian ambassador at the French Court, thus sketches this celebrated woman:— She is still in robust health, though adhering to her habit of eating so immoderately as often to bring on maladies which lay her at death's door. She is mild and amiable, and makes it her business to content all those who apply to her, at least in words, of which she is not parsimonious. She is most assiduous to business, not the smallest thing being done without her knowledge; interrupting, therefore, her meals and sleep; following the army without care for her health or life, doing all which men might be bound to do; *and yet loved by nobody.* The Huguenots accuse her of deceiving them, the Catholics of allowing these first-named to go too far. I do not say she is infallible; sometimes she relies on her own opinion too entirely; but I have pitied more than I have blamed her. I said this to herself one day, *and she often reminded me of it since,* when speaking of the misfortunes of France and her own difficulties. I know more than once she has been found weeping in her closet, *and then suddenly would wipe her eyes and show herself with a gay countenance,* not to alarm those who might judge of the march of affairs from its expressions. She sometimes will follow one counsel, sometimes another. *Every one fears her.* The King, who is now nineteen, is tall and stoops much, and from this and his pallidness one would not judge him to be strong. Public affairs do not interest him; he hears their details patiently sometimes during three or four hours in the council. In all decisions he rests on his mother, whom he honours with a respect most admirable. There are few sons so obedient; few mothers so fortunate. But this filial respect, which might be called fear, detracts from his reputation inasmuch as it augments hers; otherwise he is mild and affable to every one.—*Foreign Review.*

ZWINGLI AT ZURICH.

Born on January 1st, 1484, this noble Swiss Reformer was only seven weeks younger than Luther. Though his father was no more than an Alpine herdsman, the son received a good education, and at the age of twenty-two entered the Church. Long before Luther published his Theses on Indulgences, Zwingli saw the need of reform, and, in point of fact, became a reformer before the monk of Erfurt. He became celebrated as a preacher, and if at first full prominence was not given to all of the evan gelical tenets, he avoided as much as possible to speak about relics, images, and Romish superstitions. He was a soldier as well as a pastor, however, and this mistake of combining two professions incompatible with one another cost the Reformer his life. He went to the wars in Italy, fought the French for two days at Marignano, in September 1515, and finally fell on the field of Cappel on October 11th, 1531.

Zwingii was a more thorough reformer than Luther; and he had opposed the abuses of Rome for two years in Switzerland when the Doctor of Wittenberg commenced his great mission.

It is also remarkable that the Reformation was stimulated in the cantons by the appearance of Bernardin Samson, a Franciscan friar and seller of indulgences, who in audacity equalled the insolence of Tetzel in Germany. By purchasing the Pope's licenses to sin, all would be well both in this world and in the next; and this was so far believed that a harvest of cash was gathered for the Church. This blasphemy was boldly attacked by Zwingli, who declared that those who sold indulgences for money were 'the companions of Simon Magus, the friends of Balaam, and the ambassadors of Satan.'

ZWINGLI MORE SCRIPTURAL THAN LUTHER.

Even in the year 1516, and before Luther had published his celebrated propositions at Wittenberg, Ulric Zuinglius, an ecclesiastic of Zurich, had boldly opposed himself to the assumptions of the Roman Church, and engaged in a system of reform, which he carried on with a degree of ability and resolution not inferior to that of Luther himself. The promulgation of indulgences in the Swiss canton, by the agency of a friar named Sansone, or Samson, afforded him new grounds of reprehension, of which he did not fail successfully to avail himself; and a controversy was maintained between the Papists and the Reformers in the Helvetic states, which resembled both in its vehemence and its consequences that between Luther and Tetzel in Germany. As the opposition of Zuinglius had arisen without any communication with Luther, so the doctrines which he asserted were not always in conformity with those advanced by the German Reformer, and on some important points were directly contrary to them. In truth, the opposition of Zuinglius to the papal see was carried to a greater extent than that of Luther, who still retained some of the most mysterious doctrines of the Roman Church, whilst it was the avowed object of the Helvetic reformer to divest religion of all abstruse doctrines and superstitious opinions, and to establish a pure and simple mode of worship. In consequence of this diversity, a dispute arose, which was carried on with great warmth, and which principally turned on the question respecting the real presence of Christ in the Eucharist, which was firmly asserted, by Luther, but not assented to by Zuinglius, who regarded the bread and wine used in that sacrament as types or symbols only of the body and blood of Christ. On this subject a conference was held between the two Reformers at Marpurg, in which Zuinglius was accompanied by Œcolampadius and Bucer, and Luther by Philip Melancthon and other of his friends. Both parties appealed with confidence to the authority of Scripture for the truth of their opinions, and both discovered that an appeal to those sacred writings will not always terminate a dispute. Persevering in his original intention of restoring the Christian religion to its primitive simplicity, Zuinglius became the founder of that which is denominated, in contradistinction to the Lutheran, the Reformed Church. To this great undertaking he devoted not only his learning and his abilities, but also his life, having, in the year 1530, fallen in battle in defending the cause of the Reformers against the adherents of the Roman Church; leaving behind him an example not only of heroic firmness in maintaining his own opinions, but, what is far more extraordinary, of enlightened toleration to all those who might conscientiously differ from him in matters of faith.—*Roscoe,* ' *Leo the Tenth.*'

A PIONEER—SAVONAROLA AT FLORENCE.

Called from the seclusion of his cell, at the age of thirty-seven, to active labour in the city of Florence, Savonarola journeyed thither on foot—a dark, mysterious providence overhanging him, a disturbed world of conflicting thoughts within him, and an atmosphere of disquietude and gloom around. To what had his God called him? What meant those ceaseless agitations which electrified his soul, and burdened him as with a message from the Lord, crushing him to the earth? Subsequent events developed the foreshadowings. Just at this time Florence was at the dizzying height of its renown. It possessed nearly a thousand fortified positions. Its beauty of situation, its rich lands, its luxuriance, its wealth, its treasures of art, its libraries, its seats of learning, magnificent palaces, unrivalled advantages, and commercial prosperity, with its gaieties and worldly attractions, made it one of the wonders of Europe. If England be, as the keen satire of Napoleon has represented, a nation of shop-keepers, Florence was well-nigh a city of bankers and merchants. Being the great banking-place of the Continent, its wealth was enormous. As Corinth, under the fostering care of Augustus, and in the zenith of its commercial glory, grew licentious and proud and reckless, so Florence, under the luxurious sway of Lorenzo di Medici the Magnificent, became heathenish and viciously immoral. Savonarola's voice was soon heard in the church of St. Mark, censuring the tendencies of the age, and laying bare with merciless severity the corruptions of the Church. It must have been a strange sight to see the spare, haggard form of this pale-faced, keen-eyed, Roman-nosed monk, exciting the crowds of listeners, and overpowering them with his vigorous eloquence. There was nothing in his voice to allure attention. It was thin and weak. Nor was there anything in his manner, for he was unpractised in speaking; but his words carried weight, and each had a flaming fire-dart which pierced its way and carried conviction. His denunciations of the paganism of Florence and the gross abominations of the Church stirred the city to its depths. The friar's popularity grew and spread like living fire. Men listened and shuddered. Priests heard, trembled, and hated. The people grew enthusiastic. Salvation by faith, not by works, forgiveness of sin, not by absolution but by Christ,—these were unheard-of truths from such a pulpit, and were as welcome as they were strange. With sternness of manner he denounced the prevailing sins of the time, and with affectionate entreaty besought men, like another John the Baptist, to 'repent, for the kingdom of heaven was at hand.' Indeed, his prophetic utterances of a visitation from God were listened to with much dismay. His extraordinary faithfulness in rebuking those current sins of the wealthy to which they thought they had a prescriptive right; his personal form of address, without which no minister or reformer can hope to be successful in soul-winning; his clear evangelic utterances as to the natural state of the soul, its need of redemption, and the suitability of the free gospel of God's grace to meet that need, told upon the people. They wept, they were silenced. Men who took down his discourses were known to drop the pens from their hands. Country people walked miles to hear the great preacher; came, indeed, the night before the Sunday, and besieged the church doors at early morn, that they might be sure of a seat. Rich burghers gave them victuals, and even acted as door-keepers. The convent church was too small; nor could the cathedral accommodate more than the three thousand persons who flocked to hear the friar.—*The Sword and the Trowel.*

THE LAST DAYS OF SAVONAROLA.

A man like Savonarola, it is needless to remark, must soon have aroused the enmity of the Papacy. It was no difficulty for him to find foes; they compassed him about like bees. They were principally of the order of the Franciscans, who always hated the order of which Savonarola was a member—the Dominican. News reached Rome of the terrible power and popularity of the friar. The Pope's first thought was to conciliate so dangerous a foe. He therefore offered him a cardinal's hat. But it was declined. 'I wish,' he said, 'for no other red hat than that of a martyr, dyed with my own blood.' It was equally in the power of the Pope to grant him that favour—for which, indeed, he felt most inclined. He was then respectfully and in a most fatherly way invited to show himself at Rome: 'Beloved son! health to thee, and apostolic benediction.' But, as every one knows, the Pope's blessing was always a curse, and in this case the blessing concealed, or only partly concealed, a power that would by penance, prison, or poison, reduce the friar to everlasting silence. Savonarola was not to be caught. He knew the man with whom he was dealing. The Pope was the incarnation of all the devilry that ever escaped from hell. An abandoned wretch, guilty of scandalous crimes—who would trust him? And so wisely the friar refused to go. He did not refuse, however, to fulminate against the Pope. He, too, like most of us, could issue his little bull from his diminutive Vatican. At last the Pope prohibited his preaching, and ordered that the congregation of St. Mark should be dissolved. Such elements were, however, not really dissolved. Savonarola for a time maintained silence, but was stung into action by the Pope's Breve. 'I cannot forbear preaching,' he declared; 'the word of God is as a fire in my heart; unless I speak it, it burns my marrow and bones. It is now time,' he said, 'to open the den; we will turn the key; such a stench and so much filth will be vomited forth by Rome as will overspread all Christendom, and everybody will be tainted with it.' At last the Pope applied to the Signori to deliver up this heretic; but it was in vain. Franciscan monks were sent to preach him down; but his preaching went up. Then it was with his customary politeness that the Pope sent a gracious message, hurling his curse at his head, cutting him off as a rotten member from the Church's body, and giving him over to the powers of hell. Savonarola had his defenders in Florence, and those were among the wealthy as well as among the poor; but a host of circumstances were combining to ruin him. His friends were injudicious. His new state constitution was, as might be expected, a failure. His alliance with the King of France, who had done nothing for the Church, damaged his popularity. Plague and famine irritated the people, and as no miracle was wrought on their behalf, Savonarola was disliked. One of his friends foolishly put a controversy with the Franciscans upon the issue of a trial by the ordeal of fire. The fire was prepared in the market-place of Florence; the citizens expected to behold a notable spectacle; but the Signori and a shower of rain interfered and dispersed the crowd. The mob then turned upon Savonarola; the monastery was assailed; the once popular monk was made a prisoner; and the Pope was communicated with. Overcome with joy, 'his holiness' granted permission for the monk to be tortured. A recantation was demanded of him, but he refused. He was then stretched seven times during the week upon the rack. In the height of his sufferings he cried, 'Lord, take my spirit,' and, worn out by the tortures, he agreed to confess. When, however, he had rested awhile, he withdrew his recantation, and boldly avowed all that he had previously taught. Between the day of his trial and the day of his execution he wrote an exposition of the Fifty-first Psalm, which Luther highly prized, and published in Germany.

He was burnt, with two friends, on the 22nd of May, 1498. The bishop deprived him of his priestly garments, saying, 'Thus I exclude thee from the militant and triumphant Church.' 'From the Church militant thou mayst,' exclaimed Savonarola, 'but from the Church triumphant thou canst not.' He died blessing the people who had deserted him, and clinging to the Christ whose love had never departed from him.—*The Sword and the Trowel.*

ITALIAN AUTHORSHIP.

The low state of learning and morality in Italy in the sixteenth century may be inferred from the success which attended the writings of the profligate sycophant Pietro Aretino—1422-1557. The following passage is from Roscoe's 'Leo the Tenth:'—' It would be as disgusting to enter into an examination of the indecent and abominable writings of Aretino, as it would be tiresome to peruse those long and tedious pieces on religious subjects by which he most probably sought to counterbalance in the public opinion the profaneness of his other productions. It may, indeed, truly be said, that of all the efforts of his abilities, in prose and in verse, whether sacred or profane, epic or dramatic, panegyrical or satirical, and notwithstanding their great number and variety, not one piece exists which in point of literary merit is entitled to approbation! Yet the commendations which Aretino received from his contemporaries are beyond example; and by his unblushing effrontery and the artful intermixture of censure and adulation, he contrived to lay under contribution almost all the sovereigns and eminent men of his time. Francis I. not only presented him with a chain of gold, and afforded him other marks of his liberality, but requested that the Pope would allow him the gratification of his society. Henry VIII. sent him at one time three hundred gold crowns; and the Emperor Charles V. not only allowed him a considerable pension, but on Aretino being introduced to him by the Duke of Urbino on his way to Peschiera, placed him on his right hand and rode with him in intimate conversation. The distinctions which he obtained by his adulatory sonnets and epistles from Julius III. were yet more extraordinary. The present of a thousand gold crowns was accompanied by a papal bull, nominating him a *Cavalere* of the order of *S. Pietro*, to which dignity was also annexed an annual income. These favours and distinctions, which were imitated by the inferior sovereigns and chief nobility of Europe, excited the vanity of Aretino to such a degree that he entertained the strongest expectations of being created a cardinal, for the reception of which honour he had actually begun to make preparations.

He assumed the titles of *Il Divino* and *Il Flagello de' Principi.* Medals were struck in honour of him, representing him decorated with a chain of gold, and on the reverse the princes of Europe bringing to him their tribute. Even his mother and his daughter were represented in medals with appropriate inscriptions. His portrait was frequently painted by the best artists of the time, and particularly by the celebrated Titiano, with whom he lived in habits of intimacy; insomuch that it may justly be asserted, that, from the days of Homer to the present, no person who founded his claims to public favour merely on his literary talents ever obtained one-half of the honours and emoluments which were lavished on this illiterate pretender.'—*Roscoe,* '*Leo the Tenth.*'

LUTHERANS IN VENICE.

In the sixteenth century, Venice had risen to a great height of opulence and trading importance; and having, as M'Crie shows, resisted all attempts to establish the Inquisition, the Republic perceived that ' the concession of a more than ordinary freedom of thinking and speaking was necessary to encourage strangers to visit her ports and markets.' At one time all things seemed to promise the triumph of the Reformation in the city and her dependencies. 'The Venetian was then among Popish what Holland afterwards became among Protestant states,' says M'Crie. 'She was distinguished for the number of her printing-presses; and while letters were cultivated elsewhere for themselves, or to gratify the vanity of their patrons, they were encouraged here from the additional consideration of their forming an important and not unproductive branch of manufacture and merchandise. The books of the German and Swiss Protestants were consigned to merchants at Venice, from which they were circulated to the different parts of Italy; and it was in this city that versions of the Bible and other religious books in the vulgar tongue were chiefly printed.'

There was a large number of persons in Venice who favoured the Reformed doctrines, and some of these were afterwards numbered among the heroic band of Italian martyrs. So strong a body were the believers that at one time it was thought the Protestant form of worship would be established under the countenance of the Senate. In the year 1542 Alfieri is found writing to Luther in the name of the Venetian and Italian Churches, asking him to use his influence with the German princes on their behalf. Venice, however, allowed her opportunity to pass, and instead of standing out as a free republic, and accepting the Reformation, she allowed the creatures of the Pope to exercise all the cruelties of the Inquisition. Numbers were drowned at midnight in the Adriatic on account of their faith, showing a constancy in that faith which showed how truly divine grace had operated upon their hearts.

A complete Italian martyrology would not only show that the Reformed doctrines had made great progress among the people, it would prove to a demonstration that the popes of the sixteenth century were the chief agents of the evil one on earth. M'Crie quotes a letter written from the capital in 1568: 'At Rome some are every day burnt, hanged, or beheaded; all the prisons and places of confinement are filled, and they are obliged to build new ones.'

LUTHERANISM IN CENTRAL ITALY.

Bologna, in Central Italy, is a city of about one hundred and sixteen thousand inhabitants; and while its trade chiefly consists of costly silks and exquisite velvets, the place boasts of having been the birthplace of many men of genius. When the name of Luther was resounding throughout Europe, the Bolognese appear to have been anxious to share Lutheran liberty without identifying themselves with the Reformer's name. When the Elector of Saxony visited Charles V. in 1533, the citizens asked him to use his influence in the cause of religious freedom; and their language is very suggestive of what might have been in place of present barrenness had better counsels prevailed—*e.g.*, 'If the malice of Satan still rages to such a degree that this boon cannot be immediately obtained, liberty will surely be granted in the meantime both to clergy and laity to purchase Bibles without incurring the charge of heresy, and to quote the sayings of Christ and Paul without being branded as Lutherans. For, alas, instances of this abominable practice are common, and if this is not a mark of the reign of Antichrist, we know not what it is, when the law, and grace, and doctrine, and peace, and liberty of Christ are so often opposed, trampled upon, and rejected.' Though so commonplace in our days, this language when first used was sufficiently in advance of the times to sound unreasonable to ears unaccustomed to its use.

About a quarter of the size of Bologna, Modena is the capital of a province of the same name, the land being of great fertility, while the quarries supply the finest marble for artistic purposes. We are glad to find that in the latter days of Luther's life the Reformation had so far awakened this town, that Cardinal Maroni, in a letter to the Duke of Ferrara, says: 'Wherever I go, and from all quarters, I hear that the city is become Lutheran.' In this manner the people chose the better part, but, by means of the Inquisition and other terrific agencies, the Pope's representatives stamped out the truth to keep themselves as well as others in bondage.

Did space allow, we might linger at Ferrara, where, standing almost alone in the midst of a dissolute court, the Duchess Renée, the friend of John Calvin, sought to favour the Reformed faith. We should find that Venice was once a city of printing as well as of palaces, seeing that three thousand works went forth from its presses between the years 1465-1500. Milan is associated with the conversion of Augustine; Trent, with the well-known council, convoked by Paul III.; while many other places have traditions and histories illustrative of the conflict between Christ and antichrist in the sixteenth century.

OCHINO AND PALCARIO.

Sienna is also a small city of Tuscany, with a population of twenty-two thousand. Besides the university and the citadel, the town has a full proportion of palaces, fountains, and beautiful churches, besides which the inhabitants have attained to the distinction of speaking purer Italian than any other community. Here we find footprints of Bernardino Ochino, a natural orator of such wonderful power, that he is said to have been the most popular preacher of that age, peasants and kings being equally delighted with his utterances. Before his enlightenment he practised all kinds of austerities, but ultimately he shook off his Franciscan Pharisaism to espouse the cause of the Reformation. Contemporary with Ochino was Aonio Palcario whose book, 'Il Beneficio di Cristo,' is thought to be one of the sweetest and simplest evangelical books in the Italian language, and the popularity of which was attested by the fact that between 1543 and 1549 forty thousand copies were sold. Thus, although Sienna did not become a refuge for the Reformers, it supplied many exiles who carried on the work.

Sixty miles north-west of Rome lies Orvieto, a fortified city of about six thousand souls, and which still contains the old palace of the popes. Twenty miles nearer the 'Eternal City,' in the same direction, is Viterbo, which as a place three times the size of Orvieto is associated with the names of many Reformers, whose names we have not space to mention.

NAPLES AND JUAN DE VALDES.

The old kingdom of Naples, now included in United Italy, is one of the most fertile in Europe, just as its capital of four hundred and forty-eight thousand souls is one of the most beautifully situated places in the world. As Roman Catholicism goes, this city should be accounted one of the most religious anywhere to be found, superstitious crowds who still believe in priestly miracles thronging the churches; but common observers, nevertheless, tell us that Naples for notorious wickedness exceeds anything they have ever met with in their travels. We believe this to be uniformly the case wherever Popery has reached its most perfect development. In former times, Naples and the country around was stained with the blood of the persecuted—horrible barbarity having been practised; and to-day the city is wrapped in spiritual darkness—a sink of iniquity, so far as the lower orders of the population are concerned.

One of the most prominent characters belonging to Naples is Juan de Valdes, a Spanish evangelical teacher of the sixteenth century, and the author of the 'CX.

Considerations.' This worthy's life has been written with much skill and more sympathy by the Woburn Quaker, B. J. Wiffen, a Friend who with singular enthusiasm devoted his whole time to the work of recovering forgotten works of Spaniards who taught the doctrines of grace in opposition to the semi-pagan heresies of Rome. The Reformer's house was at a retired and beautiful spot on one of the roads leading out of Naples; and there, as Wiffen tells us, ' Valdes received on the Sunday a select number of his most intimate friends, and they passed the day together in this manner :—After breakfasting and enjoying themselves amid the glories of the surrounding scenery, they returned to the house, when he read some selected portion of Scripture, and commented upon it, or some " Divine Consideration" which had occupied his thoughts during the week—some subject on which he conceived that his mind had obtained a clearer illumination of heavenly truth.' Signor Valdes passed away to rest while the Reformation was in progress, in 1540. He was a man who in his day exercised a wide influence; and both Dr. Stoughton and Mr. Wiffen are of opinion that the Spaniard's genius partially inspired the 'Il Beneficio di Cristo' of Aonio Palearic.

FLORENCE AND HER REFORMERS.

Florence, the city of libraries, of palaces, museums, and of art galleries, lies in a country remarkable for its fertility one hundred and twenty-five miles north of Rome. In the vales and on the hills, vines and olives bear fruit to perfection in the congenial soil; while corn, rare varieties of flowers, and many other products thrive in rare profusion. Nature and art have combined to make Florence beautiful; and yet the modern visitor may sometimes realize that a little sanitary science would be worth more to him, at all events, than the superabundance of painting and sculpture which the old capital of Tuscany calls her own.

In association with Florence we name the poet Dante and Girolamo Savonarola, both of whom were in a sense reformers. The mediæval monk, while groping in the pre-Reformation darkness, set his face against prevailing corruptions, and proved his sincerity by paying the full penalty of his boldness with his life. 'That he did not reach a clear conception of the gospel, such as marked the teaching of Luther and others, must be admitted,' says Dr. Stoughton; 'nor had he a true idea of the spirituality of Christ's kingdom. He condemned the action of popes rather than the principles of the papacy, and adhered to the dogmas and ceremonial of the Church in most particulars. He was a mystic and a visionary, and indulged in dreams by which he deceived himself as well as others. But an evangelical spirit penetrated his mind; he aspired, under motives of patriotism, blended with piety, to the realization of an ideal religious republic in his adopted city; he wished to make the inhabitants fellow-citizens with the saints and of the household of God; and had they yielded to his moralizing influence, they would have become a better and a happier people.'

Dante, or 'the Bard Reformer,' as Dr. Stoughton calls the poet, was also born at Florence in 1265, a very turbulent period in the history of the city, when the differences of opposing factions were settled by the sword. The experience of the Bard was very varied; he passes before us as a student, a disconsolate lover, a soldier, a politician, and an exile. Speaking of his character generally, Mr. O. Browning says that 'whatever there was of piety, of philosophy, of poetry, of love of nature, and of love of knowledge in those times is drawn to a focus in his writings. He is the first great name in literature after the night of the dark ages.' Generally neglected two or three generations ago, Dante's fame has in these times been generally revived, and, considering the character of his writings, he is now exceedingly popular throughout Europe. The difficulty, in the case of his *Divina Commedia* at least, is to grasp the meaning of allusions which point to current abuses or to living characters of the times; and even if we accept the aid of an interpreter, the question again arises, Whom shall we follow? Mr. Browning assures us we can have 'no better guide' than Maria Rossetti; while Dr. Stoughton prefers 'Mrs. Oliphant's inartificial, candid, and intelligent comments.' On his own account the Doctor adds: 'I am constrained to regard the wonderful author of dreams touching Hell, Purgatory, and Paradise as a great reformer, full of ideas bearing on the political and moral improvement of his country and mankind. There is one idea very clearly brought out—that Rome at the time was a sink of evils, and that imperial rule was vastly to be preferred to that which was pontifical.' It was no doubt very suggestive when such a writer, living in the darkest times and not blinded by the pagan magnificence of the papacy, saw 'no pope except St. Peter in Paradise, and no emperor in Hell.' Dante also corrected the prevailing superstition when he wrote:—

> 'Tell me now
> What treasures from St. Peter at the first
> Our Lord demanded when He put the keys
> Into his charge? Surely He asked no more
> But ' Follow me.'

The names of several who favoured the Reformation also belonged to Florence. There was born Antonio Brucioli, an evangelical teacher who, besides writing a complete Biblical Commentary, prepared an Italian version of the New Testament. Then another Reformer, Pieto Carnesecchi, once the trusted servant of Clement VII., was put to death on account of his faith. There also have occurred numerous book fires, copies of works which were inimical to the so-called 'holy office' of the Inquisition. 'One day in December, 1551,' we are told, 'twenty-two penitents, dressed in cloaks painted all over with crosses and devils, marched in procession to the Duomo, and the heretical books found in their possession were burnt in the Piazza. In the spring of 1559 another batch of condemned volumes were thrown into the flames before the doors of Santa Croce.' At different times the papacy has found reason to fear books quite as much as men, and thus obnoxious volumes have been visited with martyr penalties.

THE FAMINE AT VENICE.

God only, and not wealth, maintains the world; riches merely make people proud and lazy. At Venice, where the richest people are, a horrible dearth fell among them in our time, so that they were driven to call upon the Turks for help, who sent twenty-four galleys laden with corn, all which, well-nigh in port, sunk before their eyes. Great wealth and money cannot still hunger, but rather occasion more dearth; for where rich people are, there things are always dear. Moreover, money makes no man right merry, but much rather pensive and full of sorrow; for riches, says Christ, are thorns that prick people. Yet is the world so mad that it sets therein all its joy and felicity.

No man can estimate the great charge God is at only in maintaining birds and such creatures, comparatively nothing worth. I am persuaded that it costs Him, yearly, more to maintain only the sparrows, than the revenue of the French king amounts to. What, then, shall we say of all the rest of His creatures?

Scarcely a small proportion of the earth bears corn, and yet we are all maintained and nourished. I verily believe that there grow not as many sheaves of corn as there are people in the world, and yet we are all fed; yea, and there remains a good surplus of corn at the year's end. This is a wonderful thing, which should make us see and perceive God's blessing.—*Table Talk.*

REFORMERS AT TURIN.

More than a thousand years ago Turin, a city standing in the midst of rich plains, was heard making its protest against the pagan innovation of image-worship which was then beginning to corrupt the Romish Church. The place is now more remarkable for the uncommon strength of its citadel, and the beauty of certain public buildings, than for magnitude, the population being considerably under two hundred thousand. In the year 820, when Claude the Spaniard was appointed to the see, Turin was but a small place, and, with the exception of one fragment, no vestige of the buildings of those days survives. To ordinary readers the very name of the old reformer is unknown; Claude, however, having been not so much a reformer as an opponent of degrading corruptions such as in the ninth century began rapidly to gain ground. The bishop was one of those singular examples of men who were devotedly attached to the Romish communion, and at the same time held evangelical principles. Thus he taught 'that all which is good in man proceeds from divine mercy, and that to look for salvation through human merit is utterly vain.' He taught that Christ suffered for us, and thereby justified us; that we are delivered from the law by faith in Christ; and that they are the enemies of His cross who say righteousness comes by the law, and not of faith by grace. This is directly opposed to the Romanism of to-day, which, to say nothing of superstition, is a monstrous system of self-righteousness. The soul of Claude was vexed by the sight of numberless wax figures in the churches, and by the consciousness that men were becoming more intent in adoring crosses than in securing the ascendency of Christ in the heart. The superstitious told him what any Hindoo devotee of Vishnu would tell an objector to-day: 'We do not regard as divine the images we reverence; we only pay them respect for the sake of those they represent.' The words of Claude in reply were as searching and as Scriptural as any that a Protestant iconoclast might still be expected to use: 'If you have left the worship of heathen images that you may worship images of saints, you have not relinquished idolatry, but only changed the name.' Such was the protest by a Romish bishop against the spirit of popery seven long centuries before the Reformation. Had such a man lived in the days of Calvin and Luther, he would have been one of their most devoted allies.

Turin can also boast of heroes who in the sixteenth century became attached to the Reformation. Such was Curione, who acknowledged the truth of the doctrines of grace through reading a manuscript Bible, an heirloom in the family. Thrown into prison, he contrived to escape by the exercise of a wonderful ingenuity, and reaching territory beyond the jurisdiction of his enemies, he still taught the Reformed doctrines. Equally courageous, as a disciple of Calvin, was Geoffrey Varagle, who was burned in the Castle-square, telling his judges that the Word of God endured for ever, and that wood for piles would fail rather than confessors to seal their faith. Only fifty miles from Turin, in a north-westerly direction, is Aosta, a town of about six thousand inhabitants, on the Dora-baltea river, and intimately associated with the name of Calvin. In 1536, the Reformer appears to have moved about Aosto and its neighbourhood to become instrumental in the conversion of a number of persons of position, who afterwards would give their influence to the good cause.

LUCCA AND HER EVANGELICAL TEACHERS.

Lucca produced at least one Reformer in the eventful sixteenth century who deserves to be held in long remembrance, Peter Martyr, of the Augustine Abbey, of whom Dr. Stoughton says: 'He aimed at improvements in education, and established a seminary for the study of divine truth, according to a custom then common in the Roman Catholic communion. Other scholars united with him in his work, and his department was the explanation of Holy Scripture, especially the Psalter and the New Testament. His lectures were attended by some of the Lucchese grandees. With the labours of a professor he combined those of a preacher, and during Advent and Lent gathered large congregations to listen to the gospels for the day. Not only did he occupy the pulpit, but he instituted a society for spiritual edification; and he is represented as forming a separate Church, of which he became pastor, a statement which must be qualified by the remembrance that he still remained in fellowship with Rome.' It may be, as Dr. Stoughton adds, that 'a separate church in the Protestant acceptation of the term was impossible at that time;' but still, if the followers of one man met together for spiritual edification, the resemblance was wonderfully close, considering the different character of the times. A convincing proof of Martyr's faith and successful labours is seen in the activity of opponents, which eventually led to his being cited to appear before the authorities of his order. Though no coward, Peter, instead of obeying the summons, sent back the ring he had worn as prior of the Abbey, and having by this act severed his connection with monasteries, he went to Florence, to find a kindred spirit in Bernardino Ochino, and afterwards he cast in his lot with the Protestants of Switzerland. The society he formed in Lucca more than ever resembled a separate church after Martyr's departure; and while some of the number were thrown into prison, their former teacher was able to write: 'Such progress have you made for many years in the Gospel of Jesus Christ, that it was unnecessary for me to excite you by my letters; and all that remained for me to do was to make honourable mention of you everywhere, and to give thanks to our Heavenly Father for the spiritual blessings with which He had crowned you.' Later on, under the proud and bigoted Paul IV., Martyr's 'pleasant garden,' as he called his congregation, was dispersed as a conventicle, and under fear of sanguinary penalties, some recanted. The good prior's labours in the Lord, however, were not in vain. Some of his followers left the country, carrying the truth with them; and even after the storm of persecution had spent its fury, a remnant of the faithful remained in the city. Paul IV. was one of the most despicable of the discreditable line of popes. He fostered the Inquisition, quarrelled with Philip II., until the Duke of Alva was found at the gates of Rome with a Spanish army, and in other respects lived for the aggrandisement of his family, some of whom were executed as criminals after the Pope's decease. That such a man should have plagued the faithful after he had reached the chief place of authority is not wonderful; but the fact proves that, instead of representing Christ on earth, Paul IV. really did the work of Satan.

A SPANISH FRANCISCAN.

A certain prince of Germany, well known to me, went to Compostella in Spain, where they pretend St. James, brother of the Evangelist St. John, lies buried. This prince made his confession to a Franciscan, an honest man, who asked him if he were a German? The prince answered, Yes. Then the friar said: 'O, loving child, why seekest thou so far away that which thou hast much better in Germany? I have seen and read the writings of an Augustine friar touching indulgences and the pardons of sin, wherein he powerfully proves that the true remission of sins consists in the merits and sufferings of our Lord and Saviour Jesus Christ. O loving son, remain thereby, and permit not thyself to be otherwise persuaded. I purpose shortly, God willing, to leave this unchristian life, to repair into Germany, and to join the Augustine friar.'—*Table Talk.*

DILIGENT PREACHERS.

The Reformation age had its pastors who laboured excessively hard in their studies. We hear of a man who could do sixteen hours' work a day, retiring to bed at ten and rising at four. Julius Palmer, one of the Marian martyrs, was of this character. Bishop Latimer seems to have been equally or more diligent, commencing his work at two in the morning. The 'Institutes' of Calvin were printed before the author was twenty-five years of age.

In his twenty-fourth year Calvin was at the head of the Reformation in France; and in his twenty-seventh year the 'Institutes' in their first form were published. 'Such an instance of maturity of mind and of opinion at so early an age would be remarkable under any circumstances,' says the *Encyclopædia Britannica*, 'but in Calvin's case it is rendered peculiarly so by the shortness of the time which had elapsed since he gave himself to theological studies. It may be doubted, also, if the history of literature presents us with another instance of a book written at so early an age which has exercised such a prodigious influence upon the opinions and practices both of contemporaries and of posterity.'

CALVIN AND NICHOLAS COP.

To look into the Paris of the first half of the sixteenth century is instructive, so far as the insight supplies some odd phases of human nature. The ignorance of many of the university doctors seems to have been only equalled by their conceit of learning. The spread of the Reformed doctrines created much excitement, and even alarm; and the fanatical clergy laboured earnestly to stamp out what there appeared of life in the upspringing seeds of a purer faith. Here, indeed, was a field worthy of the ability and powers of Calvin. What he would have effected had events allowed of his labouring unmolested we are only able to surmise; for a curious incident necessitated his flight from the capital. In those days certain ecclesiastical grandees, who occupied stations superior to their mental and educational qualifications, were not averse to accepting an occasional sermon in manuscript from such of their gifted contemporaries as would supply them. Nicholas Cop, Rector of the Sorbonne, was of this unhappy class, and was a gentleman who would have been learned and eloquent had eloquence merely consisted in words, and learning in pretending to know. Once, to escape a dilemma, Cop preached a discourse written by the Reformer, the occasion being important and the assembly select. As the Rector opened up his theme, the sticklers for the 'old learning' twisted uneasily upon their benches; for the sermon discomfited the Romanists by pleading forcibly for the doctrine of Justification by Faith. After so daring an assault on the enemy's position, both writer and preacher sought safety in flight; and, after their departure, many troubles fell to the lot of the Protestants. Some zealous but indiscreet friends violently denounced the pope and the mass by means of placards distributed over Paris,—a procedure which, instead of aiding the good cause, produced a reaction resulting in the death of many protestors.

FAREL AT MONTBELIARD IN 1525.

One of those highly dramatic incidents in which the chequered life of this remarkable man abounds is said to have preceded his withdrawal from the city. Happening, on St. Anthony's day, to meet, upon a bridge spanning a narrow stream in the neighbourhood, a solemn procession headed by priests chanting the praises of the saint whose effigy they bore aloft, Farel was seized with an uncontrollable desire to arrest the impious service. Snatching the image from the hands of ecclesiastics, who were little prepared for so sudden an onslaught, he indignantly cried, 'Wretched idolaters, will you never forsake your idolatry?' At the same instant he threw the saint into the water, before the astonished devotees had time to interfere. Had not some one just then opportunely raised the shout, 'The saint is drowning!' it might have gone hard with the fearless iconoclast.—*Baird.*

CALVIN AND FAREL AT GENEVA.

Geneva's break with Rome was consummated in 1535, a principal agent having been the enthusiastic Farel. When Calvin sought a night's lodging in the city, in the July of the year following, he found the great movement inaugurated, the want of the hour being men of parts and zeal to carry on the work so auspiciously begun. Farel, with glowing ardour, exerted his whole strength to relieve the gross darkness by some enlivening beams. He is thought to have been a little opinionated and somewhat intolerant; but let the failings of a man be forgotten who was manifestly influenced by so strong a love of the true faith. Though the field was not as wide as the Continent, men fitted by nature and grace to enter in and labour were sadly wanting, and consequently news of Calvin's arrival could not have come more opportunely. Exercised by a determination to secure his services, Farel, with his usual impetuosity, walked straight to Calvin's lodgings, and abruptly exhorted him to remain in a city which not only needed men of his calibre, but into which Providence had so strangely directed him. But though earnest when aroused, Calvin was not easily persuaded; and the scene which ensued, as characteristic of the times and of the men, was worthy of the pencil of a great master. When the traveller showed some hesitation, the discourse waxed vehement, and Farel invoked curses both on the head of Calvin and his studies if he dared to forsake work which God had given him. Farel triumphed, and Calvin stayed; in the first instance accepting the office of teacher of theology. In the pulpit of St. Peter, his great talents were immediately recognised, grateful crowds attending his sermons, and even following him home after them. He and Farel now earnestly applied themselves to the Herculean task of reforming the government and morals of the city; for it should be borne in mind that the Reformation had sprung out of political necessity quite as much as it did from popular love for the Reformed tenets. Even in a corrupt and pleasure-loving age, Geneva was celebrated for the easy and luxurious life of its inhabitants. Saints'-days, weddings, and christenings were a constant occasion of holiday-making, and when the prescribed order of the new Church threatened to curtail their indulgences, murmurs of discontent arose, and many expressions of deprecation were hurled at the heads of the Reformers themselves. Judging them by the standard of eighteenth century prudence, it will appear that Calvin and Farel too abruptly interfered with the ancient customs of a half-enlightened and pleasure-loving people. Their motives were good; the popular practices in too many instances were pernicious; but we question if a more cautious procedure would not have been a more potent remedy. Bells, whose musical tones had floated across the lake for ages, were taken down and cast into cannon; weddings were stripped of their gay adornings, while festivals were erased from the calendar without compromise. Moved by the best intentions, the Reformers yet misjudged the resisting power of the old Adam, and, without reconciling the people to their reforms, brought down on themselves serious troubles. The resentment of the citizens was fiercely expressed, and so high rose the indignation that the two chief pastors were banished. Of their adventures after this, at Berne and Zurich, want of space precludes our speaking. Suffice it to say, that on one occasion they would have been murdered on attempting to re-enter the city had they persisted in their design. The Genevese remained incensed against them, and ambassadors vainly sought a reconciliation.

THE LAST DAYS OF CALVIN.

God so ordered events that no human power could eclipse the faith in its ascendency. In his lifetime Calvin could count six hundred martyrs to the good cause, and not one died in vain. His last days afford a remarkable example of the manner in which burning zeal can sustain a weak body. He had never really recovered from a long illness; and at length his works were continued in spite of headaches and fainting sickness. Fasting for more than a day together, and at the best but taking a single meal in the twenty-four hours, were the remedies he himself prescribed. Then the gout joined itself to his other ailments, necessitating his being carried to the pulpit of St. Peter. Though unable to walk, tormented with stone, and weakened by spitting of blood, he yet toiled on to the very last, the Commentary on Joshua having been finished on his death-bed.

Of his closing days the surviving accounts are valuable as showing how much may be done by the weakest frame when the will to work is sustained by the grace of God. Beza vainly warned his friend of the necessity of curtailing his labour. 'What!' cried Calvin, 'would you have the Lord find me idle?' Strength and voice were failing; but his joy of heart welled up from a perennial spring. On the 10th of March, 1564, the Consistory went in a body to his house. Pale and wayworn, the pastor still sat at his table. 'I thank you, my dearest brethren,' he said, 'for your care of me, and I hope that in a fortnight I shall be among you for the last time.' True to this arrangement, he attended the next assembly. Three days after he visited the Council-house, where he thanked God for the favours received from that body. The Council showed real solicitude for the sinking pastor by sending money, which he refused, and by ordering public prayers for his restoration. Approaching death was teaching the senators the worth of Calvin's life. His wan and emaciated appearance moved them greatly, and his words—'I feel this is the last time I shall appear in this place'—agitated them still more. On Easter-day he took the Supper from the hands of Beza, in the Church of St. Peter, his countenance beaming as though reflecting the light of purer worlds. Moved by a desire to address the senators, he would have gone to the Council Chamber had not these friends insisted on attending at his own house. Calvin's last address to the Council may only be spoken of as touching and noble. Three days later the pastors of the republic also came by appointment, and to them he delivered many moving words. His last letter was one written to Farel, bidding him farewell, and dissuading him from incurring the expense and inconvenience of visiting Geneva. Crowds assembled about his door, and would have pressed into the dying pastor's chamber but for his request that they should rest satisfied with giving him their prayers. One of the last scenes of all was the annual Whitsuntide dinner, which a few days prior to his death was held in Calvin's house. On being carried from his bed and placed at table, he ate a morsel, and remarked to his guests, 'This is the last time I shall meet you at table;' and, on returning to his room, he said that the wall which separated him from them would not prevent his being present in mind. Then came earth's last stage. On the 27th of May, about eight in the evening, just after Beza had retired, Calvin's spirit quietly took its departure. He seems to have died alone, and the last struggle—too often feared more than the ills of life—in this instance exactly resembled a welcome falling into sleep.

LUTHERANISM IN BOHEMIA.

Through the whole Reformation period the sufferings of the Bohemian Brethren were exceedingly severe. They hailed the advent of Luther with acclamations; many made long journeys to greet the new apostle of freedom, and some on their return paid a heavy penalty for their temerity. The Emperor Ferdinand has been styled a just and moderate ruler, but his treatment of his Protestant subjects will not establish a claim to that distinction. One edict after another was issued against them, and the natural suicidal result of this policy was that the people left the country in bodies, to seek refuge in Poland, in corners of Protestant Germany, and especially in Moravia, whence their name of Moravian Brethren.

Those were the heroic days of the persecuted Church, and the adventures of certain actors in the scenes which ensued would seem to belong to the regions of romance. Take the case of George Israel, a pastor, who, by his subsequent abundant labours, became generally known as the Apostle of Poland. When his people saw that their leader would certainly be arrested, they implored him to flee, not forgetting to bring in their hands the necessary funds to discharge the penalty for his not answering an indictment at the Castle of Prague. Steadfast in his faith, Israel was deaf to all entreaty. The calm of his soul was a cheering contrast to the storms without. He said that he had been bought by the blood of Christ, and did not wish to be repurchased by the gold of man. Boldly appearing before his enemies on the 30th of May, 1548, he was cast into prison, where, however, he enjoyed the privilege of sending communications to his flock. He consulted with them regarding the possibility of escape, and, receiving encouragement, he determined to carry out his plans. Disguised as a common clerk, and carrying a quill, ink, and paper, he passed the sentinels unsuspected, soon to enjoy the freedom which was his birthright.

An edition of the Scriptures in the Bohemian language, and translated during the years 1571-93, is called the Brethren's Bible; but on account of the persistency with which the copies were burned, they are now exceedingly rare. Soon after the formation of their Order in 1540, the Jesuits entered the country, and on their arrival the destruction of Protestant books and the hindrance generally of true religion became an agreeable pastime. In part of the Moravian territory in 1583 the mandates of the Castellan were of that ludicrous kind which is suggestive of Jesuitical inspiration. The fine for breaking the Sabbath was three pounds of wax; for neglecting to have children baptized, a pound of wax a day; to die without confession was to risk being interred in unconsecrated ground; to eat meat on Friday cost eight dollars; and he who trifled during divine service was made a laughing-stock to more consistent people by being put in 'the fool's cage.'

A BOHEMIAN MARTYR.

Who the monk was that Holyk calls Father Ambrosius we are unaware, but we know that he was a Dominican of great learning and varied talents. When led to see the errors of the papacy he was also a theological lecturer to a number of students who appear to have attended at the monastery. On a certain day Ambrosius astonished his little audience by renouncing what he had formerly taught, and professing faith in the unadulterated Gospel of Christ. This bold step soon brought the confessor into ill odour among the brethren, and he was at once marked for discipline, a synonym in the Popish Church of that day for the most frightful cruelty. The absurdities of Thomas Aquinas were taken more account of than the teachings of Paul, and 'the mother of God' was exalted above Christ the Son. Summoned before a conclave of ecclesiastics, who had power to decide his fate, Ambrosius was required to account for his doctrines, which were so manifestly opposed to the claims of the Pope. He more boldly than ever held to the Scriptures, and again renounced what he had formerly believed. When the rage of the judges would allow of their doing so, they passed their sentence on the offender, whose only crime was that he taught salvation through faith in Christ. He was first beaten with thongs having iron stars to cut the flesh, and after this he was confined to a dungeon for some months. On again being confronted with the members of the chapter, and still holding what was so offensive, the cry went round that Ambrosius was insane; but hoping to cure such madness by harsher measures, he was, after another beating, put into a viler cell, low underground. Thrice every week he was drawn up with ropes, and was required to lie at the entrance of the refectory to be walked over and kicked by the monks; then he had to kneel in the middle of the floor, and while the brethren ate to the full of those costly provisions which were then consumed in religious houses founded to defy poverty, Ambrosius was obliged to dine on dog-cake and salt. After dinner he was lectured, or in the words of Holyk, 'sent several times to hell and the devil,' and then let down again into his subterranean hole. After a year of this experience he might have been restored to liberty had he chosen to deny Christ; but on giving a final refusal to violate conscience, he was again tortured and beaten until nearly dead, when he was confined in a prison more loathsome than either of the former. When he died we know not; but eighteen years afterwards he was spoken with for a moment or two by the historian to whom posterity is indebted for the details of a crime—one among many thousands never revealed—perpetrated by the Romish Church. A ghastly figure is seen to come forward, and then it for ever disappears in the night of the underground prison. 'I was nearly half a year in this cloister before I knew of any one being confined in its prison,' says Holyk; 'and I learned it at last from one of the scullions who had to carry food to the prisoner. In order to speak with Father Ambrosius, I sought an opportunity of approaching the aperture through which his food was let down to him. On my calling him he came forward, but I could not distinguish whether he had any clothing. His face was covered with hair and his eyes were dark. I was much surprised and startled at his wretched appearance, and asked him the cause of his imprisonment, to which he answered very sorrowfully, "I have forgotten my Latin, and am much weakened in my understanding."

I could say no more to him; for hearing one of the fathers coming down the staircase, I was obliged to hurry away.'

We are indebted to the Bohemian writer Holyk, who is quoted by the German historian Dr. Pescheek, for the above particulars.

LUTHER RELICS IN THE BRITISH MUSEUM.

The authorities at the British Museum have collected from various departments of the national library a number of treasures associated with the name of Luther and the great cause he inaugurated, which are likely to be examined with considerable curiosity by a large section of the public. It is only by bringing together these relics of the Reformation, and classifying them in some sort of order, that English citizens are enabled to estimate the extent and significance of our treasures. Buried in the hidden depths of the national archives, such things exist for little purpose if they are only brought into the daylight once or so in a century for the edification of some enlightened connoisseur who has ample leisure to bestow upon the inquiry. If they belong to the people, they ought to be used for purposes of popular instruction, for it is not too much to say that every memento of the religious revolution of the sixteenth century has a message for our own times, especially as we live in days when attempts are made by sacerdotalism to reverse the order of things and decry the Reformation itself as a gigantic mistake. It is on this account that we view with feelings of more than equanimity the flutter and misgivings which the prospect of the coming celebration has occasioned in ultramontane quarters. Jesuits abroad and even clerics at home are apparently as much afraid of Luther's spectre as their ancestors were of his actual presence. We need not be relic-mongers, nor even profess to worship the Confession of Augsburg; but we may nevertheless become daily more impressed with the fact that the Reformers delivered the world from a taskmaster as cruel and more intolerant than the mythological Nemesis. The blessings of the movement have been so far-reaching that even Romanists themselves are enjoying its fruits without appreciating their privileges. The crippled Popery of to-day is a somewhat different thing from the uncompromising priestcraft which Luther challenged; and were it otherwise, the world, by common consent, would speedily banish it from their midst as a burden no longer to be borne.

It appears that the books in the national collection bearing on Luther and his work are sufficiently numerous to have been brought together with some difficulty from their various departments; but now that they are separately catalogued and arranged in the Grenville Library, they are for the first time presented to view in a compact array. It is complained that they are not arranged in chronological order, but that is no very serious drawback if the date of each item can be readily learned. Some of the books would seem of themselves to mark, as it were, distinct epochs in the progress of the movement; and some of the earlier copies of the Scriptures in costly bindings are especially worthy of notice. The medals will be looked at with curiosity when it is remembered that the era of the Reformation was the golden age of this particular art. What are classed as modern medals date their commencement, with one or two exceptions, from the fifteenth century; and those which followed of such popes as Leo X., Clement VII., etc., were designed and engraved by eminent Italian artists. German medals are as old as the invention of printing, so that it is incorrect to infer, as was done by one journal, that the medals of the Fatherland were merely contemporaneous with the Reformation. The ordinary sight-seer, however, will perhaps be more interested in what may be termed veritable curiosities than in medals and books—things which were once the very ammunition of war to the combatants of three and a half centuries ago. Among these are Papal bulls, once veritable live thunderbolts, but now only pieces of dead parchment; a genuine 'Indulgence,' as sold by the redoubtable Tetzel, the brazen-faced Dominican, whose traffic, shamelessly carried on, at last brought on the crisis of the Reformation; an original printed copy of Luther's ninety-five Theses, and the edict of Charles V., who would have stifled the Evangelical revival if he had not been providentially checkmated by the Turks on the one hand and the jealousy of France on the other. Relics of this kind have an interest peculiar to themselves, and after them come the prints and drawings, some of which are by eminent contemporary artists, including Cranach, to whom the distinction is accorded of having been the painter of the Reformation.

Exhibitions of this kind are a fine testimony to the power of the printing-press. The invention of printing inevitably gave the death-blow to mediæval Popery; but while this fact may be generally admitted, probably few are aware of the immense number of publications with which the Christian world was inundated. Let those who despise tracts remember that it was by tracts the battle of the Reformation was fought and won. Disdaining to use any weapon save the pen, Luther was preserved from committing the error of Zwinglius, who fell by the sword. We are astonished at the immense number of Luther's publications, and after setting aside those which were intended to be only ephemeral, we still find in the residue a sufficiency to perpetuate his fame as a divine. The Reformer's entire works are about to be issued by the German Government; at the rate of three volumes a year it will take some dozen years to complete the undertaking. A complete collection of all his writings will not only make one of the most unique collections of works by one man; if chronologically arranged, we might trace in them one of the most singular examples of human development, or Christian growth, that have ever occurred. At the last he was far from being perfect as a religious teacher, but that only proved how tenaciously the old errors still clung to those who had actually groped their way to the light of truth.

We may regret that our collections of Reformation literature are not so complete as they might have been had chances of purchase been embraced in the past such as occur only once in a way; but, on the other hand, when we consider how ruthless was the war which popes and Jesuits waged against all the writings of the arch-Reformer, the wonder is that his books were not exterminated. We cannot wonder at this rage against works which had produced such effect on the world; but now that the noise of battle has died away, we can study with revived interest the weapons used by the combatants.

THE ESCAPE OF PHILIP DE MORNAY.

This eminent French statesman was born in 1549; and having been drawn to the Reformed doctrines, he narrowly escaped being murdered in the Bartholomew massacre of 1572. Visiting England after that event, he was honoured by the notice of Queen Elizabeth, and afterwards entered the service of the King of Navarre. After that monarch embraced the Romish faith, De Mornay retired from active service, and spent the remainder of his life in literary retirement, composing many religious works which found great acceptance with the Huguenots. His works were republished at Paris 1824-34; and the following description of his escape, written at the time by Madame Duplessis, was translated for the *Foreign Review* for 1834 :—

'His host was named Poret, who is still alive, a Roman Catholic, but a man of conscience. There he was sought for; he had scarcely time to burn his papers; he crept between the two roofs of the house, and did not venture out until he heard those who were in search of him depart. The remainder of the day was passed in some anxiety; and in the meantime he sent to M. de Foix, on whose friendship he placed great reliance, for assistance in the present danger; but that gentleman, not thinking his own house sufficiently secure, had retired to the Louvre.

'The fury of the mob recommencing on the following day (Monday), M. Poret beseeched M. Duplessis to flee, saying, that he could not save him, and that his continuance there might prove the ruin of both, adding that he should have disregarded his own danger if it could have secured the safety of the other. The assassins were already in the house of the next-door neighbour, Odet Petit, a bookseller, whom they slew, and whose corpse they threw out of the window.

'M. Duplessis then assumed a plain black dress, girded on his sword, and departed, while the mob were plundering the next house. Thence he proceeded through the Rue St. Martin, into an alley called Troussenache, to the house of one Girard, a law-agent, who transacted the business of his family. The way was long, nor was it traversed without some disagreeable encounters. He found the agent at his door, who received him favourably, and fortunate it was, for the captain of the watch was passing at that very moment. Girard promised to see him safely away the following morning. He fell to writing like the other clerks. The mischief was, that his servants, suspecting the place of his retreat, though he had given them no reason to do so, followed him one after another, and were observed to enter the same house. When night came, the captain of the district sent for the agent, and commanded him to surrender the individual who was in his house. The man was troubled at the discovery. At a very early hour of the day after (Tuesday), he pressed M. Duplessis to flee—a step which, however hazardous, the latter was resolved to take. He left behind him M. Raminy, who had been his tutor, and who hesitated to depart with him lest one should be in jeopardy for the other. As he descended the stairs alone (for the agent would no longer think of accompanying him out of the city), one of the clerks offered his services, saying, that as he (the clerk) had formerly been on guard at the Porte St. Martin, and was known there, he could procure egress for M. Duplessis at that gate. This assurance gave great pleasure to the latter; but on getting into the street he perceived that the clerk was in slippers only. As these were not very fit for a long journey, he desired the clerk to put on a pair of shoes; but the other thinking there was no necessity to take that trouble, he did not press it. As ill-luck would have it, the Porte St. Martin was not opened that morning, so that they were compelled to seek the Porte St. Denis, with the guard of which the clerk was wholly unacquainted. After answering a few questions, M. Duplessis giving himself out as an attorney's clerk going to spend the holidays with his relations at Rouen, they were allowed to pass. But one of the guard having observed the clerk's slippers, was convinced that no very long journey was intended by the wearer: he at once suspected that M. Duplessis must be a Huguenot, under the protection of a Catholic. After them were despatched four fusilleers, who arrested them at Villette, between Paris and St. Denis, where the carters, quarrymen, and plasterers of the neighbourhood assembled *en masse*, breathing the most furious threats. God saved him from their murderous hands on this occasion; but as he endeavoured to pacify them by fair words, they dragged him towards the river. The clerk began to be alarmed. He swore from time to time that M. Duplessis was not *a Huguenot* (such was his expression); he frequently called him M. de Buhy (forgetting the agreement they had made that the latter was to be considered an attorney's clerk), and whose house, he said, was well known in the environs of Paris. God shut the ears of these wretches, so that they gave no heed to what was uttered. M. Duplessis thus learnt that they did not know him; he therefore observed, that he was sure all of them would be loath to kill one man for another; that he could refer them to respectable individuals in Paris; that they might leave him at any house in the suburbs, and under whatever guard they pleased, until they had sent to the places he should mention to them. At length, some of the more moderate among them approved the proposal, and conducted him to a neighbouring tavern, where he called for breakfast. The most agreeable words addressed to him were threats to drown him. At one time he thought of escaping through the window, but on full consideration he ventured to trust for safety to his own assurance. He referred them to Rambouillets, even to the cardinal, their brother: this he did to delude the mob, for he well knew that fellows like them could not gain access to persons of

such distinction. In fact, they declined his proposal, but they questioned him in various ways. Just then passed the public vehicle to Rouen; they stopped it to ascertain if he was known by any individual in it, but being recognised by no one, they concluded him a liar, and threatened again to drown him. As he was said to be a clerk (so the vulgar call scholars in their jargon), a breviary was brought to see whether he understood Latin; finding that he did, they said he must be destroyed, for that he was enough to infect the whole city of Rouen. To escape their importunities, he replied that he would answer no more questions; that if he had been found ignorant, they would have judged badly of him, and now that he was proved to know something, they used him the worse; that, in short, as he perceived they were unreasonable men, they might do with him what they would. But during this altercation they had despatched two of their comrades to the above-mentioned Girard, to whom M. Duplessis had referred them with these lines:—
"Sir,—I am detained by the people of the Porte and suburbs of St. Denis; they will not believe that I am Philip Mornay, your clerk, whom you have permitted to go to Rouen during these holidays to see my relations. I request you to confirm the fact, that I may be allowed to proceed on my journey."
The messenger met with M. Girard just setting out for the palace, whom they found to be a man of respectable appearance, and well dressed. After scolding them a little, he certified on the back of the letter that Philip Mornay was neither *rebellious* nor *disaffected* (he durst not use the term Huguenot), and he signed the certificate with his name. But a little boy belonging to the house was near spoiling all by saying that M. Duplessis had been there only since Monday. In the midst of so many difficulties, we may observe how the Divine Providence watches over and for us, against

all human hope. The paper being brought back, these barbarians deemed it every way satisfactory; they suddenly changed both their looks and language, and reconducted him to the place where they had first seized him.'

INDEX.

	PAGE
Anne Boleyn's Charity	194
Anti-Lutheran Ghost at Orleans	210
Anti-Lutherans	74
Baptism of Bells, The	148
Baptizing a Jew	64
Bible and the Reformation, The	39
Bible, when first printed, The	1
Bird preaches to Luther, A	65
Birth of Luther, The	2
Birthplace of John Foxe, The	203
Bishops before the Reformation	151
Bohemian Martyr, A	251
Books and Girls	72
Burned Testaments, The	176
Calvin and Farel at Geneva	245
Calvin and Nicholas Cop	243
Catherine de Medicis in 1569	219
Chaucer's pictures of Church Life	135
Christ and His Enemies	115
Cradle of the Reformation, The	9
Death of Henry IV.	218
Death of James IV.—The Eve of the Reformation	156
Death of Luther, The	122
Diligent Preachers	242
Dr. Rowland Taylor	198
Early Days of John Foxe, The	205
Early Hardships	5
End of an Apostate	196
England at the opening of the Reformation	160
England under Edward VI.	180
English and Foreign Printers	80
English Monasteries, The	157
Erasmus	68
Escape of Philip de Mornay	256
European States, Luther and the	87
Excess of Books an Evil	70
Famine at Venice, The	237
Farel at Montbeliard in 1525	244
Florence and Her Reformers	234
France under Francis I.	217
Frundsberg	213
German Soldiers and the Pope	55
God's Providence	108
Gospel Feast, The	116
Great Pioneer, A	141
Henry VIII. and Luther	94
Holy Ghost, The	112

Index. 263

Honest Man of Eisleben, The 59
Humphrey Monmouth, Tyndale's Friend . . . 164

Italian Authorship . . 227

Jews, The 71
John Craig's Escape from Rome 197
John Daye at Aldersgate . 84
John Foxe in Prosperity . 207
John Foxe's Wit . . 208
John Kalckberner and Aix-la-Chapelle . . . 212

Last Days of Calvin, The . 247
Last Days of Latimer, The 190
Last Days of Savonarola, The 225
Latimer and the Monks . 185
Latimer's Caution . . 188
Latimer's Fall . . . 187
Latimer's Influence . . 182
Latimer the Bishop . . 189
Latimer and the Bishop of Ely 184
Latimer's Youth and Conversion 183
Lefevre, Farel, and Luther 78
Leo X. and Indulgences . 21
Leo X. and Luther . . 49
Leo X.'s Bull . . 32, 47
Life in the Wartburg . 85
Lord's Supper Degenerates into the Mass, The . 17
Lucca and Her Evangelical Teachers . . . 240
Lutheran at Meaux, A . 77
Lutheran Colporteur, A . 75
Luther and Cajetan . . 44
Luther and Charles V. . 78
Luther and Leo X. . . 24
Luther and Money . . 45
Luther and the Evil One . 62

Luther and the Fugitive Nuns 31
Luther and the Monks . 34
Luther and the Physicians 61
Luther and the Plague . 86
Luther and the Pope . . 33
Luther and the Prophets . 36
Luther and Tetzel . . 20
Luther and the Student . 65
Lutheran at Toulouse, A . 214
Lutheran Iconoclast at Paris 211
Lutheranism in Bohemia . 249
Lutheranism in Central Italy 230
Lutherans in Venice . . 229
Lutheran Works in Foreign Lands 95
Luther as a Monk . . 7
Luther as a Hymn Writer . 67
Luther a Sharp Reprover . 116
Luther at Augsburg . . 41
Luther at Worms . . 50
Luther in the Wartburg . 30
Luther, Melancthon, and Erasmus . . . 69
Luther not Perfect . . 124
Luther on Antichrist . . 99
Luther on Giving . . 111
Luther on the Bible . . 107
Luther on the World . . 110
Luther Relics in the British Museum 253
Luther still Popular—Another Reformation needed 126
Luther's Achievements . 119
Luther's Advice to Preachers . . . 103
Luther's Bible . . . 38
Luther's Books Burned in Cheapside . . . 202
Luther's Domestic Life . 91
Luther's Early Education. 6
Luther's Faith in Prayer . 58

	PAGE
Luther's Home	65
Luther's House Preserved	128
Luther's Love of Music	74
Luther's Printers and Publishers	79
Luther's Reply to the Bull	53
Luther's Style and Influence on Literature	117
Luther's Table-Talk—Its Preservation	10
Luther's Youth	4
Maid of Kent, The	178
Martyr and the Apostate, The	215
Martyr Booksellers	96
Martyrologist's Escape, The	209
Mediæval Bells	149
Melancthon's Sick-bed, Luther at	89
Minor Pioneers	146
Naples and Juan de Valdes	233
Ochino and Paleario	232
Open-air Preachers	25
Painter of Wittenberg, The	114
Patience	97
Pioneer, A—Savonarola at Florence	223
Pope Alexander VI.	130
Pope's Cooks, The	63
Pre-Reformation 'Dons' and 'Sirs'	144
Prince Eberhard of Wirtemberg	60
Prophecies of the Reformation	19

	PAGE
Queen Margaret's Presentiment	216
Reformation Promoted by Tracts, The	73
Reformers at Turin	238
Remorse, Example of	93
Rood of Dovercourt, The	177
Royal Exchange, a Memento of the Reformation	170
Scotch Martyr, A	191
Scotland before the Reformation	134
Scriptures an Unknown Book, The	7
Sirloin of Beef, The	193
Spanish Franciscan, A	242
Students' Advantages	106
Tetzel Advances the Cause	23
Thomas Cromwell's Adventures	195
Tyndale and Erasmus	163
Tyndale at Antwerp	161
Tyndale in Prison	165
Tyndale's Successors	166
Was Leo X. poisoned?	57
Why the Reformation Succeeded	132
Why Luther Succeeded	120
Worth of the Bible, The	40
Wycliffe at St. Paul's	153
Wycliffe's Bible	152
Wycliffe's Itinerants	154
Wycliffe's Teaching	155
Zwingli at Zurich	220
Zwingli more Scriptural than Luther	221

Hazell, Watson, and Viney, Printers, London and Aylesbury.

www.ingramcontent.com/pod-product-compliance
Lightning Source LLC
Chambersburg PA
CBHW031955230426
43672CB00010B/2158